Newspaper Design

EDITING AND DESIGN

A Five-volume Manual of
English, Typography and Layout

BOOK ONE Newsman's English
BOOK TWO Handling Newspaper Text
BOOK THREE News Headlines
BOOK FOUR Picture Editing
BOOK FIVE Newspaper Design

Book Five
Newspaper Design

Harold Evans
Editor, *The Sunday Times*, London

HOLT, RINEHART AND WINSTON
New York   Chicago   San Francisco

Library of Congress Catalog Card Number : 72-78099

First Edition

ISBN : 0-03-091348-9

Printed in Great Britain.

Published under the auspices of the
National Council for the Training of Journalists.

To Enid

Preface

This is the fifth and final title in my series on newspaper editing and design. It is concerned with the magical area of layout; magical because it is for most newspapermen a routine marrying of mind and metal that never loses its romance and excitement; magical because layout proceeds less by logic and more by the incantation of spells, the polishing of ju-jus and the inhalation of potions prescribed by elders of the tribe. I hope I have done some of the more primitive witch doctors a mischief; but I do not suggest that layout should be all logic and no art. I am conscious of the value of tradition (*see* Chapter 2), and I am certain that any reader who has survived four volumes is entitled to as many spells and secret formulas as can decently be circulated.

If that strikes a defensive note, it is because my prophetic ear catches already the cry of cynics either side: those who say that layout cannot be taught because it is an intuition and those who say it ought not to be taught because it is a distraction. This latter argument, which is more fashionable, is the more serious and it is one which it is the theme of this book to reject. My argument is that design is not decoration or distraction but part of the business of communication and part that we should argue constantly, for the sake of the printed word, in every newsroom from Darlington to New Delhi. For this reason I have ventured to discuss design as if there were no international frontiers; the nature of a language clearly plays a part in layout, but too many fallacies have sheltered behind an irregular verb.

And indeed it is for this reason—the belief in the relationship of form and content—that I have written a book at all.

The profession of journalism, in whose capacity for good, it will not surprise you, I have so much faith, needs sustaining by craftsmanship as well as genius. What Herbert Spencer has said of printing is true of journalism: 'No matter how great the author's wisdom or how vital the message or how remarkable the printer's skill, unread print is merely a lot of paper and little ink. The true economics of printing must be measured by how much is read and understood and not by how much is produced.'

I have expressed my general and intense debts in Book One to those who have helped throughout this series. For this volume, in addition, I must thank innumerable newspapers all over the world, for their assistance, permissions and courtesy; Don Rowlands of the Thomson Foundation for help with the international illustrations; Edwin Taylor, Director of Design at *The Sunday Times*, and Robert Harling, design consultant, both for arguing with a pencil; Walter Partridge of Westminster Press; Leslie T Owens, Principal of the London College of Printing; and Walter Tracy of Linotype for some cogent observations; Vincent Page and Terry Mead for assistance with photography; and Sheila Robinette for assistance with research.

Highgate, London   HAROLD EVANS

Contents

1 The Function of Newspaper Design

Typography is the efficient means to an essentially utilitarian and only accidentally aesthetic end, for enjoyment of patterns is rarely the reader's chief aim.

STANLEY MORISON

The great innovating Victorian journalist, W T Stead, once remarked of his editor on the *Pall Mall Gazette*: 'We disagreed on everything from the existence of God to the make-up of a newspaper.' A hundred years later newspaper make-up has shed some of its theology—serious newspapers, it is conceded, can look bright—but there is still a good deal of passionate dogmatism.

The object of dogmatism changes. Only a year or two ago no English popular broadsheet paper felt it dare appear on the streets dressed in less than an eight-column banner headline. No quality paper would let sans serif display type cross its threshold. American editors still insist on the primacy of the top right-hand corner for lead stories; English editors swear by the left-hand corner. There is wider international agreement today on certain detailed principles—for instance, that lower-case headlines are easier to read—but the millennium has not yet arrived. Newspaper design will continue to evolve.

What is important for the future of newspaper design—indeed of newspapers—is that we should understand what we are trying to do. If we can, we will be able energetically to exploit the favourable influences, minimise the adverse, and discount the transitory. And the very first essential is to realise that design is part of journalism. Design is not decoration. It is communication.

Content and Presentation

A newspaper is a vehicle for transmitting news and ideas. The design is an integral part of that process. We begin with a blank sheet of newsprint and a mosaic of ideas we want to communicate and it is the function of newspaper design to present that mosaic in an organised and comprehensible way. To do this the newspaper designer uses text type, display type, photographs, line work, white space, and a sequence of pages, in the most fitting combinations.

Typography is the basis of this craft, but it is not the whole of it. Newspaper design is more than the multiplication of a single message by printing. We can adapt the words of Walter Gropius[1] that 'whereas building is merely a matter of methods and materials, architecture implies the mastery of space.' Whereas printing is merely a matter of methods and materials, newspaper design implies a mastery of space. The problem is to communicate within the same physical context not one message but a series of disconnected messages of infinitely varying significance, and to do this with speed, ease and economy in a recognisably consistent style. It follows that newspaper design cannot begin to exist without news and attitudes to it: without something to express to a defined audience. And it also follows that newspaper news cannot effectively be communicated visually without newspaper design.

It is the failure to appreciate this inescapable reciprocity which has led to so much bad newspaper design and so much bad blood between designer and journalist. It is no good for a designer to think that a day's news or the changing sensations of a year can all fit his preconceived patterns. It is no good if an advertising agency 'packages' a new newspaper simply on the basis of an inspiration about design. It is of no help for designers to complain about the kind of untidiness which inevitably crops up in the rush of a big news story: a certain 'rawness' may be an advantage in emphasising the stridency of events. The results of the unhappy relationship between designers and journalists are noticeable at two extremes. At one end design is considered a decorative embellishment, a luxury; in the worst cases this produces a fussy newspaper, in which either decorative contrivances obscure the message, or news is forced to fit a pattern. And at the other extreme, violence is done to every rule of typography in a reaction against 'fancy design'.

Even advocates of improved newspaper design muddle things here. How often do you see the argument that newspapers must improve their design because it is their 'shop window'? It is not that. Nor is it fancy packaging. It is part of the goods. What makes the *Daily News*, New York, the *Daily News* is not just the stories and pictures. If the same content were presented on a broadsheet, dressed in Cheltenham display type, it would no longer be the *Daily News*. The design cannot be separated from the product. The format, the typography, and the printing are as integral a part of a newspaper as the words. A badly designed, sloppily printed newspaper inescapably carries with it the aura of sloppy journalism. The London *Times* has owed some of its authority over the years to dignified design and immaculate presswork. The underground papers in the United States and Europe, and the new suburban weeklies, too, are, at another level, partly the creatures of the technological revolution of photo-setting and web offset. The new clarity of printing carries overtones of credibility.

Effective newspaper design, then, cannot spring from the pencil of an artist pursuing abstract aesthetics. There is an important role, as I shall indicate, for artists, designers and typographers in newspapers, but they must be closely involved with journalists

and journalism. They must share the idea of what is being communicated and to whom.

From the artistic side there is today too much concern with the beholder's eye for beauty and too little concern for the audience of journalism. I have had the experience of offering the observation on a layout that 14pt Bodoni Bold italic caps across 88 picas for seven lines without leading is impossible to read, only to be told that this does not matter because it *looks* exciting. What an absurdity. Something that *looks* nice but is incomprehensible is ultimately as appealing as a beauty queen with the mind of a moth. The artistic imagination, set free from convention, will exploit new materials and relationships, but this must be done on the basic premise of communicating a precise content to a defined readership: a designer's flexibility of response must always stop short of the point where a reader no longer recognises his newspaper.

Tabloid versus Broadsheet
These are the fundamental bases for decisions on everything from the size of the sheet to the length of a paragraph. A format for a serious newspaper dealing in politics and social reporting will not suit a metropolitan evening newspaper offering lots of 'spice'. It is impossible for the same combination of type, text and layout to express the function of both. It is as absurd as putting a Rolls Royce body on a sports-car chassis. If the newspaper is a busy evening, published mainly for an audience of commuters on crowded trains and buses, then it should first be designed to be read by a commuter. For him, reading in conditions inimical to reflections on the nature of the universe, the newspaper will offer short spot news, sport, stock prices, and entertainment features.

The ideal format will be a tabloid, for ease of handling, and the detailed typography will accommodate lots of short reports and short paragraphs within them. If the paper, for commercial or technical reasons, is broadsheet, it will have to meet its handling problem by exploiting the larger page size: continuation stories will be avoided and the first page will be designed to have the widest possible range of appeal. So should the back page, though it is usually neglected.

Equally, a newspaper which is shared by a family at home will avoid publishing the women's feature on the same page as the sport or on the reverse side of the sports page. Or, to take a typographical illustration, a design to project major national and international news as dramatically as possible in a competitive situation, will not be appropriate for a monopoly weekly newspaper circulating in a small town: an obvious thought, but one not appreciated by the English weeklies which attempted to graft on to their entirely different product the banners and types of the *Daily Express*.

Such elementary considerations are the early framework for newspaper design. Even these can rarely be considered in isolation. There are mechanical, commercial and financial factors which impinge on the ideal editorial expression (for instance, awkward shapes produced by obtrusive display advertisements).

There is the persistent factor of reader habit, often used to justify bad old habits but neglected at one's peril. Design produces the best answer from the sum of these problems, deriving strength from the newest techniques and materials, but governed throughout by the imperatives of communication. Today we look askance at the garish assortments of types used in headline decks by the American innovators. But they were finding the right design solution with the materials then available. They were seeking to express the variety and drama of the news. As Stanley Morison said of the way the London *Times* ransacked the type cases in the first world war, 'unparalleled events were not to be expressed by tight-laced early Victorianisms.'[2] Today we do not need multi-decks of mixed types to express news values. We can do it more efficiently and more economically by using new display types, by the positioning of an item on a page, by the subtle use of white space. But however primitive by today's visual standards, the American variegated multi-decks had the essential virtue: they worked. They enabled newspapers to communicate more effectively.

If design cannot await the artist, neither can it be left to the engineer (which is the more fashionable fallacy). Photo-composition, web offset, computers and cathode ray tubes will none of them create satisfactory newspaper design; they will merely enable it to be created by journalists who know what they want to project and how to project it. Offset printing does give us greatly improved half-tone pictures, and photo-composition is freeing the designer from many limitations of hot metal, chiefly the practical necessity to work in a rigid grid of straight lines, monochrome and set type sizes. But the basic essential is still the organised communication of ideas and not the proliferation of free-form patterns. The real importance of web offset is the stimulus it should give to graphics, to selective colour and to making picture journalism more than a decorative adjunct to the text. Faced with television's coverage of the event, newspapers more and more must answer the why? and how? behind the news, and good designer–journalists will exploit filmsetting for the ease of graphic analysis (*see* page 166). The new facilities also create opportunities for abuse. To be able to print a $32\frac{1}{2}$pt. headline in purple in the shape of a bishop's mitre will not in itself be a notable advance in journalism.

Unless there is a need for such a form, for a specific act of communication, form is being allowed to override everything else, to distract from the message. But the message will remain the *raison d'être* of journalism when the cathode ray tube is consigned to the museum.

All of this may seem to be the advocacy of

a new brutalism, an end to any concern for appearances. That is not so. If there had to be a choice between efficient communication and elegance, I would certainly sacrifice elegance. But the familiar antithesis between form and function is false. A form which is superimposed will not function efficiently; and its 'good looks' will be obvious mascara. A simple example here is the stars some American papers employ decoratively to divide headline decks. But if a newspaper design seeks to express function, efficiently and economically, it will develop a form attractive to the eye: white space between decks divides attractively without distracting. The ideal is for the newspaper designer–journalist to be dominated by the desire to express function but to have a feeling (as he does) for aesthetic principles of unity, proportion and harmony. It is more difficult to analyse these, but I believe a feeling for them will develop more rapidly and surely in the designer–journalist who empties his mind of preconceived ideas of form and tries most perfectly to serve the message. Certainly, any refinement which interferes with function will destroy the basic integrity of the form.

I will demonstrate with practical examples how a better expression of function improves design—and the thought is not special to newspapers. The general point has been well put by Raymond Roberts: 'Good design in any field is a balance between form and function with function as the first consideration and driving force. If all the problems inherent in a given task are properly understood, the design solution will already begin to take shape. This is just as true of typography as it is of aircraft design or architecture, and the final solution should reveal function through its form.'[3]

The theory of newspaper design argued here will not yield that lodestone of jaded journalism, the single correct formula for newspaper format. There are many problems of message–audience relationship, so there must be many design solutions. Nor is there inevitably a single solution to a single problem. Imaginative men, and men with different technical resources, may produce several acceptable solutions to the same problem, using different typefaces, different settings, different graphic ideas. There is a large area for creative imagination, certainly far, far wider than the typical North American daily exhibits; but the area is prescribed—certainly far, far more closely than the popular French daily appreciates. It is not infinite.

Which is the 'best' solution is a matter for argument and taste, but there can be no argument that a design fails at once if it does not 'solve' the problem. If it looks good, but fails to provide enough space for text or squeezes the graphics into near-illegibility, then the design has failed. It has failed on a different scale if the design response destroys the identity of the newspaper.

This approach can give us a consistent standard for judging acceptable newspaper design. This news display type may look handsome in a magazine—but is it as easy to read after stereotyping and printing on newsprint? That 8pt black across 40 ems does add an interesting spot of colour to the page, but is it possible actually to read it? That 8-em 11-column page stimulates classified advertising revenue, but in longer editorial texts does it not erode legibility and authority? Just as the designer will have to justify his preferences by the criterion of effective communication, so the journalist will have to justify neglect of genuine design principles—or marketing reports. If, say, there is no design justification for erratic black indented paragraphs in the middle of news text—and they do not make for smooth, easy reading—then the journalist using them will have to produce convincing editorial reasons for impeding legibility. Is that paragraph in black so different in kind from the others in ordinary type that it must be expressed differently? If the journalist likes a front page carrying a lot of stories he will have to listen when the market researcher says that very few readers are bothering to follow six or seven turning stories to other pages.

There should be a continuous dialogue between designer and journalist and journalist and researcher. Ideas on form and content should interact. Theories should be tested in the market place. This has been happening too little, to the detriment of the newspaper as communicator. Newspaper design has evolved in the heat of a thousand different moments, now dependent on the whim of the printer or the taxman, now on the·passion of the crusading journalist who wants type to proselytise, now on the resources of a foundry. Even today, there has been hardly any research into what forms and styles of design attract and hold the newspaper reader. For the newspaperman it is enough that the paper is still bought; for the designer it is enough that the thing looks right. The designer is a newcomer who is only half heeded (and the market researcher on design is only faintly discernible on the horizon). Newspaper design cannot go on being so insular if the newspaper is to fulfil its role. The journalist must appreciate that the designer has more than new typefaces to contribute, that to squeeze in a maximum number of words is not necessarily to communicate more; the designer must learn to accept the primacy of the message and he must abandon his art-school condescension for the newspaper as an ephemeral product of a vulgar society.

I recognise that there may always be a certain tension between designer and writer; if the phrase did not carry overtones of failure one would say it should be a partnership of creative tension. But if the partnership, in its present context, is to begin to create there must be a better understanding beneath the arguing, of what each has to offer. I asked Robert Harling, the designer and typographer, if from his long experience he would set out his conception of a viable relationship. I give it here and will then consider how this relationship might be developed in future for better newspaper design.

The Designer in the Newspaper Office

1 As I see it, the main task of any typographical designer, graphic designer, layout artist, or whatever he calls himself, should be to present (that is, communicate) the message he is given—whether the title-page of a book, a feature in a glossy or a medley of stories in an evening newspaper—in as simple, direct, orderly and effective a manner as possible.

2 To this end he ought to be continuously on guard against the wish to 'express himself' aesthetically at the expense of that message. The main objective of too many designers seems to be to show how 'creative' they are rather than to act as the technically trained presenters of messages they are engaged to be.

3 An innate sense of orderliness must, therefore, rank high amongst the attributes possessed by the competent designer. Training can undoubtedly inculcate something of this quality, but, like taste, a high sense of orderliness seems to be a gift direct from the gods. (The more superficially minded gods, no doubt.)

4 The relative importance of the items to be included on a title-page or newspaper page must come from the person primarily responsible for the message, whether the author of a book or play, the editor or his appointed deputy. Only after these priorities have been established should the designer be allowed to show his skills.

5 Certain fundamental questions of design must also be discussed and settled before the typographer can start. Are headings or titles to be centred or set asymetrically? Is a photograph to dominate the page or to be subsidiary to the heading? Are diagrams to be part of the heading or incorporated in the text? And so on.

6 That the designer is technically accomplished should be a fact demonstrable

within half an hour. It goes without saying, therefore, that the typographical designer should be skilled in estimating required type-sizes, the most appropriate sizes for photographs, drawings, diagrams, plans and other graphic material, and so on. His literary colleagues can then relax, taking these facts for granted. Mutual confidence is thus established, to be enjoyed henceforward.

7 If the designer does his job properly, in arranging, logically and effectively, the elements with which he is presented—headlines, text, pictures—he will establish a pattern in his layout or design. The pattern implicit in this disposition may only be recognisable to himself. Why not? By genes and training he should be particularly responsive to such subtleties. If his patterns, recognised or unrecognised by colleagues, are acceptable his reward will probably be the words, 'A good page,' or 'Quite a good page.' Such seemingly laconic phrases are not patronage; they are the acknowledgment of one man's professional craftsmanship by another.

8 The designer should be able to work in easy-going concert with his literary colleagues. He should be one of a team, not an esoteric luxury. Neither should he be allowed to consider himself as an ivory-tower man who can work only when he gets 'away from it all.' The design of newspapers is a continuous and fluctuating business and the designer should be as flexible-minded (and as tough-minded) as others. They rewrite stories at the behest of a superior. He should be prepared to redesign pages.

In my view newspapers should now go farther than this. They should begin to create a new breed within the menagerie of talent, and new systems for cross-fertilisation of ideas between the verbally and the visually gifted. There should be designer-journalists, or journalist-designers—design-

ers who care about journalism and journalists who care about design. There should be experiments with the pattern of work-flow within the editorial department. For the individual a beginning could be made in two ways. Newspapers could offer design-journalism apprenticeships to young graphic artists fresh from art schools and print colleges. After three years immersed in the business of news, with the refinement of their learning rough-hewn by the raw demands of daily journalism, they would be able to make an effective contribution to design-journalism. They would be worth at least one artist plus half a deskman. And journalists and journalist-training establishments should consider how they can offer typography and design to produce the journalist-designer. The ignorance about type, even among deskmen and executives who daily command the twenty-six soldiers of lead, is unbelievably profound. Edwin Taylor, who was first a designer but is now a designer-journalist, put the general point well, though not with any noticeable response from his audience: 'To achieve more than mere "packaging" the designer must be given the opportunity to learn to understand the intentions of the editor/journalist by himself becoming a form of journalist—and the editor/journalist must rethink some of his intentions so as to make good use of the special skills of the designer.'[4]

This requires more than the creation of designer-journalists. It requires a rethinking of the traditional organisation of the editorial department. The skills of the graphic designer, the artist—and the photographer too—must be enlisted much earlier and in a different way. The general pattern is for words to be written by one set of journalists, and passed on to another set of journalists who read them and only then start thinking about presentation. The photographic editor will probably be in at the early stage when a news or features story is only an idea or assignment in the diary. But even a newspaper which can boast an artist or designer rarely enlists his aid before the words are written: most often he is called in only when the story has been allocated to a page, with its limitations of editorial–advertising shape. Worse, he is often called in when the layout has been planned and there is simply a hole for an illustration. The visually trained journalist should have an opportunity to contribute, on the contrary, at the very conception of a news or feature assignment, before the reporter goes out—before anyone develops a vested interest in the form of communication. Some stories are communicated better by drawings and photographs than by text and headline—the moon landings, for instance; very many are given a different dimension by the right combination of text and visuals. (*See* Book Four for numerous examples.) But that will not happen by chance. It must be planned from the beginning.

Given the appropriate news or feature idea, the visually trained man can suggest questions and 'angles' which will supply the right information in the right form for an illuminating chart or for a telling photographic sequence. The layout editor, forewarned, can think of matching display appropriate to the material and his actual day's editorial–advertising shapes; where the presentation requires, he has time to seek adjustments. The visual man at editorial conferences will not have a monopoly of ideas. There will be creative argument at the ideas stage and again when the research on a suitable story is completed, and again when the requirements of the graphics meet the rigours of the page shapes. But the earlier a newspaper thinks in this way about communication as consisting of many elements, the better the newspaper design, in the broadest sense, will be. Something like this happens, if one may mention Mammon, in the better advertising agencies. In the old days the copywriter wrote the message and the artist made the layout fit the words without daring to lay a hand on a single syllable. Now artists and writers argue things out first with strikingly more success. Advertising is not journalism. But it is communication. Newspapers have less time to reflect on design, and words, rightly, will always be preponderant. But we have a lot to learn.

It would be possible to go on from this point with a detailed exposition of the theoretical relationship of news presentation to design. However, it is probably more helpful if we get down to some practical examples of how function can be an effective guide to newspaper design. These will be within the traditional format of a newspaper. We can then return to general theory, international comparisons, and the possibilities for wholly new developments of newspaper design. We will conclude with the practical mechanics of page planning and a clinic for defective design. There is no point in learning the nuts and bolts until we have understood the engine.

The two practical discussions are of widely different examples—a complete redesign of *The Northern Echo*, the regional morning newspaper owned by the Westminster Press; and a redesign of the sports pages of *The Sunday Times*.

Redesigning The Northern Echo

It is worth going through the changes in detail because *The Northern Echo*, before its redesign, represented a typical classical design development, still visible, with various corruptions, all over the English-speaking world. These newspapers are all just as amenable to the application of functional principles analysed here. The solution would vary in each case with the character and content of the papers and their resources, but the revised functional format of *The Northern Echo* has something to commend it alike for solid North American community newspapers, English locals and post-colonial Asian and African dailies.

With one exception the redesign of *The Northern Echo* began by accepting the conventional format of the newspaper, news presented in multi-column display with separate feature pages. Within that framework the paper was completely redesigned both in page design and page sequence, but with great economy of resources. The design changes were made over three-and-a-half years.

It was reasoned that readers are creatures of habit and too abrupt a change might upset them. We also did not particularly want to draw attention to the editorial changes we were making: the time for that would come when and if the preliminary steps had been proved successful. Nor were all the design changes foreseen from the beginning; some developed from trial and error, and the freshest design change developed from an attempt at journalistic innovation.

The changes were built on the following functional arguments, which, I would say, have general relevance. To function properly any newspaper must do several things and it is worth noting that these requirements of function have an inner consistency. The design must:

(i) Communicate clearly and economically, i.e. with maximum legibility consistent with effective use of limited space.

(ii) Communicate with a sense of proportion, guided journalistically by the context of the news of the day and the period, and guided graphically by a sense of scale.

(iii) Communicate in a recognisable style and with such consistency as is helpful to the reader (for instance in the regular positioning of the television guide, stock prices, and so on).

(iv) Use means that are economical in time in both the printing and editorial departments.

(v) Use means that enable quick changes in response to changing news.

None of these requirements was properly met by the 1961 design. It was not easy to read; it wasted time and space; there was only rough proportion in news display and none in graphic scaling; and the result was unredeemingly ugly (illustrations 1-3).

First, let us examine the main constituents of the page design.

The Type

Text type was Intertype Royal, which was satisfactory, set at 11 picas in 7pt. Towards

the end of the design development the text type on page one was increased to 8pt. News headline type was Bodoni with some Tempo. Sport was in Tempo, features in Goudy, Tempo and Bodoni. The redesigning had to be carried out without buying any new headline type, and this was not really a limitation. The first essential was to assign a specific display type to each section to give sections an identity and unity.

The two sans types used occasionally on the news pages were therefore banished so that all display type on the news pages was Bodoni. The weaker of the two sans types (*see* Reserves Drop, column 5 of the Macmillan page) had been lost in the page and the heavier (Late News) was abrasively harsh when mixed with the elegant Bodoni. Tempo was also banished from features display, so that it appeared only on the sports pages. The women's page was based on Bodoni Modern, the lighter face, and the leader page on Goudy.

Each section then had a display-type unity and identity. But each section needed further detailed attention. First the news pages:

The Headlines

These failed in several ways to meet the basic functional requirement of legibility. Lines of type were jammed in without adequate white space, so that it was like trying to read by candlelight. Headlines down page were frequently too small to distinguish in the grey text, especially since these, too, were not lit by white space (**2, 3**).

Where the headlines were in decks—as were all page leads and some down page too —the separate decks of headlines were squeezed together, again without proper differentiation.

In page leads, the width and pattern of the headlines created visual difficulties. The spread of the headline was often so wide (for instance (**1**): Join vanguard of movement towards greater unity in the free world) that it proliferated letters and the eye just could not cope with them. Furthermore,

decks staggered drunkenly about the page in a way that was hard to follow. In the second deck of the first page one illustrated (Join vanguard . . .) the eye is expected to traverse first five columns then three columns, then negotiate a hairpin bend into a double column. This second deck is quite unreadable.

The same straggle and squeeze was apparent in all the main news headlines inside but without the benefit of any consistency in treatment. Sometimes the main deck was set across 5, 3, 2, sometimes it was 4, sometimes 4, 3, 2, and so on, changing for no apparent editorial reason. I call these headline shapes 'dog-leg' shapes.

The detailed headline typography itself was also functionally at fault. Throughout the news pages there were headlines in caps, many of them also in italic and so even harder to read.

In no way at all did the economy factors offer compensation for these deficiencies in legibility. On the contrary, the design wasted time and sacrificed flexibility. Multi-deck headlines clearly take more time to write and more time to set; and they consume more newsprint. In *The Northern Echo* they not only appeared in lead positions but also littered the entire page.

Reports of no more than 3in. long were dressed up in decks of two lines of 14pt caps followed by two lines of 12pt lower-case, offering a unit count far in excess of that needed to signal the rather simple stories.

The loss of flexibility of the old design lay basically in the headline shapes. Their complication imposed a pattern. Consider, for instance, changing the Macmillan lead story quickly between editions for a new story or a bigger new picture.

The ideal solution for a quick change is to be able to cut a simple shape in the existing design which does not have repercussions on the rest of the page. This is not possible here. Any new shape would mean cutting new column rules over six columns and adjusting the lengths of the stories in the six

columns under the main headline. The deskman would be forced in fact, to copy the existing lead shape, writing three wordy decks of headline to the same pattern as the Macmillan lead—though the new story might suggest an entirely different word pattern.

The deficiencies suggested their own solutions. Headlines must be rectangles, simple in shape and simple in constituents. We needed to abolish straggly dog-leg headings and also the proliferation of multi-deck headings. We needed to concentrate on lower-case headings. And all headings had to have sufficient white around them to be legible. This led gradually to a policy of lower-case news headlines throughout, set left to introduce white on the right within the headline space and to avoid headlines clashing.

The Pictures
The old *Northern Echo*, it was felt, was failing to exploit picture journalism, and especially the possibilities of strong pictures of genuine regional news. The opportunities were largely lost both by the picture policy and by inadequate sizing and display. Policy was in the tradition of local newspapers—as many local faces to the square inch as possible—and it understimated several factors: the reader; the real news-picture possibilities in the region; the capacities of an excellent team of photographers; and the ability of *The Northern Echo* to make and print outstanding half-tones. The new design of the newspaper had to do more than allow for adequate picture space: there would have to be a positive policy of building page design around strong half-tones.

The Layout
The functional policies for text, headlines and pictures had now to be related to each other. The simpler style might save time and be more legible but could it express the variety of the news? What should the size

of headlines be and where should they appear on the page? It was now time to look at the page as a whole. Certain additional functional defects were at once apparent. Individual headlines were not merely jammed in; they were allowed to abut and run into each other in adjacent columns: see, for instance, Britain's application to join Common Market, and Three North-East Men Die (3). Again there was a loss of legibility. Aggravating the over-crowding of headlines in one area of the page was a dearth of typographic colour elsewhere. Where there was too much headline colour the reader was confused by too many signals competing for attention. Where there was too little headline colour, mostly down-page, the news was inadequately signalled.

This seemed a simple weakness to remedy, but it raised a fundamental issue. How does a newspaper most fittingly express its estimate of the relative worth of news on a page?

Let us, for the moment, accept that the function of a news-page design is to project a range of wholly different news items in a coherent and consistent order. There are four ways in which, within one page, display type can be used to indicate to the reader the relative importance of the item:

(i)   The size of the headline.
(ii) The weight of the headline.
(iii) The spread of the headline.
(iv) The position of the headline on the page.

There should also be a relationship between the length of text and the newspaper's judgment of the importance of the news. Normally the biggest headline at the top of the page and the longest text should signal to the reader the most important report.

Of course there will be exceptions—for instance, the late important new lead rushed in with only a few paragraphs—but the general rule would be that the longer the text the bigger the headline, so that a journalistic judgment (length of text) marches

harmoniously with a design projection (weight and position of headline). There is thus an internal proportion between headline and text and an external proportion relating the worth of one headline-text unit to another. Failure to observe these proportions lay behind some of the worst visual confusion of the old *Northern Echo* pages.

There was no sense of scale and hence no clear expression of values; or perhaps it was the other way round: there was no clear sense of values and hence no expression of scale. Stories were allowed to run too long under small headings. Relatively small news was appearing high up the page with a small heading. Despite the small heading, the effect of position was to exaggerate the importance of the news. The worst effects of all were in the use of the eye-catching 'shoulder' position: the space below the right angle created by double-column setting of an intro; in terms of emphasis this shoulder position ranks only just below the double-column headline itself.

It was decided, therefore (4), to scheme suitably important stories in the shoulder positions and assign an appropriate headline weight: a 24pt in the shoulder of a 36pt double-column headline. Generally an 18pt had been used (too small) and sometimes a 36pt (too big) had been schemed in the shoulder of a 30pt double-column. For other headline–text relationships, a scale was laid down: a story which editorially was worth four to seven paragraphs would rate two lines of 24pt heading; a story worth only two paragraphs would rate an 18pt headline, and so on. A single-column story with 10 or 11 paragraphs would rate a four-line 24pt. We would not, therefore, scheme a 3- or 4-line 24pt single-column near the bottom of the page, and the effect was to shade down the single-column headings as one came down the page.

But why 24pt for a four-paragraph story? What should govern the scale of display values? Editorially the two limits are set by the most important story of the year, and the most dispensable paragraph. The most dispensable paragraph should have a headline just sufficient to stand out from the grey text: say a minimum of 10pt bold on this broadsheet paper setting in 7pt. So much for the lower limit. The upper limit needs more judgment. I said the most important story 'of the year' because a newspaper should always have something in reserve.

It should be able to respond to a major event by increasing the type size of the lead or its weight and spread or both. Using the biggest available type every day puts an unnecessary limit on the doctrine of flexible response. And there is a limit to the inflation of type faces. We are disciplined by the size of the sheet; by the feasibility of writing an intelligible headline in the limited unit count of a monster type-size; generally, by what type is in the case-room, and by the sheer space consumed. This last point was important for *The Northern Echo* (based then on an average of twelve pages a day).

The largest size available in Bodoni was 48pt. This seemed to accommodate an adequate scale of values by size: upwards from 10pt there were seven type sizes to 48pt. *The Northern Echo* was signalling the varying worth of the main lead story, if not with much consistency, by varying the spread of the 48pt and the number of decks. As I have already indicated, a simplified heading unit was chosen for the redesign, but for the lead there had to be a basic decision whether to opt for a banner headline across eight columns. We rejected the concept of the banner for these reasons:

1 It was associated with popular morning newspapers in Britain and we did not want to imitate anybody since we were a regional newspaper offering a distinctive service. It seemed clear to me then that the aping of the *Daily Express* banner was foolish; that papers like *The Times* and *Guardian* which occasionally went to a banner would have to find a better alternative; and that even for the popular daily the stylised banner, day in, day out, was questionable.

2 If we did not compete with the popular nationals in comparable size of banner, ours would look weak. If we did compete we would use a good deal more space on display than was really justified: not only the banner but all the other headings would have to be sized up in proportion.

3 The large banner headline invites absurdities in wording because it accommodates very few letters.

4 The larger banner takes so much space at the vital top of the paper that it means the picture of the day can easily be pushed below the halfway fold of the page. This seemed to me a serious defect, especially in view of our new policy of projecting pictures boldly.

So a banner was ruled out; and so was imitation of the *Guardian*, *Telegraph* and *Times*, then with a fixed, restrained double-column lead headline every day. We wanted to emphasise the lead story, especially when it was a late lead story which would have missed the regional editions of our competitors printed in London and Manchester. In all the developments of main news display, it seemed to us that an element of projection had been neglected: vertical emphasis with a bold multi-line headline in a heavy face in one deck (**4, 5**).

This could be striking and flexible and it had several other advantages. By making our main headline emphasis vertical rather than horizontal we were always able to have our main picture firmly above the fold. This is a marginal factor in casual sales.

A secondary advantage followed. The picture, placed to the right of the main news lead, prevented a clash of headings in adjacent columns at the top of the page. There was one weakness: 48pt Bodoni lacked impact as the main heading. We therefore experimented with Century Bold Extended as the lead headline, and as finally developed it brought welcome colour in a limited space without jarring with its companion Bodoni. (I made the mistake initially of keeping the lead headline in caps and never followed the logic of the lower-case headline policy to the lead headline. My successor, Mr J D Evans, had the courage to carry this through with handsome effect, though on the page shown, headlines have become inflated below the fold (**5**)).

These were the basic changes, every one

springing from function. Other things followed. The Stop Press was abandoned altogether. It was a move that seemed reactionary in the extreme, but it was simply a recognition of editorial realities. For any important news there was time between editions to replate page one; and any late trivial news should not be given the breathtaking prominence of a Stop Press, often simply for the sake of having something there. The release of the Stop Press space created the possibility of an arresting horizontal display at the foot of page one. This apart, we decided to scheme fewer multi-column breaks down page (whether headline or picture) because the device had been overworked. But the multi-column headings retained were made to do their work by an increase in type size which adequately reflected the newsworthiness of a multi-column position and also prevented the page sliding into greyness.

Perhaps the most awkward problem of effecting the whole redesign was achieving the right amount of white space in headings. A standard was laid down but sometimes it looked wrong. When, for instance, there were not ascenders and descenders between two lines of headline the standard whiting looked excessive. We learned on these occasions to trust our eyes. Spacing should not be uniform. It should be *visually* correct.

When all this had been done, the old title for the page with its gothic blackletter and 'earpiece' advertisements seemed even more out of place. Its antique quality did not express what we hoped was the surging spirit of the newspaper and the region it served; and the directors of the Westminster Press were prepared to agree to the extent of abolishing the 'earpieces' which had brought in £2,000 a year. There was one additional gain from the new logotype designed by Bert Hackett: it saved in depth one-eighth of an inch across eight columns, thereby producing a valuable extra inch for news.

Leader Page

The leader page is where the voice of a regional newspaper should speak clearly and authoritatively for the region. Instead the old *Northern Echo* led (7) with theatre and cinema ads filled out, when these fell short, with crudely designed house advertising and even on occasion an undertaker's 'tombstone' which completed the funereal appearance. The editorial column was

The Northern Echo
Saturday, September 25, 1965

THE WIDE EYE

THE RADICALS

The £32,000 haul by the ram gang in Tottenha... the biggest of an increasing number of wage g... cusses the security measures being taken b...

Sad — but right

Bright green dye to beat the bandits

TODAY'S REFLECTION

My philological studies here satisfied me that a gifted person ought to learn English (barring spelling and pronunciation) in thirty hours, French in thirty days, and German in thirty years.

MARK TWAIN

A PASSAGE TO INDIA — 2

The Wear at Sunderland

6

Across the river in this picture is J. L. Thompson's shipyard. On the right is the Fish Quay, with the Corporation Quay beyond.

headed with a quotation and an ugly clutter of type, purveying a variety of information, and the leader itself was set in short jerky paragraphs, reverse indent, the same size as other articles on the page, 8pt.

Much more space and emphasis needed to be given to editorials. We decided **(6)** we must begin with editorials; they must be in larger type (9pt) which meant wider setting. Double-column setting was the obvious solution, but we managed something better. Double-column setting would have conflicted with another need—to introduce more white space between columns and do away with column rules on a page which, with few items, could reasonably well be organised without them. By setting the new editorials 4 ems short of double-column we achieved something most useful. We were able to set material for the leader page at ordinary single-column news measure (a great aid in standardising production and in moving appropriate text, such as letters, between pages) and use the

---

HEAR ALL SIDES

Planning: my fears for our city

The County Planning Officer, in his report in The Northern Echo, has all the right principles and knows some of the reasons for the failures to build places which are fine to be in. Then why is there so much bad building in Mr. Atkinson's area?

County Hall, for instance, owes everything to the County Council's direction but shows no excellence at all. Surely by Mr. Atkinson's standards such nullity is actively bad, not merely waste?

When neither buildings entirely in nor those partly out of the Council's control show imaginative design what hope have we that the redevelopments in the city will not be similarly characterless, that the challenge of river frontages will not be shuffled off as tarred margins, but that these will be exciting places and not just extra commerce?

We want buildings which fill all our needs and extend our experience: apart from Design Centre litter bins and some pleasant patches, can the Planning Officer make his standards affect the big decisions?

R. S. HUGHES
Neville's Cross College, Durham.

Over to England for NH teeth

Mr. Sam Winckup (The Northern Echo, September 22) not only has my sympathy, but demonstrates one of the unjust and nonsensical parts of our own free National Health Service.

Mr. Winckup, or his insurers, have to pay for his medical treatment while his Canadian counterpart visiting this country gets everything free. Fifty-four Canadians had free treatment in Newcastle last year, with 63 USA citizens, 31 Australians, 44 Germans, 54 Greeks, 18 Norwegians, 17 Portuguese, 14 French, ten Spaniards and 17 from Eire.

In all, 742 visitors from abroad to Newcastle got treatment as temporary residents, and the total of temporary residents registered numbered 4,719.

The cost per head during the year was £6 1s 2d, so our visitors to one city alone may have cost us £5,000. Incidentally my French onion vendor regularly brings his wife to this country to renew her false teeth and her spectacles!

Like Mr. Sam Winckup, I think this is nonsense, and visitors from countries who do not give free treatment to our nationals should be charged, except in an emergency.

IAN BRANSOM,
Prospective Conservative Candidate for The Hartlepools.

Doors Diary   September 24

ARE OF A DUCKING

er banks are often bordered by graceful trees, the precise nature of which offers a species, for they hybridise very freely. onally the timber from which cricket bats the white willow, is planted in many places England, where it sends its fine white to the water.

ouring trees may well be specimens of the w, which has coralled rootlets. This tree branches with ease and those misguided have tried to perform acrobatic feats on hanging over water have found this out to

upper dales of Yorkshire, wet hollows are nised by, the leaved willow with its own twigs and long leaves with a surface and green leather. This species is rather distribution and you'll not usually find it orkshire.

E.M.H.

Tom Little is on holiday this week and instead Jack Fletcher contributes

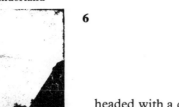

View from the Hartlepools

I AM a cuckoo in the Little nest.

It seems fitting, therefore, to start with an apology to all those who look forward on a Saturday morning—me among them—to the wide smile and lively mind of my Newcastle colleague, Tom Little.

For better or for worse, Tom's absence on holiday—why didn't he pick this kind of weather?—has temporarily switched the view.

Normally, my personal confrontation is confined to the sports pages. And it is consoling to think that in this column, if I'm careful, I may not get into so much trouble.

At least I shall not be writing about a Hartlepools United match which so many other people never saw. I don't mean that they weren't there. But it turns out on a Monday morning that there were actually two games—the one I saw and the one they saw.

That's why I have to keep a stiff upper lip every other Monday. The scorn is withering. "And where were you on Saturday?" they ask with that smile which soccer's superior intellects reserve for the humbler breed.

"How on earth could you make Joe Blank the man of the match? He was chronic. Not a clue."

All this must be borne with fortitude, good humour and restraint. Hence my strained air on a Monday as I battle to give these virtues full play.

Very occasionally, of course, some simple fellow comes up and says: "I liked your match report."

We need more of these people. They are the salt of the earth.

Outside the bright lights

AS a cool quarter of a million changes hands in the La Dolce Vita deal, I have a question for the North-East's night club moguls. Why isn't the colour of our money at the Hartlepools as good as anyone else's?

Hartlepools people are ready to gaze, feed, drink, and gamble with the same enthusiasm (and moderation?) as the rest. But they have to go ten miles or more to do it.

Newcastle, Sunderland, Stockton, Darlington, Middlesbrough, even South Bank, all have night clubs. Yet here in a prospering —I repeat prospering—area of 100,000 souls we remain bereft. We don't even possess a steak bar.

I know that local estate agents had an inquiry many months ago about premises suitable for conversion into a night club. That seems to be as near the glitter as we have got.

I believe this is an important matter for the Hartlepools. The battle of the image is on. You can hold your hands up grandma, but night clubs and steak bars are integral to the new social structure.

In their own way, they have become status symbols.

When Foster Wheeler's "prospecting party" came up to run the rule over West Hartlepool in July one of their young married craftsmen told me he liked the look of the place, but before electing to move with the firm he would want to know what

entertainment there was—what it was like at night.

This is the way the new Elizabethans think. Bingo, beer and bamboo shoots are not enough. They want the champagne, too.

Unwritten law

IN the reading room at West Hartlepool's public library there are three rules—no smoking, no noise, and no monopolising a paper for more than ten minutes.

Like most rules in our rule-ridden world, they occasionally get broken. There is the tell-tale smoke spiral from the crafty cigarette, the involuntary snore from the magazine benches.

But the ten-minute limit is the rule that suffers most. The regulars will have none of it.

It was a big help, of course, when some years ago the Library Committee stopped the punters' timeless studies by blacking out the racing columns. But there remain those for whom the clock stands still as they browse happily through the news.

In the brotherhood of the reading room it seems to be an unwritten law that the ten-minute rule is never invoked. Though they breathe down your neck, they'll never tap your shoulder.

"Excuse me, sir, your ten minutes is up." However respectfully put it would take a lot of courage.

Quite apart from the tense situation arising from a possible rebuff, the great danger is that such an argument would ensure that both parties would be ejected under the rule against noise.

Chin up, Zak

POOR little Zak, the mini-Beatle. In the age of reason I cannot think he is going to be too pleased with his dad, Ringo.

I suppose it's as good as Ted or Bill for a nickname. But not for real. Imagine the quizzical looks and the questions later on. How tired he is going to be of insisting that it's Zak on his birth certificate.

That's the trouble with Christian names. You're stuck with them. It would make the documentation of life too complex if they were temporary till, say 16, and you then picked your own.

Still, let's count our blessings. I was tal...ing the other day to a West Hartlepool woman whose husband is one of four brothers called Zachariah. Ishmael, Shadrach and Isaiah. I am glad my father was not of quite such a religious turn of mind.

Just average

HOW are your maths? Shaky as ever? Consider this one. Thrower and Spinner are the village cricket club's star bowlers and, before the concluding game of the season, both had the splendid average of 28 wickets for 60 runs.

In the final match, Thrower took four wickets for 36 runs and Spinner one for 27.

So Thrower has come out on top. But has he? Look at the final figures: Thrower, 32 wickets for 96, average 3.00; Spinner, 29 wickets for 87, average 3.00.

Any questions?

8

9

4 ems saved on the leader column as vertical white space throughout the page.

The clash of heavy sans with Goudy was ended by standardising on Goudy (except for the editorials) and the Goudy was given a chance to show what it could do by generous whiting. Again no new type was bought and all the changes were made with the maximum size of Goudy at 36pt.

The theatres were pulled down-page and grouped below the editorial. The Country Diary could be moved out of the leader column when editorials were exceptionally long.

Home Page

The women's features had been assigned a regular six columns which were laid out (8) without reference to the advertising on the page. The result was that when advertising did not fill the remainder it was open for news. The confusion is obvious. The mix of Goudy, Bodoni and Tempo for headlines, varying from day to day, compounded it. Given the shortage of display faces, Bodoni Modern (9) was chosen as the basic headline type (to distinguish it from the news page Bodoni Bold). A further attempt was made to identify the page by the use of a Home Page logotype. Again, the picture treatment was big, bold and simple. More white was introduced around the headlines, and the text setting was indented a nut on the left; at the old measure, without column rules, the text type from one column ran too close to the next for visual comfort.

Two other new pages were introduced on Saturdays: the Entertainments Guide and the Country Page.

News Focus

The news pages of the redesigned *Northern Echo* stayed within an eight-column format, accepting the traditional treatment of news and features. There were occasions, however, when this seemed a strait-jacket and the editorial impulse led to an experiment in design which is illustrated here as another example of function determining form (**11**).

The problem was this. There was, say, a complicated set of facts and arguments to relate about whether fluoride should be added to the water of twenty towns in the North-East of England. The paper had to tell the reader what the latest news was from each of the twenty towns, each making up its own mind. But in addition to giving the latest news we wanted to serve the readers with an impartial presentation of the arguments for and against fluoride so that they could themselves take a part in the debate. Finally we wanted to give our own view. The traditional solution would have been one long feature with headline and pictures, with the paper's own editorial comment on the leader page; a news story, separated from a background feature, in turn separated from editorial comment.

Given the complexity of the subject, the first traditional treatment offered an article too long and tangled for *Northern Echo* readership; and the second treatment fragmented a single subject. We therefore decided that all the facts and all the opinions, but each clearly differentiated, should be assembled on one page, clearly sub-divided into reasonable lengths, and that the paper's own editorial comment should appear with this material. Given these editorial ideas, their design expression begins to shape itself: the page begins to look the way it does because of the job the journalist is trying to do. The weight given to one side of the question must be seen to be similar to that for the other. Hence there must be similar headline display throughout.

Since the tone was one of dispassionate analysis, the headline treatment would also be restrained.

The page must begin with the latest news, to set the scene, and end with the paper's own conclusions. Bodoni Bold, the paper's news type, was retained for headlines because the material was related to current news; it was an attempt to put the news into focus (hence (**10**) the logotype News

Focus). Since all the material was related, the type was set indented and column rules left out. Each sub-section was set off with an overline label set left in 14pt Bodoni italic caps and an active news heading set left.

This was made a standard style so that the reader became familiar with the aims and methods of presentation.

Another example of the way design can

12　　　　　　**13**　　　　　　**14**

be used to serve an editorial concept is the treatment of the second escape from prison of a man convicted in the famous mail-train robbery. The news and background treatment were pulled together on a single page under an eight-column pica rule broken by the label 'The World's most astonishing crime serial.' An economical eight-column 'film-strip' of highlights of the robbery emphasised the unifying effect of the pica rule and evoked some of the original excitement of the story **(11)**.

Each sub-section of the serial was signalled with a 14pt Bodoni italic caps strapline: the first escape, the failure; the second escape; the story of the robbery; and a picture panel on the fates of all the other people implicated in the crime.

Sequence

The final act in redesigning *The Northern Echo* was to change the page sequence. The 'newsier' opening of the paper is shown in the 'before' **(12-17)** and 'after' **(18-23)**

18　　　　　　**19**　　　　　　**20**

15

16

17

sequences here. Such a reorganisation is elementary compared with the thought needed to make sense for the reader of multi-section newspapers such as the *Los Angeles Times,* and the *New York Times* and indeed most metropolitan American dailies. However, even the most elementary considerations of page sequence were widely neglected.

The paper opened not into news but into classified advertising. (When this fell short news was used as a filler in the classified.)

On the inside pages there was a jumble of international, national, and local news.

After the redesign the reader could be sure that the main inside pages were retained exclusively for regional news and pictures, except for a self-contained Parliamentary report. The TV programmes were moved from the middle of the newspaper to the *outer edge* of the foot of page two. Here the reader did not need to open up the whole newspaper but only make a half-fold of page one.

21

22

23

24   25   26

The Sunday Times Sports Pages

The Sunday Times sports pages of 1966 **(24-26)** served reasonably well, after the pattern of sports pages of most newspapers. They made the same assumptions and, within their class, the same appeal, so it was not surprising that the design solution was similar also. The basic difficulty was that there is no evidence for the fundamental assumption that the reader of the sports page is prepared to read all the content and is equally interested in all of it. Sports readers are, arguably, discriminating; and even the sports omnivore has priorities whose satisfaction requires clear signalling from the newspaper designer.

The result of the traditional assumptions is sports pages which are almost everywhere in the world a higgledy-piggledy mixture of different sports and in which the minor sports reports are treated as expendable filler paragraphs, popping up here, there, everywhere and sometimes nowhere (to the bewilderment of the minor-sports follower). These defects had been aggravated in the old *Sunday Times* by a decision at some stage to abandon column rules on some pages.

The page achieved a clean look but at the expense of failing to organise the content in even the most rudimentary fashion. In the illustrations of the old *Sunday Times* pages, the racing features, news and results tumble down the page out of control over seven columns, with no column rules, to mingle with cricket and tennis **(25)**; women's hockey is squashed under Old Boys' Rugby **(26)**; paragraphs on lacrosse, hockey, squash, and road walking pop up inconsequentially all over the place. Such signalling as there was (in Century Bold Extended cap overlines) was neither clear nor consistent.

The difficulties for the reader in the jumbled sports pages were obvious. Behind the simplicity of the various solutions found **(27-29)** lay a series of editorial decisions which set the route for the design solution. First the new design had to accommodate a decision to exploit the writing skill of the *Sunday Times* writers by giving more space to fewer reports and more emphasis to the Henry Longhurst column at the foot of the back page. Secondly, an attempt was needed to set all the main sport of the week and

27

28

29

especially Saturday in a context. This was assigned to a writer who was briefed to summarise and comment on the main sport —to set it all in perspective.

David Hillman's design solution to all this was to emphasise order by rules and rectangles. First, the sports summary column was stripped across the top of the back page above the main reports. Its shape and

THE FUNCTION OF NEWSPAPER DESIGN

colour provided a strong horizontal stress. Second, each main sports report was concentrated in a clearly distinguishable and self-contained shape, preferably a clear rectangle, with an economy in headline depth and spread. Each sport was signalled by a bold strip block of white on black: on that page all reports for that sport would be self-contained under this signal. The dif-

ferentiation of separate sports was further emphasised by reintroducing rules between sports, only this time decisive 2pt rules. This created uncompromisingly clear divisions for the reader. Fillers as such, of course, were forsworn. Fans of minor sports should not have to scour the columns for droppings. Minor sports paragraphs were grouped together in the same end-column position each week, each under its appropriate label: headlines here were considered wasteful and they were avoided as often as possible on reports of scheduled events where all the reader requires is a clear signal (a platform number rather than an itinerary).

The Sunday Times sports pages were prepared each week within this basic grid; but it was not rigid. When there was a major event requiring dramatic treatment it could still be arranged boldly and cleanly within the requirements of order and consistency. The World Cup page and the London *v.* Clay fight (**30**, **31**), are examples of flexibility.

2 How Design Developed

One of the reasons for the sterility of design in many areas of printing in the later 19th and early 20th centuries was the strength of the book tradition. —MICHAEL TWYMAN

The change in the appearance of newspapers over the last 100 years or so tells us a great deal about the changes in society—the convulsive effects of war are apparent in the convulsions of newspaper design. Newspaper display also reflects the changes in taxes, tastes, invention, and the advent of broadcasting, as well as the increasing part the newspaper began to play in everyday life. There are many lessons in the contrast between (1) the *Herald Tribune* of 1963 and (2) *The Morning Chronicle* of 1847. It is worth going through the files of any newspaper, and there are three major books for browsing.[1, 2, 3]

The Tyranny of Column Rules

The historical insights we gain are a bonus for journalist–designers because there is so much to learn from the files about how newspaper design can respond to the news and how it is influenced by custom and technology. Type-revolving presses used in the 1840s and 1850s, for instance, required type to be locked into the formes by wedge-shaped column rules. For the type to stay in place column rules had to run from the top of the forme to the bottom and so headlines running across more than one column were impossible. The rotary press and the curved stereotype plate made horizontal layout feasible[4], but vertical layout persisted.

The newspaper files reveal how improvements can cross national frontiers, while for a time worthwhile new ideas are held back by domestic barriers of competitive jealousy and snobbery; how innovations develop into tendencies and tendencies into conventions; and how what is frequently thought to be sanctified by tradition has

comparatively shallow roots.

Newspapers at the beginning of the nineteenth century made no effort, in their vertical display, to put a headline over the main story or to make sure that the main story began at the top of a page. Early American and Canadian colonial newspapers (such as Quebec's *Morning Chronicle* of 1847) were copies of English papers but, with the war against Mexico and the gold rush, American display began to respond with bigger headlines and more of them—single-column, of course. The American Civil War was a new stimulus, especially to illustration (but *see* Book Four) and big news began to be head-

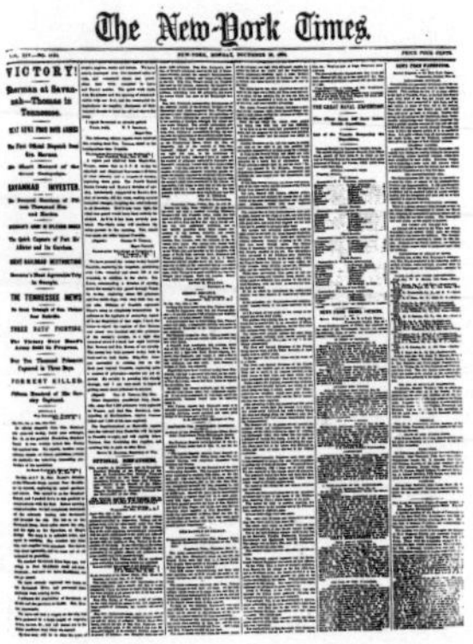
The New-York Times.

VICTORY!

3

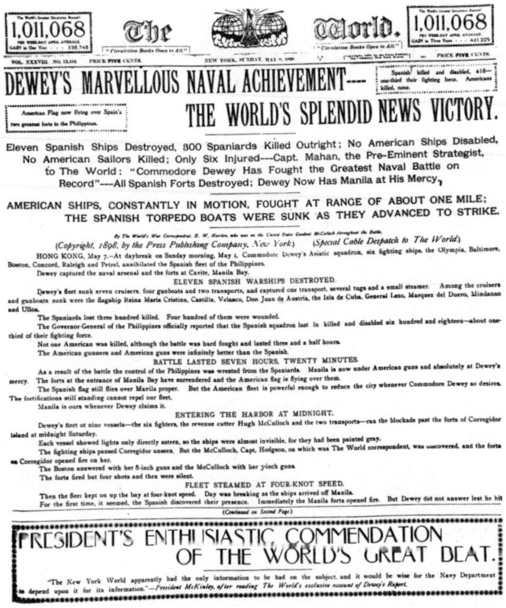
1,011,068

The World.

1,011,068

DEWEY'S MARVELLOUS NAVAL ACHIEVEMENT---
THE WORLD'S SPLENDID NEWS VICTORY.

American Flag now flying over Spain's two greatest forts in the Philippines.

Spaniards killed and disabled, 618—one-third their fighting force. Americans killed, none.

Eleven Spanish Ships Destroyed, 300 Spaniards Killed Outright; No American Ships Disabled, No American Sailors Killed; Only Six Injured---Capt. Mahan, the Pre-Eminent Strategist, to The World: "Commodore Dewey Has Fought the Greatest Naval Battle on Record"---All Spanish Forts Destroyed; Dewey Now Has Manila at His Mercy.

AMERICAN SHIPS, CONSTANTLY IN MOTION, FOUGHT AT RANGE OF ABOUT ONE MILE; THE SPANISH TORPEDO BOATS WERE SUNK AS THEY ADVANCED TO STRIKE.

(Copyright, 1898, by the Press Publishing Company, New York.) (Special Cable Despatch to The World.)

ELEVEN SPANISH WARSHIPS DESTROYED.

BATTLE LASTED SEVEN HOURS, TWENTY MINUTES.

ENTERING THE HARBOR AT MIDNIGHT.

FLEET STEAMED AT FOUR-KNOT SPEED.

(Continued on Second Page.)

PRESIDENT'S ENTHUSIASTIC COMMENDATION OF THE WORLD'S GREAT BEAT.

4

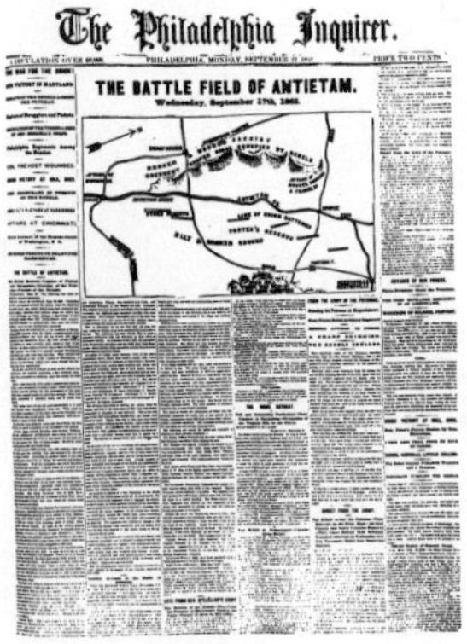
The Philadelphia Inquirer.

THE BATTLE FIELD OF ANTIETAM.

Wednesday, September 17th, 1862.

5

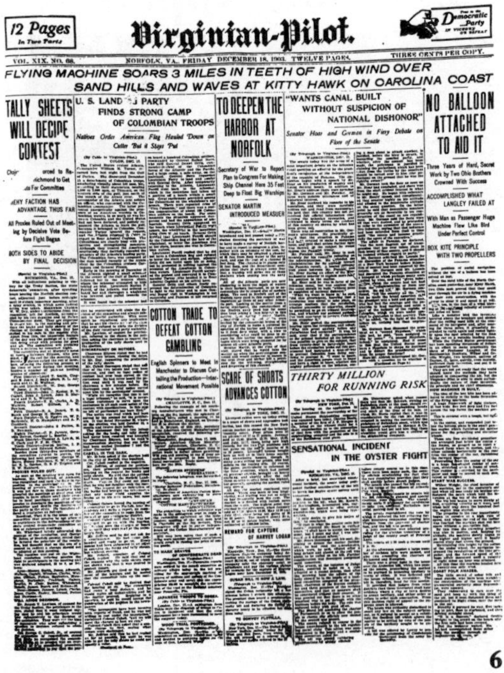
12 Pages In Two Parts

Virginian-Pilot.

FLYING MACHINE SOARS 3 MILES IN TEETH OF HIGH WIND OVER SAND HILLS AND WAVES AT KITTY HAWK ON CAROLINA COAST

TALLY SHEETS WILL DECIDE CONTEST

U. S. LAND PARTY FINDS STRONG CAMP OF COLOMBIAN TROOPS

TO DEEPEN THE HARBOR AT NORFOLK

"WANTS CANAL BUILT WITHOUT SUSPICION OF NATIONAL DISHONOR"

NO BALLOON ATTACHED TO AID IT

COTTON TRADE TO DEFEAT COTTON GAMBLING

SCARE OF SHORTS ADVANCES COTTON

THIRTY MILLION FOR RUNNING RISK

SENSATIONAL INCIDENT IN THE OYSTER FIGHT

6

lined in ten or more decks of single-column headings, beginning in column one.

Horizontal Headlines

The *New York Times* **(3)** of December 19, 1864, announced Sherman's capture of Savannah in fifteen decks. Efforts were now beginning to be made to place stories on the page in some kind of order of importance. The *Philadelphia Inquirer* front page **(5)** of September 22, 1862, is notable for having five major displays, and the main heading is one of the first horizontal headlines. The circulation war between William Randolph Hearst's *New York Journal* and Joseph Pulitzer's *The World* coincided with the Spanish-American war and produced upheavals in display. Dewey's victory at Manila was announced in *The World* on May 8, 1898, in a page **(4)** still astonishing by any standards—two decks of banner heading, two more decks of headline spread across the page, and then large text-type and headline spread across the whole page and running its full depth. The horizontal revolution had arrived, and it was taken up around the world, so that by 1903 a non-metropolitan paper like the *Virginian-Pilot* was making full use of the page for multiple display **(6).**

In the next ten years the main advance was in the development of stronger display types, accompanied by a preference for symmetrical layouts: **(8, 9)** the *San Francisco Chronicle* of November, 1916, and the *Daily Chronicle* of London of May 14, 1915, mark the trend. The foundations of modern broadsheet display are apparent. The next revolution was the arrival of the tabloid picture paper, of which **(7)** the pioneering *Daily Sketch* of London is a good example in display (and incidentally in war hysteria).

American newspapers, both morning and evening, developed boldness much earlier than British newspapers. There had been no horizontal double-column headline in any London morning newspaper until 1901. The *Evening News* had presented a streamer in 1895, but English development

was held back by a feeling that morning newspapers should look like *The Times* and for long *The Times* was in the design doldrums. It was not until the late 1930s that the influence of broadsheet design began to drift the other way across the Atlantic, with the London *Daily Express* being admired and copied as it was later in France.

In the following section we complete the story with a glance at the changes in the last fifty years in the English *Daily Express*, *The Times*, the *Daily Mirror*, and in two American newspapers, the *Washington Post* and *New York Daily News*.

1908

1918

1928

1938

The Washington Post

1908: The *Washington Post's* eight-column banner in 72pt caps backed by subsidiary double-column headlines and text was years ahead of the 36pt banners of the *Daily Express* in London, revolutionary by British standards then. The other *Post* headlines, all verbally active, are vertical and notably well whited in up to six decks. The sixth deck is a masterpiece of verbosity (fifty-five words in the New York story). The headlines are in classical American 'narrative' style, attempting to sum up all the points of a story and not only the main theme. Perhaps the most noticeable feature of this 1908 page, by American standards, is that the lead story is run down the left-hand columns.

1918: The lead has moved to the right; and has stayed there ever since. The banner has developed into two lines, stepped, in Cheltenham. At this time even three-line banners had appeared in America (for the fall of Petrograd to the Russian Bolsheviks in 1917 the *New York Times* had a three-line banner supported, in a purely symmetrical page, by three single-column tops each with no fewer than six matching decks). In this 1918 *Post* there has been little advance in text typography. The paper is in eight 12½-em columns, well broken by sub-heads, and distinguished by bold double-column setting—especially in columns 7 and 8 here—which helps in the absence of illustrations.

1928: The stepped banner is in Century Bold and the single-column headlines have been standardised on the sans with fewer decks and tighter wording. A new feature is a weakly headed column of brief comments in column 1. The text type is clearer but the column has begun a process of shrinking; it is 12 ems now.

1938: The headline dress is standardised on Bodoni Bold upper- and lower-case with the top deck set left and the second set right. The second 'decks' here are really a development of the narrative style of headline—each line tells a separate point of the story. In column 1, for instance, the lines say:

General 64 Retires
Fears Dictatorship
Sees 'Sinister Motive'
Army Regrets Words

Some attempt has been made to match single-column headlines but there is nothing to compare with the rigorous symmetry of the *New York Times* of this period, and there is a horizontal headline below the fold. The 60pt streamer is unusual. It is centred, not stepped, and has a second deck in contrasting italic.

1948

1948: The streamer has reverted to decks of stepped roman lines, in wordy 48pt. Bodoni Bold remains as the dress but decks have virtually disappeared, remaining only on the tops. The second decks are now self-contained headlines. The bottom of the page has come to be supported by three groups of double-column display headlines of identical size and treatment, 24pt set left with Bodoni Black kickers (or overlines).

1958

1958: The biggest change is the column width—down to a mere 10 ems. The stepped streamer is up in size to a less verbose 60pt and better organised and there has been an increase in horizontal display, with even an introduction set across two columns leading to single-column.

The Washington Post

Times Herald

92d Year — No. 23   SATURDAY, DECEMBER 28, 1968   Phone 223-6000   10c

Apollo 8 Lands Safely in Pacific After Epic Flight Around Moon

Jubilant astronauts gather on deck of the Yorktown at close of historic mission to the moon. From left, Borman, Lovell, Anders.

Fiery Re-entry, Splashdown Are on Target

By Thomas O'Toole
Washington Post Staff Writer

HOUSTON, Dec. 27—The explorers of Apollo 8 took their places in history alongside Columbus and Magellan today, when they landed their spacecraft in the South Pacific three days after completing man's first flight around the moon.

Living Costs Rise; Buying Power Off

By William Greider
Washington Post Staff Writer

U.S. Lists 6 As Plotters With Spock

By John P. MacKenzie
Washington Post Staff Writer

World Heaps Praise on Apollo

19 Die of Flu In City Home For Elderly

By Carl Bernstein
Washington Post Staff Writer

China Sets Off Bomb No. 8

U.S. Sells Jets to Israel; Delivery Is Speeded Up

By Warren Unna

Navy frogmen stand by the unmanned Apollo capsule as the carrier approaches to pick it up.

Apollo 8 Crew Likely to Become First to Land on Moon

1968

1968: The column width has widened somewhat to 10½ ems but most of the page is made up without rules to link text on the Apollo story. The Bodoni Bold streamer is up to 84pt but headline treatment has been still further simplified: two of the horizontal headlines are single lines without kickers. Pictures are generously treated, a space requirement which has meant turns to other pages for all but one story on the page. The layout is now asymmetrical.

1908

1918

Daily Express

1908: The *Daily Express and Morning Herald* had been the first English daily with front-page news in 1901 and the first with a double-column horizontal headline. The eight-column front page of 1908 was greyer for the loss of De Vinne bold heads but remarkable journalistically for the column-1 summary of the rest of the news inside the paper. None of the other morning papers of the time approached the *Express* in American-inspired daring.

1918: The *Express* had borrowed the American streamer—in 36pt De Vinne and ruled off from its text—and also the style of heads alternately in bold and light. The streamer's wording is notably active. The page is now narrower, in seven columns, instead of eight, and the column-1 news summary has gone. But there is a campaigning panel (The Censorship—Abolish it).

1928

1938

1928: The streamer, in caps now, has been given more air, if less weight, and Cheltenham has given way to Bodoni Bold for the main decks. If the words did not fit the headline pattern then the *Express* might set part of the head a lower size (column 4, Diplomatic Storm Over Driver). But the most striking change is the use of illustration.

1938: In the middle of the design revolution by Arthur Christiansen (Editor 1933–57) which began to be copied round the world; an effort is being made to project the news dramatically all over the page, but by a simplified heading style. The main head is a modified two-decker, but otherwise decks have vanished in favour of active multi-line heads set horizontally, many in lower-case and all without full points. Century Bold has been introduced but not yet standardised (it is mixed with Bodoni Bold—*see* Helen Wills Moody, column 3).

1948: The classical *Express* banner in Century Bold Extended with the text in column 1. The page is standardised on Century, Cooper Black in the picture bonnet and Bodoni italic as the only headline variant, and is back to eight narrower columns. Pictures have begun to be properly exploited.

1958: A most striking return to an economical vertical layout. Apart from the banner there is only one horizontal head on the page and that in 18pt at the foot of the page. The typographical innovation is the use of Gothic Medium Condensed in column 5 to give kick to a single-column position—the famous sans kicker.

1968: A simpler, cleaner page with a single banner without subsidiary decks or overlines and the lead brought boldly down the centre of the page in 10pt (compare 1958 with the lead still in column 1). The text is more legible with column white and the heads, too, are better whited.

1908

1918

Daily Mirror

1908: Founded in 1903 as 'The First Daily Newspaper for Gentlewomen' the tabloid *Mirror* was the first newspaper to exploit half-tone blocks. It gave its front page to news pictures, usually on the same theme, but the 1908 inside display was traditional. There were four 15-em columns, with dignified single-column heads in decks.

1918: The front page had not changed its style in ten years but the *Mirror* was exploiting the centre spread for picture features. Apart from the pictures of women candidates, the other pictures are unrelated.

1928: The inside page is still broad gauge, but a horizontal streamer has appeared. All the other heads are in Clearface Bold (first produced in 1907 by American Type-founders, a spotty face all the more noticeable for the profusion of decks even on down-page fillers).

1938: The basis of the modern *Daily Mirror*, laid by Harry G Bartholomew, editorial director from 1934, with the help of an American advertising agency. The Bartholomew revolution was to direct the paper at a new audience, the lower and working classes, with smaller articles, bigger headlines and more pictures. The

tabloid revolution started by the *New York Daily News* had been slow to reach England. The *Mirror* is still in four columns though the text is clearer, but the restrained composite picture display on page one has been replaced by insistent heads in 72pt Gothic Condensed with Ludlow Tempo Medium and Cooper Black. The old banner title has been replaced by a small box title leaving the top of the page open for news display.

1948: The typical 9-em tabloid column in a 7-column *Mirror*; it whispers by comparison with 1938. The front page has been squeezed, boiled and squeezed again to cram in news during newsprint rationing. The title letter has been given more strength.

1955: After newsprint rationing the *Mirror* reverted to more open design with one, two, or three stories boldly projected on the front with a large picture. This was conventional tabloid technique. The real innovations of the Fifties and Sixties were developments by Hugh Cudlipp which took campaigning journalism into a new dimension. Pungent advice to princesses, primates and prime ministers is expressed in steam-hammer blows of poster-size Gothic and reverse blocks. In the best examples the metal perfectly catches the mood of the message. Directness of language is expressed in directness of

design: no verbal equivocation, no gilded serif, no clutter of words, no proliferation of display type. The philosophy is to say one thing and say it loud. It is not all exhort-ation. The same technique is used to explain the balance of payments. In one 1956 issue the *Mirror* departed from its customary simplicity. For dramatic effect it printed its tabloid front and back pages sideways to form one horizontal flash, in an attempt to make people sit up and notice its warning that the Prime Minister, Anthony Eden, was preparing for war at Suez. The year before, the *Mirror* got into hot water for using its front page as a poster for a view on Princess Margaret's possible marriage: Come on Margaret! Please make up Your Mind!

1960: A front page is used as a rude retort to the Russian Prime Minister Khruschev who had been visiting Britain. Similar blasts against Britain's own politicians, whether of Right or Left (both Mr Macmillan and Mr Wilson suffered in their turn) appear on the front or front and back and in the double spread at the centre. As the *Mirror's* readership has grown more educated, so have the *Mirror* blasts become more sophisticated.

1968: This blast, the one against Mr Wilson, was one of the reasons for the fall of its author, Mr Cecil King, then chairman of the Mirror group.

1928

July 14, 1928   THE DAILY MIRROR   Page 3

MISS SAVIDGE "NOT COERCED"—MAJORITY FINDING

The Police Vindicated in Main Report, but Censured by Mr. Lees-Smith

GIRL'S STORY REJECTED BY TWO MEMBERS

"Childlike but Acute" Witness—Minority Belief That Public Rights are Imperilled

ANSWERS BY GIRL "NOT MISCONSTRUED"

Majority Acquit Inspector of Any Improper Conduct

"NO DEMONSTRATION"

"THROUGH HER PARENTS"

MASTERS AS PARENTS

DANCE EPISODE CONTROVERSY

Lady Denman Explains Daughter's Presence

DINNER GUESTS

Party Who Went on to Lady Ellesmere's Ball

HEAT WAVE TO LAST FOR THE WEEK-END

Dear Anti Cyclone's Happy Weather Premise

M.P. RIVALS THE GIRLS

SIR LEO SILENT

SEASIDE RUSH

Motor-Coaches in Bathing Costume—Huntington Girls

EXPRESS DERAILED

Child Killed and Eleven Passengers Hurt in France Accident

COTTAGE FIRE SEQUEL

Mother and Son Account of Burning While Daughter and Grandchildren Slept

NEWS ITEMS FROM ABROAD

1938

Daily Mirror

FAMILY BIBLE AS WITNESS

FOR GIRL BRIDE

ALL THE BEST FOR 1939!

CAR KILLS SOCIETY WIFE

Offered to Bring Bible

Grab-No Oil

Strip Tease Stops Panic

BEATEN NAZI CHIEF HAS "RELAPSE"

VANISHED ARMY OFFICER SACKED

1948

Daily Mirror

FORWARD WITH THE PEOPLE

THESE TWO HAD EVERYTHING—BUT HAPPINESS

TITO DUBS STALIN LIAR—'DISGUSTED BY YOUR INSULTS'

Quads fund flops, only £10 in 9 days

"Loton Honey" the Premier called it

Hear Hear

DOCKERS BACK TODAY —GOVT. WON'T USE ITS CRISIS POWERS

BRITAIN MOVES TO SAFEGUARD TRADE AGAINST JAPAN

Coal exports beat target

Sacred chalice is seized by Customs

NO PAY INCREASE —UNION BARS OVERTIME

BOY MISSING FROM SCHOOL

"Drene leaves my hair shining with glamour"

drene

Daily Mirror

FRI. AUG. 19 1955

1½ FORWARD WITH THE PEOPLE

No. 16,077

- The Princess is 25 on Sunday.
- Will she wed? When will she announce her decision?

COME ON MARGARET!

FOR two years the world has buzzed with this question:

Will Princess Margaret marry 40-year-old Group Captain Peter Townsend?—OR Won't she?

Five months ago, Group Captain Townsend told the Daily Mirror: '. . . the word cannot come from me. You will appreciate it must come from other people . . .'

On Sunday the Princess will be 25. She could then, if she wished, notify Parliament direct of her desire to marry without first seeking the consent of her sister the Queen.

She could end the hubbub.

Will she please make up her mind?

Your favourite centre!

14 milk chocolate caramels! 6d

CARAMETS

NOW ON SALE EVERYWHERE

Please make up your mind!

Daily Mirror

Tuesday, May 17, 1960

No. 17,547

Mr. K!

(If you will pardon an olde English phrase)

DON'T BE SO BLOODY RUDE!

PS

Who do you think you are? STALIN?

1960

Daily Mirror

Friday, May 10, 1968

No. 20,022

ENOUGH IS ENOUGH

By Cecil H. King

Chairman of the International Publishing Corporation

DISASTER AT THE POLLS FOR LABOUR

THE results of the local elections are fully confirming the verdicts of the opinion polls and of the Dudley by-election.

Mr. Wilson and his Government have lost all credibility: all authority.

The Government which was voted into office with so much goodwill only three and a half years ago has revealed itself as lacking in foresight, in administrative ability, in political sensitivity, and in integrity. Mr. Wilson is seen to be a brilliant Parliamentary tactician and nothing more.

DECLINE

If these disastrous years only marked the decline of Mr Wilson and the Labour Party the damage to our political self-confidence would be serious enough, but the Labour Party came into power with such high

CECIL H. KING, Chairman of the International Publishing Corporation. The Corporation publishes the Daily Mirror, the Sun, The People and the Daily Record and Sunday Mail in Scotland.

The Tories storm to victory in thirty towns

—SEE BACK PAGE

Continued on Page Three

Illustrated Daily News

GERMANS BLOCK SIGNING OF TREATY

Newport to Entertain Prince of Wales in August

1919

New York Daily News

The *New York Daily News*—'New York's Picture Newspaper'—set the pattern for American tabloids. Its design history can be studied alongside the London *Daily Mirror's*. The style of the 1919 front page is similar to the *Mirror's*, but while the *Mirror* has developed a front page of headline, text and pictures, the *Daily News*—followed by other American tabloids—went for a poster front page and has demonstrated the versatility of this form. On big days the whole front page, as in the 1941 example, is entirely given up to a news flash, in big Gothic black headlines or full-page picture. The January 14, 1928, edition sold an extra million copies with a sensational full-page picture of a woman being electrocuted ('this most remarkable exclusive picture shows close up of Ruth Snyder in death chair at Sing Sing as lethal current surged through her body at 11 : 06 Thursday night'). The page on the moon landing in July, 1969, speaks for itself. There is an intermediate standard of display where the page, though given to a single story, is shared between main headline, subsidiary headline and photograph (Kennedy's assassination and Stalin's death). And there is a cooler poster style where (*see* 1962 and 1966) the poster page may announce separate news items in headlines and pictures.

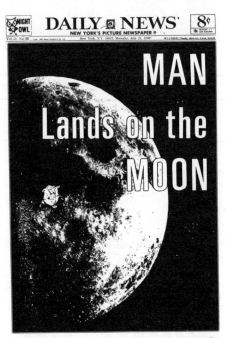

1969

JAPAN AT WAR WITH U.S.

Hawaii, Philippines Bombed; 104 Killed

CONGRESS TO ACT

1941

DEATH, TRIUMPH & A BUS STRIKE

1962

LBJ TO KREMLIN: Y'ALL COME

Gallashaw Found Not Guilty

1966

The Times   **1908**   **1918**   **1928**

1908: This left-hand centre page (later the main news or Bill Page) shows *The Times* of Northcliffe at a standstill in design, differing very little from *The Times* of 1850. The headline type is indistinguishable from text type; there are no cross-headings; and nearly four of the six columns are advertising (the front page of course was wholly advertising).

1918: The excitement of the war produced many more headlines and headlines in decks proliferated from a double-deck in 1910—one story attracted eight decks in 1915. But the headlines were always labels and never across more than one column in a mixture of faces (Caslon, Bodoni, Cheltenham Bold Condensed and others). This centre page has now become the main news page facing the leader page. There are cross-headings and reverse indent setting in 9pt for the text of the lead. Half-tone blocks had begun to appear in 1914.

1928: The entire paper except the leader page had gone to seven columns at 14 ems from 1921. The headline fount is now an exaggerated 'modern' face. The layout style is still tombstoning: a line-up of cap headings in single columns with no strength below the fold, but the heads are better whited and there has been some attempt at balancing the changes in style at the top. By the end of 1923 the alternating of columns with light and heavy headings had become a regular practice. Perhaps more importantly by 1929 *The Times* had stabilised its most important features in placing and in typographical display. It had taken ten years to do this and Stanley Morison's view[5] was that without the revisions of 1909–22 *The Times* would appear to the present generation as an enlarged parish magazine: 'Because *The Times* is read, re-read and consulted time and time again, the constituent articles must possess a consistency of treatment of placing which will automatically assist the reader to make rapid references.'

1938: After the 1932 redesign supervised by Stanley Morison. On October 3, 1932, *The Times* had been completely redressed. It had been given Times New Roman text types by the Monotype Corporation ranging from 5½pt to 9pt and six designs of headlines, based on the same new face, light, heavy and extra, all in narrow and wide dimensions and all in a range which ran, in some cases, from 7pt to 48pt. The headlines were in every case heavier versions of the capitals belonging to the new text founts. 'Thus the whole range of founts, text and headline, used on October 3, 1932, bears a family likeness which guarantees harmony but, owing to the variation in width and weight, avoids monotony.'[6]

The bold provides a striking but dignified colour contrast with the text. Tombstoning survives, with text type turning to the top of a column, but as Morison intended the blackness of Times Bold at the bottom of the page helped the reader select what he wanted to read. The heads at the top are still not quite successfully balanced against each other. There had also been a revolution on the front page: a roman caps title replaced the Gothic after furious arguments among *The Times* staff.

1938

1948

1948: In 1932 Stanley Morison said 'If ever *The Times* accepts double-column headings, it will not be because they are necessary but because a generation of readers has been habituated to them by reading journals less scrupulously conducted.' Readers had been offered much more daring innovations elsewhere. There was little change between 1948 and 1958. The top of this 1948 page is finely balanced, the heads in columns 3 and 5 pivoting on the bold head in column 4. Times New Roman 327 (the original light face of this extensive range) is used as relief in column 7.

1966

THE TIMES

SAVUNDRA ARRESTED AT HOME
In court on two charges today

China accused by Mr. Kosygin
Aggravated relations 'are no fault of Russia's'

TROOPS OUT IN ADEN RIOTS
General curfew ordered

PRISONERS REVOLT IN SECURITY BLOCK
Durham cells barricaded

Walkout stops production at Vauxhalls

Gypsy's share in Roberts cash reward

Mr. Brown for Moscow in May

1967–8

THE TIMES

BIG GUERRILLA THREAT IN SOUTH AMERICA
Strongly fortified Castro-type base in jungle

Rail bonus dispute gets amber light
Settlement basis agreed

Taxi protest stops the traffic

MR BROWN KEEPS ADEN SECRETS
Farce in emergency debate

New shots in Riots

Inter-cities helicopter project

Move to end U.S. radio strike

April bonus

Wednesday October 7 1970
No. 57,990 Ninepence

THE TIMES

Tory Strategy for a Century, page 8

Strike pickets clash with public as some councils try for local settlements

Pickets clashed with people trying to dump rubbish at a council tip at Newport, Monmouthshire, and a picket was injured. Mr Maurice Gaffney, chairman of the G.L.C. Public Services Committee, said that 2,000 to 3,000 volunteers came forward by the weekend to man sewage pumping stations, strikers could be told to " get lost ".

Nearly all London's ambulancemen

begin a series of 24-hour strikes today in which the use of ambulance cabs will be restricted and administrative work halted. Local shop stewards will decide on emergency coverage.

As the council workers' strike entered its eighth day yesterday, London hospitals faced the prospect of a 24-hour token stoppage on Monday by several hundred Health Service manual workers.

Walkout threat at hospitals

Striking workers outside County Hall, London, yesterday protesting in support of their pay claim.

Life sentences for Hosein brothers

By Clive Borrell

Government will face strong pressure to end Rhodesia sanctions

From David Wood
Blackpool, Oct. 6.

Canada refuses to ransom British diplomat

From Our Own Correspondent
Ottawa, Oct. 6.

Cathedral statue must go

Mr Maurer hurt in car crash
Vienna, Oct. 6.

US call for jets from Britain

Washington, Oct. 6.

Talks on Concorde's future

By Arthur Reed
Air Correspondent

Air Force bombs palace in Bolivia double coup

La Paz, Bolivia, Oct. 6.

Grenades found at BOAC air terminal

Bishop Huddleston may leave public life

King Faisal

The rest of the news

Discover how the fastest, easiest way to learn a new language is the way you learned your own.

Send for this FREE record.

Linguaphone for languages.

1966: News on the front page at last. The double-column style for the lead story has been carried forward from the Bill Page—but now it is in lower-case. So are several other headlines. *The Times* moved to lower-case for the main headings, abandoning the splendid Titling caps, following the report by Christopher Poulton (*see* Book Two) on the greater legibility of lower-case. There is another horizontal headline. The vertical *Times* has gone for good.

1967–8: After the merger with *The Sunday Times*. The columns have been increased from seven at $13\frac{1}{2}$ picas to eight at $11\frac{1}{2}$ picas. The lead has been strengthened into three columns and for this position Titling caps (332 rather than 328) have been restored, providing unambiguous emphasis. There are introductions set across two columns, creating a display position in the shoulder. The headline style then was still a mixture of all caps and upper- and lower-case, but in 1968 lower-case became standard, and the sizes were increased on main stories: 60pt made its appearance. The 9pt text type was extended from page one to inside (another Poulton recommendation).

1970: The fourth main change since front-page news in 1966. *The Times* moved to a wholly modular layout of horizontal stress and dramatically deflated the size and range of headlines. News headlines were standardised on Bold 334 u/lc and contrast was obtained by juxtaposition of sizes. But the range of sizes was limited at 14 to 36pt. At the same time the inside text type was reduced from 9pt to 8pt. (Incidentally, advertising/editorial quotes became tighter too, when the *Business News* section was later brought into the main paper.) The deflation of displays was a courageous move when competing newspapers such as *The Guardian* were blowing up headline sizes. It has its critics, and its difficulties—notably in the fragility of 8pt Times Roman, in the loss of picture display, and in the wordiness of 334. The British trade journal *Press Gazette* carried a cartoon of a sub-editor interrupting a reporter: 'Could you possibly let me have a few more facts? I've run out of words for the headline'. It is easier to write a sensible narrative headline, provided nobody is worried about lines ending with a preposition, and fitting for a serious paper to have headlines that mean something; but the wider headlines produce so many letters that the headline is delayed in its appeal and impact on the mind. The compensation for all this was an increase for *The Times* of about 10,000 words in

editorial space, and despite misgivings the modular layout proved easy to arrange and sub-divide **(11)**. The designer, Jeanette Collins, insisted on a horizontal stress. 'Because there is only one headline type-face the necessary contrast will be obtained by juxtaposition of sizes. It is very important for this reason and also to achieve a strong layout to group horizontally two or more headlines. To be avoided is the make up that looks like an upturned brick wall.'[7]

The Times Business News, first printed as a separate section, had already moved to lower-case **(10)**. As Allen Hutt has noted, the lower-case style can present problems in a horizontal layout. Caps were the only conceivable style in 1931 when the type was designed, and the condensed lower-case, blown up from the original Times Roman text and its duplexed bold, gives a letter count so generous as to produce wordiness at multi-column lengths.

The *Business News* headlines alternated attractively between the black Times Bold 334 and the light Times Roman 327. The Women's Page, introduced in 1966, immediately broke away from *Times* and indeed newspaper conventions **(12)**.

3 The Context Today

That we may not omit any Material Part of our Intelligence etc. for the future, or lessen the Use and Value of our Paper in the Opinion of ANY of our Readers, we shall, whenever press'd for Room, print the same, as at present, on larger Paper, in four columns, without raising the Price to the Public, notwithstanding the extraordinary Expense to ourselves.
—The *Daily Journal*, January 19, 1728

The editor or printer of the *Daily Journal* was an original theorist of newspaper design and something of a pioneer. This was probably the first newspaper venture into four columns. He responded as a designer should do to consumer reaction, and the paper returned permanently to three columns after a few weeks: 'the Method of Four Columns, in which we have of late been often obliged to print this paper,' had been found 'inconvenient by many of our Readers.'

It is rare to find the design assumptions of the early newspaper stated like this. Many of the design practices were carried into newspaper printing from craftsmen accustomed to book printing. Design practices of the successful newspapers set the style for others: the position of the leading article in the middle of the English-language daily derives from imitation of the *Morning Chronicle* of 1770. The *Chronicle* sold as much of its front page as it could, then followed it with the foreign mails, and thirdly London Intelligence, where announcements by the paper were made.[1]

The Growth of Advertising

The growth of advertising precipitated this comment to the centre of the newspaper. Of course, there is a certain prudence in plagiarising the style of the successful, but the style which suits one may inhibit another; and then, as now, tradition was invoked to justify what was only a temporary fashion.

The earliest newspapers had news on the front page, and it was only gradually displaced as the column-one advertisement grew. Yet when Chester Ives, formerly of the *New York Herald Tribune*, founded *The Morning* in London in 1892 with front-page news, it was regarded as un-English and his successors restored front-page advertising which alone, they maintained, made it look like a morning newspaper instead of a vulgar evening.[2] Mr Kennedy Jones, who introduced a full-page banner headline to the London *Evening News* in 1895, thought it was only permissible in an evening newspaper: a morning paper must look like the successful *Times*.

The twentieth century has recognised a similar taboo. The most hideous blackletter titles survive around the world from Victorian days because they are 'traditional,' but in fact the earliest titles, such as those of the first daily paper, *The Daily Courant* (1702), and the first evening, *The Evening Post* (1710), and America's *New England Courant* (1721) were all in good bold roman lower-case. And for many years newspapers priding themselves on being serious or quality have shunned sans-serif display type, tabloid formats, large half-tones, and white-on-black headings as being the work of demon sensationalists. Of course these latter developments were first exploited by sensational newspapers, but the modern designer's attitude should be that of the Salvationist when told that some hymns were based on the melodies of drinking songs: why should the Devil have all the best tunes?

It is not easy to rid one's mind of prejudice. An automatic acceptance of all that is new is no guide. In communication as in politics, a convention may enshrine the wisdom of the ages and a current fashion may be a mere artistic petulance. Our basic reading habits are not open to instant innovation. In the West we can comfortably read lines set from left to right in lower-case roman serif letters with the lines not going beyond a certain length and the type not falling below a certain size (*see* Book Two).

Arguably the newspaper designer need not follow the standards developed through centuries of experience as rigorously as the book designer, since newspaper text, editorial or advertising, is not intended for hours of continuous reading. But clearly there is a limit to what the newspaper designer may legitimately do with text setting: and what he does should be related to the practical problems of his own readers rather than to any fancies of his own.

Web offset printing, for instance, offers the chance for superbly printed text, but also for colour. Some of the conventional offset newspapers, but especially some of the underground papers, have seen this as a chance to present a new art form. The *Chicago Seed* will print text in green, brown, blue or purple on a porridge of psychedelic colours, and set 8pt text of this hue across an eyeball-stretching 40-odd picas. As a gesture of revolutionary defiance, it is fine; as a flash of colour on a grey landscape, it is defensible; for prose it is a non-starter. You cannot read the words.

Newspapers which want all their text to be read have to work to physical limitations. They have to contend with the fact that readers want text they can read in a hurry or in bad light or a moving vehicle, or that readers may not be as willing to chase continuations of text over many pages as they are in the different format of a magazine.

There is a whole series of such factors affecting newspaper design, beginning with the basic choice of format (and, for the moment, limiting that word to the shape and size of printed sheet).

1 Basic Choice of Format

The designer must be aware of the finite possibilities offered by the existing range of machinery and processing, but certain general principles can be explored.

On what area of paper should the messages of the multi-paged newspaper be printed and published? The largest page size ever used[3] has been 51 in. by 35 in. for *The Constellation*, printed by George Roberts as a Fourth of July celebration in New York City in 1895. The smallest recorded page size has been $3\frac{1}{2}$ in. by $4\frac{1}{2}$ in., by *El Telegramma* of Guadalajara, Spain.

But we can take the question further than saying that the physical size of the sheet should be somewhere between these extremes. A newspaper fulfils different functions from a poster or a book. Its purpose is to print a variety of disparate information for a multiplicity of individuals. On the assumption that advertising remains the commercial basis of the newspaper and that this is needed in volume, the newspaper must be able to offer space and prominence for advertising. It must be capable of being printed and distributed at speed in large quantities and with optimum economy. It must be easy for the average reader to handle, so that both the news and advertising messages may be seen by a large number of readers.

These criteria set limits for the theoretical size of the sheet, leaving aside the question of machinery. A newspaper might be able to print a variety of information on two sides of a 51 × 35 in. sheet, but it would be exceedingly awkward to hold and even to read pinned up. It is more than four times the size of the modern broadsheet. Experience suggests that the convenient size of sheet is considerably smaller than this, and much smaller also than the largest page size printed in the Sixties, the weekly *Nantucket Inquirer and Mirror's* 30 × 22 in. sheet. (How that compares with three familiar papers is seen in the comparative picture **(1)** at the start of this chapter.)

Indeed, confining ourselves to the simple fact of the muscular comfort of the reader, the ideal sheet would clearly be much nearer to the book than to the large poster. The larger broadsheet papers, such as, say, the $22\frac{1}{2} \times 18\frac{1}{2}$ in. *Cape Argus* of South Africa can be tiring to hold (remember that the $18\frac{1}{2}$ in. wide page is 37 in. opened out); and these papers are difficult to manipulate in a crowd without provoking a breach of the peace. But, of course, physical comfort for holding is only one factor. A newspaper on the format of a small paperback book would be physically convenient to hold, but it would not yield its information as quickly or economically. It would begin with greater unit costs. Additional page margins would consume more paper; a news paperback of any size would require some elementary binding.

The journalistic difficulties are more serious still. The paperback format would be unable to exploit picture journalism in an age when visual journalism from television is challenging newspapers. It would be unable to offer instant assessment of news priorities by page display. In so far as it was able to guide the reader through its volume by a full index it would be consuming additional raw material and time, thus adding to its basic diseconomies.

And its display advertising potential is as restricted as its journalistic display potential. Some of these objections still apply if the paperback format is increased to a more realistic size, such as the news magazine size of $10\frac{1}{2} \times 8$ in. (*Newsweek*), or 12 × 9 in. (*The Economist*) where fifty pages or more are stapled together. Many columns of classified advertising (on which papers have come to depend and readers to expect) would produce a news magazine of unacceptable bulk;

turning over scores and scores of pages would easily become an irritation. The journalistic limitations of a news magazine remain in the limits on display and the use of a bigger page to express priorities.

But there is one fundamental to keep in mind: the purpose of the newspaper. That can change. If daily newspapers retreat from communicating instant news of a series of disconnected events, because they are beaten to this by broadcasting, and if instead they concentrate more on treating selected news in depth, then the news-display limitations of the smaller format will disappear. It is possible to envisage a daily news magazine whose content is fashioned in part to satisfy the interest aroused by the day's television and radio programmes of all kinds. It would have a section of news summary, and its own news exclusives, but its emphasis would be on news analysis and features with colour and diagrams.

Tabloid versus Broadsheet

Grading upwards from the news magazine we come to a range of more feasible sizes for the newspaper as we understand it. These I propose to discuss under the term tabloid, meaning a size of sheet and not a style of content. There are no precise dimensions for a tabloid; the size depends on the mechanical dimensions of the rotary cylinder. When the rotary press is used to print a broadsheet paper, the depth of the printed page is fixed by the circumference of the rotary plate cylinder. It is the cut-off point of one complete revolution of the cylinder. The depth of a broadsheet newspaper varies from about 21 in. to 26 in.

If you imagine this broadsheet laid on its side and folded in two—which is what tabloid printing does—the depth limit for broadsheet becomes the width limit for the tabloid. Therefore a rotary cut-off of 23 in. will give a sheet 23 in. wide for tabloid, which is an effective page of $11\frac{1}{2}$ in. wide. The conventional tabloid size is about this width, and about $14\frac{1}{2}$ in. deep: the London *Daily Mirror*, the Chicago *Sun-Times* and many others. The (London) *Times Educational Supplement* is also a tabloid at $11\frac{1}{2}$ in. wide but 17 in. deep, and *Le Monde* really comes into the tabloid dimensions though it is a large tabloid at $13\frac{1}{4}$ in. wide × $19\frac{1}{2}$ in. deep (compared with the typical broadsheet of $14\frac{1}{2}$ in. wide × $23\frac{1}{2}$ in. deep). The tabloid and large tabloid are certainly convenient for the reader to hold, scan, fold, and carry. How far do they meet the other objections to the newspaper of smaller format?

The editorial possibilities of a tabloid, especially filmset, web offset, have yet to be fully explored anywhere. The tabloid newspaper really began with the *Daily Mirror* in Britain in 1903, but experiment has been inhibited in Britain by the idea that the tabloid shape for a daily newspaper necessarily means a sensational or low-brow content. It is an historical accident that has nothing to do with national newspaper design but the association of ideas will have to be broken in any future attempt to produce a serious tabloid daily or national weekly in Britain. There are a number of non-sensational tabloids in North America (the Chicago *Sun-Times*, the Middletown New York *Times Herald*, the *Village Voice*, Long Island's *Newsday*) and the tabloid format does have distinct attractions for editorial.

It greatly assists the clear and coherent organisation of content. It is easier to departmentalise editorial (and advertising) because the smaller tabloid page is a more flexible unit—if foreign news needs five pages that is an awkward two-and-a-half on broadsheet. It is easier to design an individual tabloid page. And it is easier, throughout, to devise sensible advertising shapes and hence workable editorial shapes. Clive Irving, in his discussion of the newspaper of the future[4], envisaged a 36-page serious tabloid with the use of integrated editorial colour and the ability to 'bleed' across margins and spreads.

The broadsheet retains three editorial attractions. First, it can carry more text without continuing to another page. Some of the newer tabloids offering longer text strain the reader's patience. The *Village Voice* of New York will jump fifty pages as a turn over or sometimes to four separate unadjacent pages. Second, the broadsheet page affords a bigger base for projecting on one page a wide range of news at one time in an obvious order of priority. This is a service which readers may be prepared to forgo as newspapers, having lost the monopoly of hard news, turn more to interpretative reporting. But in its third advantage the broadsheet will always remain superior to the tabloid: it can publish bigger pictures and graphics. Tabloids can exploit a centre spread—many fail to do so—but no tabloid newspaper or magazine, using any combination of spreads, can compete with the display possibility of a broadsheet front page. To take one example, nowhere in tabloid was there anything to touch the colour picture of the Earth, with the Moon in the foreground, published as one whole page broadsheet in the London *Times* in January, 1969.

This was a brilliant exploitation of broadsheet picture journalism (the colour was web-offset fed into the newspaper presses from preprinted reels), which web offset has made technically feasible as a service to daily journalism.

This point about broadsheet having better possibilities for dramatic projection carries a rider. A newspaper which very rarely, if ever, needs to communicate dramatic news does not need broadsheet and might positively be handicapped by broadsheet. Weekly and small-town newspapers come in this category. The smaller tabloid sheet is the more appropriate scale for the small events. Many weeklies produced on broadsheet feel impelled to fill out the broadsheet acres with big headlines and display on what are inevitably less than earth-shaking events. The sense of discord this produces has certainly been one influence behind the movement among weekly newspapers in Britain from broadsheet into tabloid.[5]

Tabloids or Broadsheets

The choice of format must always begin and end with editorial purpose, but the decision must be taken in the light of prevailing technology, and the economic environment of the paper. The tabloid usually wastes more paper on page margins. Every time a sheet of newsprint is folded into two pages of tabloid there is a loss of about 11 in. in the gutter compared to printing broadsheet. The tabloid, breeding more pages than broadsheet, loses time in hot metal page make-up and justification and stereotyping, and also in filmset production. The comparative costs of transmitting pages by photo-facsimile for printing in other centres have also tended to favour broadsheet. And there are two advertising drawbacks. The tabloid offers an inferior range of display possibilities, and in multi-paged tabloids (50 and more) the advertiser fears low page-traffic beyond the centre fold.

There are, however, some economic gains for the tabloid. First, it is more flexible in total sizing. A broadsheet, faced with editorial–advertising pressure on space, has to go up in size by two pages and often prefers to go up by four pages for ease in printing (avoiding the loose sheet which can be troublesome mechanically as well as bothersome for the reader/handler). This two- or four-page increase will decrease the rate of profit if most of the extra advertising quota cannot be obtained. The tabloid's two- or four-page jump, on the contrary, represents only half the investment, so there is more chance in a tabloid of achieving an optimum balance of editorial–advertising requirements at lower cost.

Secondly, advertising rates 'page' for 'page' are lower in a tabloid; there is a chance of attracting more advertisers who want a page to themselves. The web offset paper's hope of attracting self-contained full pages of colour advertising will be easier to realise in tabloid, partly because the charge for a full page will be less than for comparable broadsheet, partly because the costs of preparing a colour ad will favour tabloids since they can conveniently share an ad already sized for colour magazine schedules.

The final physical-commercial factor in deciding the size of sheet is bulk. In papers with minimal pages, tabloid should be preferred to give a feeling of value for money. This is especially so when a high-priced weekly or small daily is circulating in the vicinity of fatter metropolitan broadsheet papers. But there is a point at which bulk becomes an embarrassment. The 36-page broadsheet is a 72-page tabloid, and it is hard to find your way in a 72-page paper with one section, or to divide it among several members of the family. Readers may have stood back in awe from the record *New York Sunday Times* of October 17, 1965, which was fifteen sections of 956 pages; but imagine that as a 1,912-page tabloid.

Of course tabloids can be packaged in separately-folded sections, but not as conveniently as broadsheet papers, and somehow with not as much conviction. The usual device is to mark certain pages of the large tabloid as a pull-out section; publishing the pages upside down is one way of reminding the reader.

The innovating tabloid, *Newsday* of Long Island, has found a still better way. It is produced in one clump of 100 pages or more, but three sub-sections have been designed to be separated from the main paper by simple thumb tab cut-outs. The thumb tab cut-outs are made by a patented process developed by *Newsday* and first put into operation in 1964. They are made from special dies mounted on the presses and require careful synchronisation and placement. (The most troublesome problem is carrying away the tiny punched-out pieces of paper in an elaborate vacuum arrangement leading from the presses to a hopper located outside. The paper thus retrieved is resold as waste.) This ingenious device effectively guides the reader to the women's section or the opinion section, so that it is the work of a moment to extract these and leave the main news–sport section intact.

This discussion has assumed a simple choice between broadsheet and tabloid. Bulkier newspapers of wide appeal can combine the advantages of broadsheet and tabloid by combining a main broadsheet newspaper with tabloid sections separately folded or inset inside the main paper. These tabloid sections can be regular editorial; distinct editorial such as a television guide, or magazine; or commercial supplements (jobs, cars, boats or supplements sold off to a single advertiser). The Boston *Herald Traveller*, basically a broadsheet, produces several attractive tabloid editorial sections (Books, Sport, and so on) and commercial supplements as well. The daily *Bangkok Post* folds a tabloid sports section of sixteen pages inside its two- or three-section broadsheet.

Newspaper design begins with the format, and the decision on that is a mixture of technical, physical, commercial and editorial considerations. Design within the format, once fixed, turns on (i) the nature and quantity of advertising, and (ii) editorial ideas.

2 Influence of Advertising

A newspaper can no more be designed in isolation from commercial influences on the press than it can from the demands of journalism. The most important commercial factor, and the only one which need concern us here, is the presence of advertising. Nobody has yet come up with a formula which will free mass daily newspapers from their dependence on advertising; and I suspect that if anybody did, newspapers would still wish to carry advertising for the variety and interest, and often vivacity, it injects. Advertising is here to stay, and the sensible designer will not resent it as an alien in his perfect world. It is another form of communication in print; indeed the newspaper designer can learn from the imaginative

range of answers to visual problems offered by the best display advertising.[6]

There are, however, areas of proper concern for the designer. The first is the volume of advertising and its ratio to editorial content. It has to be recognised by journalists and managements that there is a point at which the newspaper begins to lose its character and its utility as a vehicle for the communication and interpretation of news.

It is a matter of judgment and argument where the line is drawn between a newspaper as a communicator of news, supported by advertising, and a newspaper as a merchandising catalogue supported by editorial. It seems to me unarguable that large number of American newspapers have gone over the brink with editorial quotas below 30 per cent, and sometimes below 20 per cent in bulky papers, presenting the reader in search of news with a physically daunting task.

This is the judgment of American newspaper readers: it is not the only reason, but it must certainly be one of the reasons why the American newspaper sells fewer copies per head of the population than either the British or the Japanese. The American newspaper is cheaper (as a percentage of income), but where British newspapers have been selling 49 copies a day to every 100 of the population, the Swedes about 45 copies, and the Japanese 44 copies, the American sale is only 32, and in the past quarter-century the number of newspapers taken per family has dropped by 18 per cent.[7] At the same time there has been an increase in paging from an average of 27 in 1940 to 50 in 1965, and of these 23 extra pages no fewer than 20 have gone to advertising. The result too frequently justifies Mr Cecil King's judgment: 'After the first page or two, in the typical American paper, all you get is a rivulet of news flowing sluggishly by a wide meadow which has been leased to some departmental store or supermarket'.[8]

This is not inevitable. There are several successful American dailies where advertising does not run amok. But that great newspapers like the *New York Times* and the *Washington Post* (2) or the *Los Angeles Times* can be reduced to the tokenism of 2 in. ribbons of editorial across a page of 22 in. depth, or a single column out of eight, is endorsement of how far things have gone Good design can direct the reader to such morsels of news on the top of the supermarket double-page spread, but winning back readers who have deserted to television, radio and magazines for their news requires more fundamental action. The over-bulky newspaper has to establish a new equilibrium where profits are maintained but journalism has a chance. Publishers who gradually increase display advertising rates, persuading the advertiser to tell his story in shorter space (which does not mean reduced response if everything else is scaled down), can hope to maintain revenues with reduced bulk and so give the news reasonable space and display. There are also savings in newsprint costs.

Where newspapers are competing for advertising there are, of course, limits to which the individual paper can go, but in North America, the only part of the world where bulk is already a problem, competition is rare. Where you have prosperous monopoly newspapers the problem, as Carl Lindstrom observed, is not to stay in business. It is to stay in journalism.

The second area where commercial considerations impinge on the designer is the disposition of advertising. This is discussed in detail in the mechanics of design, but some principles should be set out here. The designer must provide space for display and classified advertising which will produce results for the advertisers. He must exploit the commercial possibilities of the newspaper—but he must stop short of the point where commercial influences erode the distinct editorial character of the paper.

The reader must be enabled at all times to distinguish between bought space and editorial space. Editorial space carries with it the authority of the newspaper, years of

2

expensively acquired authority; it cannot be sold overnight. No advertiser should be allowed to imitate the newspaper in typographic presentation. Secondly, the advertising should not be so disposed that the editorial message, though identifiable, is hampered. Any policy which consistently breaks these two canons is self-defeating, for it will undermine reader-confidence, circulation, and commercial viability.

The quality of the host newspaper, as much as the quality of the advertisement itself, determines the success of advertising. When advertising imposes an arbitrary pattern, it is adversely affecting the quality of the newspaper.

Controlling Ad Shapes and Sizes

No advertiser or group of advertisers specifying pages and shapes should be able to predetermine the sequence and arrangement of the pages of a newspaper. That can only be decided on the day and hour by hour by journalists responding to problems nobody could anticipate.

Classified advertising is no trouble here.

It makes both commercial and editorial sense to group at least similar sections of classified advertising together. It is a service to both reader and advertiser, for instance, to have all the job advertising together, and the designer must organise the content accordingly. And classified is flexible in its shapes. It can be prepared in full pages or clear sub-sections.

The problem is with display advertising, first the barring of certain pages and sequences to editorial, which sometimes occurs; and almost everywhere the random shapes of individual display advertising. Ideally, newspaper design should begin with the designer deciding, in the light of the news content, the shape and space required on a page, and allocating the remainder to be sold to an advertiser. But it is the other way round in newspapers. The tradition (and there is good reason for it) is that advertisers buy space and editorial fills what is left: the stuff between the ads, in Lord Thomson's picturesque phrase.

The resultant shapes have only accidental relationship to the editorial purpose of the page. Sometimes the editorial can be adequately expressed in the shape available; sometimes it has to be contorted. This is bad for the reader and bad for the advertiser, since the whole purpose of the advertiser specifying 'NRM' (next to reading matter) lies in the notion that the stuff between the ads will draw and hold a lot of people.

Most magazine editors no longer have this problem. Magazine advertising, to the apparent satisfaction of advertisers, is grouped in whole-page layouts or sub-sections making up a full page. Tabloid newspapers can hope to copy magazine layout for advertising display. Display space can be sold in units of full page; half-page; or quarter-page to be shared with other quarter-page advertisers. The enormous gains for newspaper display by this kind of rationalisation are evident in Long Island's *Newsday*. Broadsheet papers have a bigger problem, since fewer advertisers can afford full broadsheet pages, but there is no reason why the existing anarchy should prevail, with shapes varying from 2 × 2 in. up to 16 × 8 in., all bought at random and all supposed to be located in the same newspaper. Of course, except for special supplements and early feature pages, it is not possible to end this by deciding to design a page editorially and selling the appropriate advertising space afterwards.

Ads in most countries are not generally prepared for individual papers, and even if there were time to sell an individual space the editorial requirement on that page might have changed as the news changed. The answer for broadsheet pages is not this Utopia of designing the page first—or totally empty pages—but to work for clear rectangles for editorial, whatever the shape of the individual advertising making up the interlocking rectangle. Display advertisements should be invited to conform to a grid so that both editorial and advertising on the same page occupy separate squared-off shapes. This is to the benefit of advertiser, reader and editorial. The advertiser could be offered the opportunity to exploit new positions: a shallow horizontal box, say, running across the gate-fold the entire width of the sheet. In its separate squared-off grid this would be eye-catching without destroying the viability of the remaining editorial shape.

Of course, in most countries this clean-up would need co-operation between individual newspapers and with advertising agencies, because agencies generally prepare the same display ad for insertion in a variety of papers. Since it is so much in the interests of both to improve the effectiveness of press advertising and maintain newspaper circulations, there is some hope that even the most intractable traditions will yield to modest reform.

In the meantime, let us examine some examples of the way newspapers cope with 'difficult' advertising. Too many newspapers curl up and die without making a design effort to offset awkward shapes and colours.

3

4

5

6

7

Bad Advertising

(3) Our basic rule is that editorial and advertising should be distinct.

The *Daily Telegraph* of London has allowed an advertisement in column 8 in the same body type and setting style as its news stories. Compare, for instance, the headline in column 8 with that in column 3.

(4) The page from the *Tampa Tribune*, in the Egyptian type mixed with Bodoni, is confusing. All the items below the reverse block Wining, Dining, Dancing and Entertainment, are all advertising. So is the panel above about a free race at Golden Gate speedway; and perhaps there is an advertising association with the bowl game.

(5) This page could have been rescued, in the relationship between advertising and editorial, if the *Idaho Statesman* had insisted on a clear white space between the editorial at the top of the page, or a 2pt or 3pt rule.

(6) But these are trifles compared with the absurdity of 'house' promotion material for classified ads dropped, deliberately, in the middle of news text.

(7) This is a different problem—a full page advertisement but laid out in the style of a newspaper. There should be two regulations for this type—that the advertisement is not run in the display type of the parent newspaper; and that the identification word 'advertisement' appears at the top. There is one consolation for layout men— these advertising agency imitations of a newspaper rarely look like the real thing.

8

(8) A second practical rule must be that editorial is given the top of the page and must never be lost in advertising (it is in the advertiser's interests, too, since page traffic is higher when there is more to read). The first of the illustrations is from the *Financial Times* of London. The six-column display advertisement on a left-hand page is poised on two smaller display advertisements and six editorial items, all crammed in like emergency props for a sinking building. The editorial items stand little chance of being read and the arrangement might give the impression the paper does not care whether they are or not.

(9) In the illustration below, the *Fort Worth Star Telegram* of Texas has managed to lose one of the most important editorial services. The TV programes for the evening and next day are buried beneath fish and cigarette display advertising.

9

10

(**12**) If there is a heavy display advertisement, it should be offset by editorial of a lighter and more open nature. And editorial display should be set out asymmetrically to the advertising display, when this is irregular, so that the advertising does not divide the page.

The page with the large display advertisement headed 'Oops!' is from the *Rockford Register-Star*, Illinois. This is a difficult enough page, with such a large display ad, but the layout man has made it worse by putting a five-column top on the five-column ad and so emphasised the advertisement and bisected the page. There is white space in the editorial, but what this is doing is hard to see. It is not being used, as white space should be, to illuminate a black display feature. It is scattered around a caption, which for some reason has been set away from the picture it is supposed to serve.

Ads in clear rectangles, preferably horizontal, are best for editorial display. By some absurdity, horizontal ads are banned in most American papers, but while straining at this tasteful butterfly innumerable nasty wasps are swallowed. The conventional America textbook teaching and practice is to group ads in a pyramid building up to a point on the right-hand side of the page. The *Los Angeles Times* spread (**10**) has advertising in a typical pyramid, and would be commended for leaving editorial in the top left corner of the left-hand page. Edmund C Arnold calls it the primary optical area, POA, for editorial display.[9] While one would accept that the left-hand side of the front page is more likely to be read first than the right, is it true of broadsheet spreads? Does the eye really go as far left as it is expected to do in the *Los Angeles Times* example? It must be doubted, and it is at least arguable, that the eye is as likely to be attracted by editorial appeal just off-centre of the spread. The spread certainly looks better, if editorial supporting editorial is concentrated at its centre. That is how I have refashioned the left-hand page in the accompanying dummy (**11**).

(**13**) Good use of white space is shown in the spread from the *Tampa Tribune*, which has to cope with the large factory warehouse sale display advertisement. Though one can argue about the white on the left-hand page, it does give relief from the grimy emphasis of the right-hand display,

and the editorial display on the right-hand page is asymmetrically set off from the display ad. The white is generally correctly distributed around the headings and tinted rule, and succeeds despite the one awkward corner around the advertisement.

13

48

(14) A picture feature on the fiftieth anniversary of the end of World War I. The headline and story type is Franklin Bold and it all seems to work quite well.

(15) But now the ad is placed: it uses a stronger, bigger sans face which quite overpowers the picture feature. Despite the bold rule, the editorial and the ad merge. It is an ugly and confusing clash. What can be done? It is too late to change the ad.

(16) The attempt made to minimise the ad's effect on editorial. The editorial picture is fully boxed in, and the ad is left to drift, without rules, in the hope of dissipating its competitive force. The panel for the editorial feature is a 9pt rule with a 1pt inside. The place names and dates, too, are boxed in within two parallel white rules. Finally, the Franklin of the text is changed to the lighter face, Record. There is no doubt the distinctive treatment for the editorial feature helps; but, of course, it is more a salvage operation than a rescue.

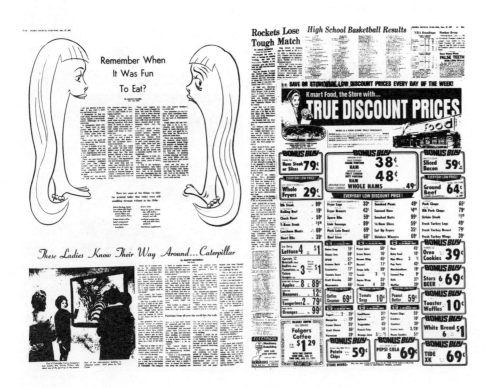

(17) The spread at left with the two large line drawings is from the Peoria *Journal Star*; it, too, has the effect of providing a relief from the savage display ad on the right-hand page. Unfortunately, on the right-hand page itself ultra-small type has been allowed unattractively to come to the top of the page and the struggle for the reader's attention has been lost.

18

19

20

But reaction also flourishes. The illustrations **(18-21)** are of an invention called Flex-Form advertising, of which anybody with a care for design should have warning. Flex-Form advertising offers the advertiser *any* shape on the page, with or without colour, with editorial left to fill in the irregular holes. It has been used in the *Peoria Journal Star* (Illinois); the *Joliet Herald-News* (Illinois); the *Buffalo Courier-Express* (New York); and in the Southam newspapers of Canada. It destroys the editorial integrity not merely of the page but of the whole newspaper, yet such is the confusion in the United States over the proper role of the advertiser that an authority like Edmund C Arnold, who is chairman of the graphic arts department of the school of journalism, Syracuse University, says 'the newspaper designer must applaud the imagination and daring that gave birth to the new concept.'[10] Delete applaud, substitute deplore.

3   Format and Editorial

The size of sheet and the attitude to display advertising are two of the elements of the design structure of a newspaper. The third is the editorial philosophy. What is the newspaper's view of its role and how should the designer–journalist reflect it with the series of rectangles (hopefully) open to him on a sequence of pages? Judgments on all three elements of design structure interact; we take them separately here only for ease of

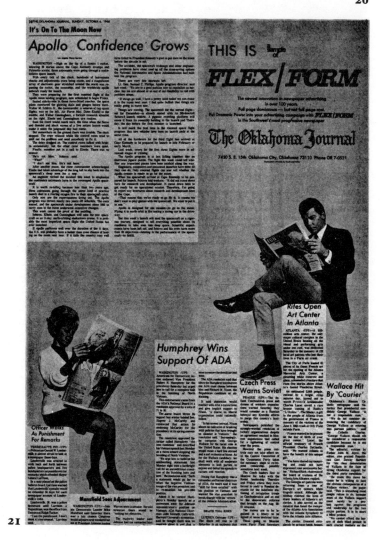

21

discussion. The design reaction to editorial philosophy ends in the detailed layout of a story on a page for a particular edition (Chapter 5), but it has to begin further back with some basic judgments.

I have argued earlier (pp. 1–5) that design must respond to content, projecting what is selected in the form suited to the readership. This is as true of a paper like *Le Monde* as it is of *Rolling Stone*. It is sometimes said by *Le Monde's* more fastidious admirers that it does not bother about such vulgarities as design. It does not use half-tone photographs, it is true, and by comparison with the run of French newspapers its display style is austere. But *Le Monde* has not escaped basic design judgments. The renunciation of photographs, the sizing of headlines, and the whole arrangement of the paper are all in themselves attempts to accommodate, in logical design, the editorial philosophy of being a paper of serious news and interpretation rather than a paper of 'spot' news, surprise and entertainment.

It is arguable whether, in detail, the layout and typography of *Le Monde* is the best expression for the editorial philosophy; it is unarguable that every editorial philosophy has to have an expression in design, good or bad. The design will always stand a better chance of being good if it is consciously related to the editorial philosophy and its assumptions. For most general newspapers, the first simple assumption must be about the readership today—that, unlike the nineteenth-century newspaper reader, the twentieth-century reader will not regard the search for news and ideas as a satisfaction in itself. The audience is no longer captive.

That is one side of the design problem. The other is the richness of material the newspaper is now able to communicate to readers wanting to read—instant news on the price of Australian nickel and the level of a Paris hemline and the reasons why one is going up and the other coming down, and what has been happening in Oregon and Omsk, and the likely course of political developments in Greece, and what won the 3.30. In most parts of the world the newspaper no longer has a monopoly of news, but it has even greater possibilities for exploiting its unique capacity to transmit many details at speed in permanent form. Television arouses new interests which newspapers can satisfy: a national trade union secretary is now known to more people far better than ever Gladstone or Lincoln were. Television may offer the telegraphic news but it would take six hours to broadcast the editorial contents of a morning's London *Times*.

Every newspaper must be quite clear about its own role here, its own priorities between news in depth, comment, interpretation, and fun. And, to optimise the service it provides for the uncaptive reader, every newspaper must have some understandable system for presenting that mass of disparate information and ideas. The common system which has evolved is to use the pages as more or less self-contained units for the presentation of a content sub-divided into subject units called stories, the latest or most dramatic subject units being retained for the front page.

There is nothing sacrosanct about this. The first page could conceivably be simply the first page sent to press. It could record the earliest news of the day and the other news could follow chronologically on other pages as in a book. That would be wasteful of space because news 'dates' news, but it would have a logic.

Nor need the newspaper's opinion be distinguished by a separate page or section. Comment, where appropriate, could be appended to a news report. (By this I mean a newspaper's considered opinion and not the mere mixing of fact and opinion so that you cannot tell one from the other—once called propaganda, then news analysis, and now rediscovered by the underground press as 'free' journalism.) The sub-division of each page into subject units can be questioned, too, and will be later when we look at layout in detail. But whatever the system of division and sub-division, it should not distort meaning, and its sense should be apparent to the reader. If possible it should also be attractive and flexible, but sense and order come first.

Organising the Content

We can get a bit closer to what this means if we consider the editorial elements that design has to organise. They divide into four broad groups: (i) the wholly unpredictable—spot news in words and pictures which divides into local, national, foreign and so on; (ii) journalistic developments of (i), the explanation of developing news by text and graphics; (iii) the expected—stock market prices, weather forecasts, TV programmes, art criticisms, sports reports, the paper's comment and (iv) irregular features.

Order requires first that the predictable content (group iii) should be in predictable positions. Television and radio programmes, share prices, weather, births-marriages-and-deaths announcements should all be anchored in the same place day after day. Predictable content with high 'traffic' (such as TV or weather) should also be readily accessible.

The *New York Times* anchors the position of the News Summary and Index, obituaries, editorials, book news, crossword puzzle, contract bridge column, financial and business news, television and radio programmes, shipping news and weather report, and the daily weather map. The London *Times* anchors the position of its famous Letters column and crossword.

Secondly, where unpredictable news (i) is organised in departments (foreign, sport, business, etc.) these should appear in approximately the same position in the newspaper every day. The space will vary according to the news and the size of the paper, but the page should not change from day to day.

There is still room for variety in the way a newspaper organises its sections, its news and features sequences; in how it divides the

content into sub-divisions, in the detailed treatment of a page. If the layout treatment is distinctive, a columnist or a cartoon can be slotted regularly on a serious page, a clearly signalled feature interview can be set in a box on a news page. And having news organised in departments does not mean sealing departments within the paper so that a sports story or a business story can never appear on the front page of the first section. A paper can be consistent in broad pattern and still give huge scope for imagination. The curse of so many newspapers is the absence of both. The disorder you see is not the debris of inventive energy; it is the tidemark of inertia. The uncontrolled arrangement of editorial inside many one-section British evening and weekly newspapers which so unfailingly goads judges in the Newspaper Design contest is not the result of any theory that the newspaper should be a kaleidoscope of life. It just happens.

The cornucopia of chaos in the multi-sectioned multi-paged American newspapers is not the badge of a bountiful society. It is the banner of anarchy. There should be a clear identification of news departments, of sections and sub-sections. And the identity of the newspaper should remain plain throughout. It should begin on the front page. It is possible to succeed with a sky-liner—a headline or headline and story stretched over the newspaper's title and so beloved of newspapers in North and South America (**22**). But it needs to be rarely used to have effect, it needs to be well whited, and altogether it must not crowd or shout down the newspaper's title, its first asset. Ninety-nine times in a hundred such conditions are not met. Body type comes fuzzily to the top of the page; the title and date are lost in greyness; and sometimes, worse still, the sky-line headline type is indistinguishable in style from the newspaper's logotype. This is so with (**23, 24**) the *Chicago Daily News* and the *Idaho Statesman,* but there are bigger sinners.

22

23

24

25 Overseas News

BIG DAY IN SPORT
THE FA CUP (Semi-finals)

BIG DAY IN SPORT
THE BOAT RACE

26

THE LOWELL SUN

the *Suburbs*

Billerica · Chelmsford · Dracut
Tewksbury · Tyngsboro

February 1, 1971   Page 15

27

MOTORING GUARDIAN

28

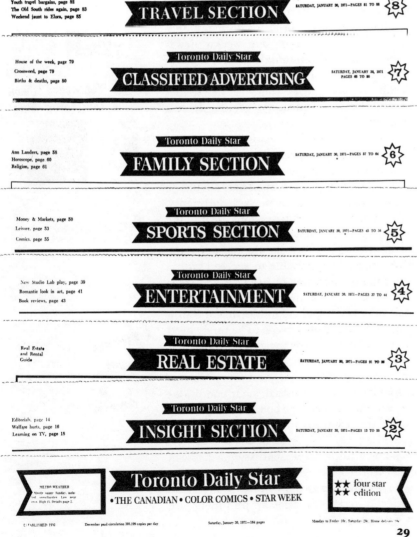

Youth travel bargains, page 82
The Old South rides again, page 83
Weekend jaunt to Elora, page 85

Toronto Daily Star
TRAVEL SECTION
SATURDAY, JANUARY 30, 1971—PAGES 81 TO 88   **8**

House of the week, page 79
Crossword, page 79
Births & deaths, page 80

Toronto Daily Star
CLASSIFIED ADVERTISING
SATURDAY, JANUARY 30, 1971
PAGES 65 TO 80   **7**

Ann Landers, page 58
Horoscope, page 60
Religion, page 61

Toronto Daily Star
FAMILY SECTION
SATURDAY, JANUARY 30, 1971—PAGES 57 TO 64   **6**

Money & Markets, page 50
Leisure, page 53
Comics, page 55

Toronto Daily Star
SPORTS SECTION
SATURDAY, JANUARY 30, 1971—PAGES 45 TO 56   **5**

New Studio Lab play, page 39
Romantic look in art, page 41
Book reviews, page 43

Toronto Daily Star
ENTERTAINMENT
SATURDAY, JANUARY 30, 1971—PAGES 37 TO 44   **4**

Real Estate
and Rental
Guide

Toronto Daily Star
REAL ESTATE
SATURDAY, JANUARY 30, 1971—PAGES 21 TO 36   **3**

Editorials, page 14
Welfare hurts, page 16
Learning on TV, page 18

Toronto Daily Star
INSIGHT SECTION
SATURDAY, JANUARY 30, 1971—PAGES 13 TO 20   **2**

METRO WEATHER
Mostly sunny Sunday, milder and cooler temperatures. Low near zero. High 15. Details page 2.

Toronto Daily Star
· THE CANADIAN · COLOR COMICS · STAR WEEK

★★ four star
★★ edition

ESTABLISHED 1892   December paid circulation 389,109 copies per day   Saturday, January 30, 1971—384 pages   Monday to Friday 10c. Saturday 20c. Home delivery 50c

29

Section Signals and Logos

Labelling news departments inside a newspaper is desirable, and achievable, for any size of newspaper, as this page shows.

For single-section newspapers, the pages or parts of pages only require a modest labelling in scale with the layout (25–28), though preferably set off in white space, a panel or reverse block, and preferably in the same place on every page. For papers divided into sections, the identification on the front of each section must be bolder, the paper's logo must be repeated (since sections are meant to be read apart), and if the content itself sub-divides that, too, should be indicated on the section front. It is obvious: the bigger the paper the better must content be divided and signposted. *The Toronto Daily Star* (29) has the scale of things right. Here are eight sections each clearly introduced by a white-on-tint reverse block across the top of each front page.

The sub-division of content inside is indicated in the same title banner, but without crowding. The identification of *The Toronto Daily Star* is maintained throughout. The content is not always 100 per cent true to the section labelling; occasionally the back pages fizzle out indiscriminately into news fillers. But the reader knows where he is with *The Toronto Daily Star*. Every large paper ought to equal this, yet many of the largest newspapers with the most resources exhibit an unbelievable indifference to the

convenience of the reader. On Sunday that thrusting newspaper the *Los Angeles Times* may deliver sixteen bits of separately folded paper to its readers, yet it fails to maintain the paper's identity throughout or clearly to signal content. An issue in 1971 is taken (above) as an example.

Section A: Twenty-eight pages of national and international news but thin index to this section or to others.

Section B: Seven-column display ad running to within 1½ in. of the top dominates the front page of this section. Underneath a weak single-column logo *The Times*, it indicates, in body type, that there are two foreign stories. Is this then a foreign news section? No. For pages 4 and 5 are about California politics and, worse, they are a continuation of a story begun in the first A section and then jumped!

Section C: A different logo introduces an unidentified section C. The reader might guess it to be a state and local section, but the section includes a Norwegian plane crash and a Philadelphia strike.

Section D: Yet another logo introduces a handsome front page. It does not say so in the logo, but it turns out to be a woman's section. There is, at least, a good index at the foot of the front page, and the type used for the section title is a good Bodoni.

Section E: Yet another typeface for the section title—but this section at least is true to its sports identification.

Section F: Back to another untitled, inadequately labelled and confused section. We are invited to turn to page 5 for a story that the Department of Health, Education and Welfare has picked a South Texas school district officer for a pilot effort to counter discrimination against Chicago schoolchildren, and to page 10 for: 'There was a great variety of musical instruments being used at the story of Christ.' Yet the column-one story edged into the front page here with a seven-column display ad is a foreign story; it gets three single-column legs on three pages, each with a seven-column display ad. The story about musical instruments has two single-column legs on similar display-ad pages and then turns a few inches to the foot of the back page.

Section G: Yet another typeface for the title, and a feeble one at that. The subdivision of the section is indicated, but not the pages to turn to.

Section H: The Outlook typeface is repeated for the Opinion title, but the detailing and placing of the box is different.

Section I: Another ragbag. The box introduces a section about Hanoi—and Charleston, South Carolina. And inside, unannounced here, there is chess.

Those are the main broadsheet editorial sections.

Calendar (30) (page 54) is a tabloid arts section, well designed in itself, but lacking in design identity with the main paper.

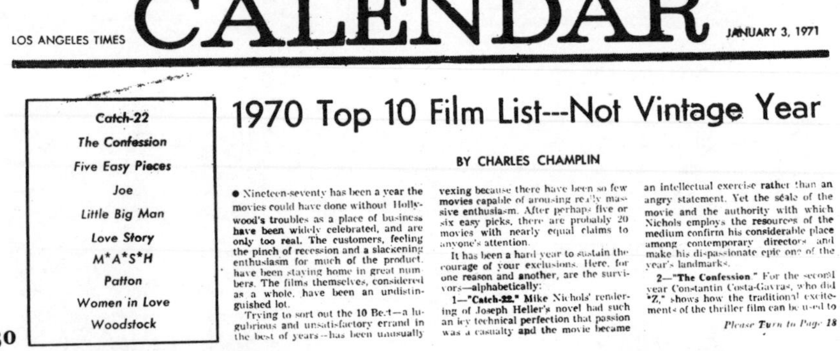

LOS ANGELES TIMES **CALENDAR** JANUARY 3, 1971

Catch-22
The Confession
Five Easy Pieces
Joe
Little Big Man
Love Story
M*A*S*H
Patton
Women in Love
Woodstock

1970 Top 10 Film List---Not Vintage Year

BY CHARLES CHAMPLIN

● Nineteen-seventy has been a year the movies could have done without. Hollywood's troubles as a place of business have been widely celebrated, and are only too real. The customers, feeling the pinch of recession and a slackening enthusiasm for much of the product, have been staying home in great numbers. The films themselves, considered as a whole, have been an undistinguished lot.

Trying to sort out the 10 Best—a lugubrious and unsatisfactory errand in the best of years—has been unusually vexing because there have been so few movies capable of arousing really massive enthusiasm. After perhaps five or six easy picks, there are probably 20 movies with nearly equal claims to anyone's attention.

It has been a hard year to sustain the courage of your exclusions. Here, for one reason and another, are the survivors—alphabetically:

1—"Catch-22." Mike Nichols' rendering of Joseph Heller's novel had such an icy technical perfection that passion was a casualty and the movie became an intellectual exercise rather than an angry statement. Yet the scale of the movie and the authority with which Nichols employs the resources of the medium confirm his considerable place among contemporary directors and make his dispassionate epic one of the year's landmarks.

2—"The Confession." For the second year Constantin Costa-Gavras, who did "Z," shows how the traditional excitements of the thriller film can be used to

Please Turn to Page 18

30

Los Angeles Times, January 3, 1971
HOME
AND THUS THE MINI LIVES ON—A BIG TRIUMPH FOR TODAY'S ACTIVE CONSUMER

31

PRICE 50 CENTS
Los Angeles Times
Sunday Morning, January 3, 1971
Win a Cruise to MEXICO

32

LOS ANGELES TIMES CLASSIFIED ADS
JUBILEE '71
SUNDAY, JANUARY 3 / OVER 15,000 IDEAS
JOBS—HOMES—BEACH AND RANCH PROPERTIES
CHOICE RENTALS
MOBILE HOMES
YACHTS AND BOATS
ANNOUNCEMENTS
INVESTMENTS
MERCHANDISE
AND AUTOS

33

OBSERVER
7 MAY 1972/CONTENTS PAGE 7

34

The magazine *Home* (**31**) carries the title *Los Angeles Times* in a barely visible but poorly reversed white-on-black line. It is left to the comic section (**32**) and classified (**33**) to have any conviction about the paper's title. Contrast the *Los Angeles Times* magazine cover with the bold manner of the London *Observer's* magazine title (**34**).

There can be excuses for dullness. There can be none for disorder. Any size of newspaper and any production system can be used to produce rational organisation of editorial and classified advertising within sections and sub-sections. A one-section newspaper should realise that it can occasionally exploit some of the advantages of multi-sections by devising the page sequence so that a natural pull-out section develops which the reader can extract and keep separately for reading and reference. This might be a four page pull-out in the centre to exploit a major news event or collate election results. Another idea is a wrap-round. The *Northern Echo* dealt with the death of Winston Churchill by devoting the outer four pages to a commemorative news and picture supplement. When these were removed the reader had his ordinary newspaper, with the front page and the normal newspaper title.

Back-page Potential

Back pages are widely neglected editorial potential in broadsheet newspapers. They are a second 'front page.' Editorial should not lightly sell them off to advertising. Tabloid newspapers do better with their back pages, but often fail on using the two centre pages as a single middle-spread with print across the gutter.

The designer faces four basic questions: Is it orderly? Does it strengthen the identity of the paper? Does it use the sequence of spaces well? Does it serve the reader? As has been said, one should, for instance, avoid the mix of editorial sections likely to appeal to different sections of a family. The *Utica Press* once reported a number of family quarrels because a serial story, popular with women, had been put on the back of the sports page so that it was impossible to split the paper amicably.

Observation and market research can help here. The kind of thought it is worth giving the reader's requirements is illustrated by an account of the reasoning behind a change of layout in 1968 in the *Financial Times* of London. The *Financial Times* had listed Stock Exchange prices on the back page some years earlier, when they filled less than a page. When the service was extended it was continued on to the penultimate page 'with the result that the paper had to be read backwards like a Chinese or Arabic book.' There was the prospect that, with still further growth in prices coverage, there would be a third 'Arabic' page. A further drawback was that the *Financial Times* system gave prices actually appearing on the back page unmerited prominence over those inside, which included many of the most active stocks. The paper therefore decided to put the two prices pages in the logical order by giving them the last double-page spread: each page had equal prominence, the prices were in the right order, and there was room to expand to a third (the back) page.

The change was obvious and simple, but the *Financial Times* reported:

'We discussed the change with some of the stockbrokers who make the most intensive use of our prices, to test their reactions. Some of them tear off the back page to keep, and find it convenient to have all the prices on the two sides of one sheet; they will now have to tear off two pages and we apologise to them. Others prefer to be able to keep the paper open on their desks and will now be gratified to find that they do not have to keep turning the page as they switch from share to share.

'The rush-hour traveller will benefit because he will be able to open his paper at the prices and simply turn over the folded sheets instead of having to open the whole paper again to move from the first to the second prices page.'[11]

Page Sequence

In addition to the orderly arrangement of editorial and advertising, the newspaper must try to consider the effect from page to page on the casual reader. Magazines take care to have an exciting opening to each editorial spread, but in newspapers pre-occupation with isolated page design allows page sequence to be neglected. Some general principles can be set out:

1 Early right-hand pages can be regarded as key positions. Reader traffic has been shown by many surveys to be consistently high on right-hand pages and highest at the beginning of the paper.

2 Page sequence should be used to vary the pace of the paper, especially in a one-section paper of general appeal. A series of packed pages should be broken with a more open feature page. But if producing this change of pace means introducing inconsistent and muddled categories of news, orderliness takes priority. (This problem of priorities arises only on the one-section newspaper: papers in several sections can cater for different audiences without worrying so much about retaining the whole variegated audience from page to page.)

3 There are untapped dramatic possibilities in a sequence of pages planned on a related event—a big news story which requires several pages or a feature series. Clive Irving[12] has likened the technique, when exploited with pictures, to the 'cutting' of a film director in editing the frames of his film—zooming from a general scene to a close up.

Day-to-day production will suggest many other ideas on page sequence and the proper arrangement of editorial and advertising. But they should all constantly be related to the changing habits and needs of the reader. In every office which recognises that the world changes there should be an annual reassessment of the assumptions on which the newspaper's design is based. Nowhere is this more necessary than the front page.

EXTRA

RACING RESULTS-ENTRIES

Los Angeles Times

LARGEST CIRCULATION IN THE WEST, MORE THAN 960,000 DAILY; MORE THAN 1,320,000 SUNDAY.

THURSDAY FINAL

SAN FERNANDO VALLEY EDITION

VOL. LXXXVII   ELEVEN PARTS—PART ONE   F   THURSDAY MORNING, JUNE 6, 1968   174 PAGES   Copyright © 1968 Los Angeles Times   DAILY 10¢

KENNEDY DIES
Succumbs to Assassin's Bullet

LISTENED ON STETHOSCOPE
Wife Was Reassured by Heartbeat Sounds

BY PAUL HOUSTON
Times Staff Writer

A physician who wanted to reassure a distraught Mrs. Ethel Kennedy at Central Receiving Hospital early Wednesday handed her a stethoscope so she could hear the beat of her husband's heart.

"Her face just lit up, she was so elated, because she knew there was genuine hope," said Dr. Victor Bazilauskas, 53, who helped revive the dying Sen. Robert F. Kennedy on his arrival from the Ambassador.

"This woman was as distraught as any wife could be," the physician said. "Her husband was brought in breathless, pulseless and lifeless. He was comatose.

Closed Cardiac Massage

"We gave closed cardiac massage and then placed him in a heart-lung machine. We administered oxygen, inserted a tube in his mouth to facilitate breathing and gave adrenalin to the muscles.

"We were ready to give adrenalin to the heart, but we found we didn't need to.

"Mrs. Kennedy pleaded with us to do something—something gentle, not real rough or violent.

"But at a time like that we had to act quickly, and some violence was required.

"So I kind of roughed him up a

A PLEA—Mrs. Ethel Kennedy as she frantically shouted for crowd to move back from husband moments after he was felled by gunman.

little like this, you know," the weary physician related, slapping his own cheeks as he lay resting in a darkened room at the hospital.

"I didn't shake him—but patted his face, trying to get a response.

Please Turn to Page 2, Col. 1

Yorty Reveals That Suspect's Memo Set Deadline for Death

BY JERRY COHEN
Times Staff Writer

About three weeks ago the young Jordanian refugee accused of shooting Sen. Robert F. Kennedy wrote a memo to himself, Mayor Sam Yorty revealed Wednesday. The memo said:

"Kennedy must be assassinated before June 5, 1968"—the first anniversary of the six-day war in which Israel humiliated three Arab neighbors, Egypt, Syria and Jordan.

Sirhan Bishara Sirhan, 24, police said, missed his deadline for shooting the senator by a mere 20 minutes.

The shots which felled the Democratic presidential aspirant were fired at 12:30 a.m. Wednesday—June 5, 1968.

Sirhan, described by acquaintances as a "virulent" anti-Israeli, was seized seconds later, and a .22-caliber revolver was wrested from him.

He would tell police nothing, not even his name.

Hold Hatred of Israel

But as the day wore on, investigation and disclosures from persons who knew him best revealed Sirhan, a Pasadena resident, as a young man with a supreme hatred for the state of Israel.

Sen. Kennedy, it appeared obvious from what Mayor Yorty and others said, became a personification of that hatred because of his recent pro-Israeli statements.

The memo, said the mayor, appeared in one of two stenographer's notebooks found in Sirhan's home at 696 E. Howard St., Pasadena.

Each, said the mayor, contained "18 to 20 pages" of anti-Israeli, pro-

Please Turn to Page 12, Col. 1

KENNEDY STORIES ON INSIDE PAGES

Reagan hits word mongers, Page 3.
New security orders, Page 3.
Suspect's gun traced, Page 2, Part 1.
Eyewitness report, Page 2, Part 1.
Mystery girl sought, Page 13, Part 1.
Busboy's crucifix, Page 12, Part 1.
Suspect in court, Page 12, Part 1.
Scene at hospitals, Page 3, Part 1.
Youths' hopes fade, Page 1, Part 2.
Minorities' sorrow told, Page 1, Part 2.

HELD IN KENNEDY SHOOTING—Sirhan Bishara Sirhan, 24-year-old Jordanian refugee, in the Hall of Justice just after he was arraigned Wednesday. Sirhan was identified after revolver was traced.
Times photo by Frank Q. Brown

Senator Fails to Rally After Undergoing Surgery on Brain

BY DIAL TORGERSON
Times Staff Writer

Sen. Robert F. Kennedy died at 1:44 a.m. today of bullet wounds inflicted by an assassin at the Ambassador early Wednesday.

The announcement was made by the senator's press secretary, Frank Mankiewicz, after eight hours of silence about the stricken senator's condition.

The short announcement was made at 2 a.m. outside Good Samaritan Hospital.

Mankiewicz said: "I have a short announcement to read which I will read at this time. Sen. Robert Francis Kennedy died at 1:44 a.m. today, June 6, 1968. With Sen. Kennedy at the time of his death were his wife, Ethel, his sisters, Mrs. Stephen Smith, and his sister-in-law, Mrs. John P. Kennedy.

"He was 42 years old," Mankiewicz said and left the podium.

Kennedy was shot down at a moment of triumph.

Police said he was shot by a young Jordanian who was described as a possible pro-Nasser nationalist seeking revenge over what he felt were the senator's pro-Israel stands.

Mingled With Crowd

Investigators said the gunman mingled with the tumultuous throng celebrating Kennedy's presidential primary victory early Wednesday at the Ambassador, then fired point-blank at him as he sought to leave through a hotel kitchen.

The shots rang out as the throng in the Embassy Room was still chanting "We want Bobby! We want Bobby!"

The 42-year-old senator slipped to the concrete floor, blood gushing from a wound in the head. Aides grappled with the gunman. More shots were fired and five other persons were wounded, less seriously.

Captured and turned over to police, the man was identified as Sirhan Bishara Sirhan, 24, a native of what was Jordanian Jerusalem prior to the Israeli occupation.

Mayor Sam Yorty said police found at Sirhan's Pasadena home notebooks with statements about assassinating Sen. Kennedy, including one saying:

"Kennedy must be assassinated before June 5, 1968."

Wednesday was the first anniversary of the beginning of Israel's war with Jordan and other Arab nations.

Kennedy was taken to Central Receiving and then to Good Samaritan Hospital, where he underwent a 3-hour, 40-minute operation to remove a .22-caliber bullet from his brain.

At 2 p.m. Wednesday, in the last official bulletin of the day, his condition was still said to be "extremely critical."

Said Kennedy press aide Frank Mankiewicz:

"The team of physicians are concerned over his continuing failure to show improvement over the post-operative period."

A physician told a county official that it seemed doubtful Kennedy could survive.

Vigil Begins at Hospital

A vigil began at Kennedy's bedside at the intensive care unit of Good Samaritan—a vigil which was observed in the hallways, by newsmen outside, and by thousands of circling cars which passed up and down Wilshire Blvd., many of them bearing newly printed bumper stickers which read:

"Pray for Bobby."

To the hospital came those who hoped to comfort Kennedy's wife, Ethel, who is expecting their eleventh child in January.

Mrs. Martin Luther King came late Wednesday after a flight from Atlanta.

Sen. Eugene J. McCarthy, the man Kennedy defeated in the greatest political victory of his quest for the Presidency, came to the hospital from his Beverly Hills hotel.

Mrs. Jacqueline Kennedy flew

Please Turn to Page 15, Col. 1

Kennedy Marks Up 46% Vote; Rafferty Victor Over Kuchel

BY RICHARD BERGHOLZ
Times Political Writer

California voters dealt out the news to political aspirants Wednesday as returns trickled in from the state's primary election.

Ironically, the news that Sen. Robert F. Kennedy won his bid for the Democratic presidential nomination came as his life hung by a thread after he was shot during an election victory rally at the Ambassador.

Kennedy rolled up 46% of the California vote, backed by a strong showing in Southern California, and was awarded 172 California delegate

votes at the party's nominating convention.

State election officials issued an informal opinion Wednesday that the pro-Kennedy slate of delegates, headed by Assembly Speaker Jesse M. Unruh, will represent California

State and county returns on Page 8; Southland returns on Page 20, Part 1.

at the nominating convention regardless of the outcome of Kennedy's fight for life.

Asst. Secretary of State H. P. (Pat) Sullivan said if Kennedy is unable to continue his quest for the nomination, the Californians will be free to vote for another candidate.

For Sen. Eugene J. McCarthy, Kennedy's chief rival here, Tuesday's vote was bad news — and possibly a knockout blow in his

Please Turn to Page 19

THE WEATHER

Cloudy nights and mornings but fair afternoons today and Friday. High today and Friday near 71. High Wednesday, 67; low, 61. Complete weather information on Page 58, Part 1.

4 The Front Page

The first items in the press to which all men turn are the ones about which they know already...for rational beings to see or recognise their experience in a new material form is an unbought grace of life.

—MARSHALL MCLUHAN

The front page is not merely an act of publishing. It is an act of marketing. It is only the first of many pages of editorial, but it establishes the identity, character and freshness of the newspaper by its title, its display treatment and content. The public is induced to buy it, or pick it up and read it. This dual function of the front page requires that it should be predominantly editorial. A front page of classified advertising is a front page of classified advertising. A newspaper must daily renew its relevance. It must surprise the reader or promise to explain his yesterday. A newspaper which reserves the whole front page for classified, as the London *Times* did until 1966, makes every day look the same. It may survive on its quality or on buying inertia, but it must not confuse an accident of history—the spread of column-one classified announcements—with a theory of design.

Traditionally, the front page has met both editorial and marketing requirements by being reserved exclusively for spot news—what we classified as group (i) editorial in the previous chapter: the wholly unpredictable spot news in words and pictures. 'The Latest News! By Telegraph' as the *Charleston Daily Courier* proclaimed in February, 1861. Two interpretations of this function as the urgent conveyor of news have developed, and hence two different design solutions; but, lately, with the development of electronic news media, the purpose of the front page has had to be reconsidered. What if the news, excitedly received by telegraph, has already been piped into the reader's home? Detailed layout cannot begin until the newspaper has decided what function it sees for the front page. In the examples that follow, let us try to concentrate on the function and ignore, for the moment, the patterns on the page.

The Signal-and-text Front Page

The 'signal-and-text' type is the classical modern front page where a selection of the items judged most important in editorial group (i) is signalled both by headline and positioning in a clear scale of priorities and supported with text. Other items of editorial group (i) of less importance or freshness are placed inside the newspaper. Opinion and features of interpretation or entertainment are also placed separately inside. No effort is normally made on this kind of front page to indicate the existence, content or placing of these inside-paper items. Most broadsheet newspapers still follow this style—the *New York Times* and the London *Times*, the *Hindu* and *Daily Express* (3), the *Scotsman* (1), the *Bangkok Post*, and indeed nearly every newspaper in the West; and *Pravda*, too. The text on this kind of front page begins at the beginning and goes on to the end, preferably on the same page. It is not a summary of a fuller article elsewhere; if the text does turn to another page, this is merely because of the exigencies of trying to signal five or ten or twenty stories on the front page.

Occasionally, the broadsheet signal-and-text front page will be given exclusively to one shattering piece of news—such as this example of the *Los Angeles Times* splash (2) on the assassination of Senator Robert

3

58

4

5

of the most thoroughgoing poster pages.

Here is another (5), which was never printed. It is the London *Times,* as proposed by designers consulted by the newspaper in 1965 when it first contemplated changing the front page from classified to news. The page cross-refers to twenty-six items—but it demonstrates just how quiet a poster page can be.

The designers also produced a poster page without illustrations, which was remarkably lively for a page without a scale of priorities (6).

The designers commented: 'If there is an advantage in having news on the front page, it is that the reader gets his news quickly. In the case of the sensational paper, there is the other consideration of headline appeal at the point of sale. But this does not apply to *The Times.* It seems logical, therefore, that the front page should carry as much news as possible: that it should be arranged for easy reading; and that, to cover as wide a front as possible, news should be in breadth rather than in depth, provided it is dealt with in depth elsewhere.'

Kennedy. But signal-and-text papers have not changed their nature when they do this. The most important story is signalled and continuous text immediately supports it.

The Poster Front Page
The idea of the front page as the urgent conveyor of news is carried to a logical extreme by publishing as many group (i) news signals as possible—to the exclusion from the front page of supporting text. This detail is carried inside with the other editorial categories. France and Latin America provide the commonest examples of the front page as a poster; the page from the Paris evening *Le Parisien Libéré* here (4) is one

6

This is a fair statement of the case for the poster front page. It is a response to the increased richness of news available, and it optimises the chance of casual sale.

The choice between a poster front page and a signal-and-text page, with the variations possible with both forms, turns in part on the format of the newspaper. The poster front page is better suited to the tabloid. The tabloid which sticks to the classic signal-and-text front page can display few stories and is forced to turn stories to the back and/or inside, perhaps to several pages inside, always a bad thing; and its point-of-sale pull is weaker. There is also a negative reason: it is easier to manage the typographical display of a poster tabloid than of a poster broadsheet. A broadsheet with a pure poster page one requires careful typography—and it wastes much more space than the poster tabloid. Everything has to be repeated inside; there have to be identifying headlines for the text. This is not a serious drawback for a fairly plump tabloid, but it is one for any low-paged newspaper whether it is tabloid or broadsheet.

Variations and Combinations

Of course the two front-page styles can be moderated in varying degrees. The extreme French style can be muted by giving a short text summary with each headline—a self-contained summary rather than the beginning of the full story.

Some European newspapers do this, such as Germany's *Morgenpost* (7). This at least reduces the problem of publishing a page of headlines which, in the mass, become unreadable.

It has to be said, though, that the thoroughgoing poster page need not be as

7

8

9

unreadable as the French extreme, where type is mixed indiscriminately and where there is no realisation of the importance of white space to illuminate display type. Long Island's *Newsday* offers a poster front page which is a model of cool clarity (8—not 9).

The signal-and-text front page can be moderated by introducing a poster element. The index paging sections, TV, crossword, classified, and so on, is a poster element, but it is a paltry one. A real change in the nature of the signal-and-text front page requires a decision to use part of the front page every day to encapsulate the main news and features presented inside. The device is called a summary index in the United States, where it is a fairly frequent element of multi-paged newspapers.

It can contain capsules of news and features which are dealt with in full inside; or the capsules can be self-contained. The *Financial Times* of London runs two columns of summary index (10) mixing of both forms. The Florida newspaper *Today* and the *Seattle Post-Intelligencer* too are good examples of the summary with page cross-

references (11, 12). They have the advantage over the *Financial Times* news summary of clear classification—I like the logical impudence of *Today* which, selling in the Cape Kennedy area, adds 'In Space' to the traditional categories of The Area, Florida, The Nation, World. The specialised London weekly, *The Times Educational Supplement*, anchors a summary index at the foot of its large tabloid page (13).

There are advantages to the summary index, and it is odd that so few tabloid newspapers have experimented with the possibilities. It provides a useful summary for the busier reader, and a good signpost for those who are prepared to explore some text thickets, but not all. And it offers the opportunity, graphically, for colour and a change of pace on a page. There is no reason why it should not contain small half-tones or drawings, or a different typeface from the main news headline face. But within itself the summary index should have consistent display type and style and it should always be anchored in the same place—across the top of the page, down the left- or right-hand

10   **11**   **12**

columns, or across the foot of the page. The summary index in the middle of a front page is an awkward obstacle when there is a first-class news picture.

Beyond the News

All the front-page styles discussed—poster, modified poster, signal-and-text, and signal-and text with summary index—have been discussed on the assumption that the newspaper has maintained a monopoly of spot news (group (i) in our classification). In many countries television and radio rob at least the morning newspaper of the surprise of announcing the unpredictable. Is there any point in a front page made up of tele-graphic headlines, with or without support-ing text, when news is no longer news by the time it is read? If there is not—and it is a matter of debate which in part turns on the nature of the newspaper's competition and its readership—then the newspaper's front page can change and ought to change in content, and hence in design. For instance if a community or a nation is convulsed by the news of a legal judgment (as America was by the judgments in the My Lai mas-sacre), then a front page which merely announces the news details almost every-body knows is useless.

If what is wanted is comment, interpre-tation, discussion, then that, it can be argued, is what should be given as a priority on the front page—without turning aside to the 'feature' or 'opinion' pages. And that kind of content needs different headline wording and different display treatment; the head-lines, their wording, and the display style for hot news will not do. They are too crude, too unsubtle.

Again, the right 'mix' of content and dis-play for a front page depends on the circum-stances. A major issue may require all the front page, certainly of a tabloid. The signal-and-text treatment on *Newsday's* front page of the anxieties over the invasion of Laos in 1971 is one logical solution. **(9).**

The front-page poster treatment of a

THE TIMES
Educational Supplement

FRIDAY FEBRUARY 26 1971   NUMBER 2910   FIRST PUBLISHED 1910   PRICE 5p

From deadlock to breakdown

The majestic progress of Burnham towards deadlock reached another stage on Tuesday. Next week should see the formal breakdown. The course of events continues to be dictated from outside. The Management Panel's offer and the teachers' response are controlled by the Govern-ment's n+1 policy, as modified by the equivocal results of the Pearson, Scamp and Wilberforce tribunals.

The public interest demands a sharp reduction in the level of salary increases from the 13 per cent achieved last year to something nearer to three or four per cent. It is obvious that this will not come about by voluntary restraint while prices are rising steeply as a result of last year's increases. The Government have eschewed the temporary expedient of a statutory freeze for ideological and for practical reasons. All that remains to them is to bear down on wage offers in the public sector (and to lean on the private sector, too) and resist the inflationary demands of one group of workers after another with a series of formal confrontations.

So far the policy has failed. The Government got a black eye over the dustmen's settlement; a broken nose from Wilberforce. It is already clear that the postmen will get more than the eight per cent they were offered before the strike; by the time both sides get off the hook it could be into double figures.

What the Government have managed to do is to make sure it pays no union to settle freely by agreement. There is always something to be scrounged beyond the formal breakdown. always some sort of *douceur* to restore nor-mal working.

The effect of this is now to be seen in Burnham. The teachers have been offered a pay increase of nine per cent plus the first instalment of the new salary structure which adds an additional .7 per cent. This is " without preju-dice " and is only available as an inducement to an agree-ment. If the issue goes to arbitration the offer reverts to the earlier eight per cent (8.8 including the structural payments). If the Teachers' Panel were to negotiate on the basis of the latest offer they could probably squeeze out a little more juice. which would at least mean a rise that more or less keeps pace with prices. But why should the teachers' leaders settle for this, at this stage, while other. more powerful unions are still in there mixing it with Mr. Carr ? What have they to lose ? The offer already made will stand and a month from now the Government's wages policy may be in even greater ruins.

Of course things could go the other way. A collapse of the n+1 policy could lead *faute de mieux* to a statutory freeze which could catch Burnham on the hop. It might be a lot wiser for the unions to prepare to fall back on arbitration, which could well be a great deal more promising than some people believe : arbitrators have a natural dis-taste for appearing to be Mr. Heath's poodles, and this time this could be worth one or two per cent.

But all this neglects the key question of the salary struc-ture. The Management Panel's offer is tied to their own structural proposals. An important minority of the tea-chers' panel like these ; the N.U.T. remains opposed. But all agree that, whatever the merits of the new pattern, the money available is not enough to pave the way for its introduction. If all this were to be referred to anyone outside the Burnham Committee it would require an ad hoc inquiry (there no longer being a Prices and Incomes Board). This, with a payment on account, is probably what Mrs. Thatcher (and the N.A.S.) would like. But it could only postpone the negotiated settlement which, as the law now stands, has to take place in Burnham. And the truth is that it is not differences of opinion but shor-tage of money which prevents this from being thrashed out in Burnham.

No comment

" *The Department is able to maintain the polarities between disciplines within the areas of study, but does not preclude working between these activities*"—*from a Prospectus Supplement on the Department of Fine Art at Norwich School of Art.*

Mr. and Mrs. Sidney Ponting have kept Radley Primary School clean for twenty-five years. After the gates shut, page 31.

This Week :

Burnham reaches deadlock

After three days of negotia-tions between teachers and local authority representa-tives, no settlement to pay talks is in sight pages 3 and 5

Youth orchestra money crisis

The National Youth Orches-tra appeals for cash to ensure its survival and development
page 13

Race relations row

Race Relations Board clear Haringey of prejudice in clas-sifying E.S.N. children.
page 5

Crossing barriers at 11

Caroline Moorhead visits Bristol primary and second-ary schools and discovers an alarming gulf between them : teachers in one sector seldom venture into the other page 4

Student loans in America

Yale starts a new scheme in-volving student loans : foreign news also covers signs of an anti-student revival in Italy, Swedish lock-out of teachers   pages 14, 15

T.E.S. Extra : history

Eight special pages of articles on using museums, examina-tions, changing American perspectives, industrial archaeology and new books
pages 37-44

Student in the classroom

In the second article in our survey of school practice, a correspondent suggests that some of the most encoura-ging developments in teacher training are in this part of the course   page 10

Poetry competition winners

Winning entries in the two age-groups of the poetry competition are published this week   page 16

Review front : adventure

The " old-fashioned " adven-ture for children : Aidan Chambers talks to Malcolm Saville on his seventieth birthday   page 19

13

14

single feature is, of course, the normal magazine cover; the underground front pages are really magazine covers on newspaper formats (**14**).

And again the front page can be used for a combination of news and features—more precisely for a mix of group (i) and group (ii) editorial. One design for the evening newspaper the *New York Times* contemplated (**17**) in 1967 would have boldly married these two kinds of editorial content on the front page: the 'Lessons of Vietnam' on the signal-and-text front page here is the kind of content American and British newspapers would normally reserve for their opinion sections; so are the features on Florence and hippies. But the rest is spot news handled in the traditional way on this theoretical dummy.

There was a stimulating mixed approach from Peter Palazzo when he was charged in the mid-sixties with giving a radically new look to the Sunday edition of the *New York Herald Tribune* (**15** and pp. 184–6). The front page of the *Tribune* in 1961 was not very different from that of the 1940s—telegraphic news signalled by headlines in Bodoni Bold in several decks with text in eight columns. By 1962 there was a change with rather more analysis on the front page, and columns 1 and 2 had been given up to a double-column news summary, under label headings (The Nation, The City, Sports, etc.).

In the 1965 example the summary index has been retained, though the 18pt Bodoni heads now say something, but the emphasis has shifted to the large graphic presentation of single news story in a feature-magazine style. This panel was often a poster, a tempter for a fuller story inside. The setting of the type in the panel might change from week to week, depending on the illustration and whether the story was self-contained or acting as a poster. But it would always change within the rectangle of the panel. There has never been a more elegant presentation of the mixed page than Palazzo's—mixed in its combination of spot news and feature. (And one might note, in the light of

15

16

Vol. 1, No. 1 © The New York Times Company

Letter From Italy

Florence Calls It A Miracle

By PETER CARVELL

FLORENCE—Eight months ago this was a dead city. Today the miracle has happened: the city has been saved. "Florence is ready once again to receive its guests," runs the publicity—and it's right. But the scars are here still. And sometimes the optimism seems to run away with itself.

Florence is lucky to have been loved. Not only by the people who live there, who worked with their bare hands clearing away the Arno's muck. But also by the world, which has poured in money and encouragement since last November's flood. Other towns, like Grosetto, still lie largely forgotten. Villages farther down the Arno, like the one whose factories produce leather soles for most of Italy's shoe industry, were almost completely destroyed and are still in chaos. Their tragedies are given no newspaper glamour, and no countries clamor to help them.

But Florence uniquely belongs to the world, and when I returned to the city for the first time since last November it was difficult to remember what it had looked like then. A few days after the long day of Nov. 4, the streets were still deep in mud; every wall and statue was lined with naphtha fuel from broken tanks; and the whole city smelled damp and decaying.

But now 6,000 shops have been refitted, nearly 250 hotels redecorated, 60 roads repaired, thousands of walls scrubbed. The Ponte Vecchio is half open, the Uffizi has a special display of works saved from the flood, the Excelsior has a new deep carpet in its foyer.

"Florence will be better than ever," the city dignitaries say, and they're right. The Government gave only $840 to each shopkeeper and businessman, however big his premises, but the banks lend money at only 3 per cent payable in 10 years, and most people have taken advantage of the destruction to turn their scruffy old places into something more civilized.

"Florence is discovering it lost far fewer art treasures than it thought," one restorer said to me. The Cimabue Crucifix lies in the art hospital set up in the Limonaia, once the lemon hothouse in the Boboli Gardens, and one wonders if more people haven't seen it in the last eight months than in the previous 600 years.

Down the hospital ward another 150 paintings on wood lie drying out and carefully picked at with knives, daubed with cotton wool, caressed with

Continued on Page 27

Bullet Kills Girl Driver

A bullet killed a 17-year-old girl as she drove along the Belt Parkway in Brooklyn in rush-hour traffic this morning.

Nancy McEwan of Garden City, L. I., was alone in her car, driving to a summer secretarial job, when the bullet struck her in the head at about 8:30 A.M.

Her car, headed west in the Plum Beach area, between Sheepshead Bay and Floyd Bennett Field, veered into the roadside bushes and stalled. A man driving behind her telephoned the police.

She was taken to Coney Island Hospital, and died three hours later.

A tow-car operator told the police who converged on the scene that, about an hour before the fatal shot, he had seen a man by the roadside taking pictures of a girl with a gun.

The low-car man, George Heffran, said that the photographer, about 26 years old, had a goatee and sideburns. The model, about 21 years old, held a rifle, he said. There was another girl with them, holding a reflector.

Mr. Heffran said the three were being questioned by a policeman. Parked near them, he said, was a 1963 Buick hardtop.

This was about a block west of the point near the parkway's Knapp Street exit, where the shooting occurred.

Miss McEwan was described as a dark-haired, lively girl. She was the youngest of three children. This was her first week of summer work at the James A. McEwan Corporation, a machine-moving company at 250 64th Street, Brooklyn, owned by her father. In Sovergreen, she would have entered her senior year at the Garden City High School.

WEATHER: Sunny, mild today; fair tonight; partly cloudy tomorrow. Temp. range: today 77-59, Sat. 76-60. Temp. Hum. Index 72, Sat. 70.

This is an experimental newspaper printed by The New York Times Company

KNIGHTED: Queen Elizabeth II dubs Sir Francis Chichester a knight at

VIEWPOINT

The Lessons of

George Ball Deplores 'Creeping

By GEORGE W. BALL
Former Under Secretary of State for Kennedy and Johnson

Our experience in Vietnam has taught us that there is clearly a point of no return beyond which national options tend to fade and disappear. Once America passed beyond that point in Vietnam, its only course was to go forward; otherwise, it would have disclosed its weakness rather than demonstrated its strength—and this could have serious political consequences all over the world.

The deeper lesson, of course, is that we must be at all times aware of, and on guard against, the process of creeping involvement; we were not drawn into the Vietnamese trouble quickly but by a slowly accelerating process of absorption.

The best example of this is the bombing of the North. I think it was a mistake for us ever to begin bombing North Vietnam, yet we did not begin that bombing as a systematic air offensive. The first attacks were made as a reprisal for specific acts of terrorism and sneak assaults at a time when South Vietnamese morale was appallingly low and drastic measures were felt necessary to sustain it. Unfortunately bombing offensives tend to develop a life of their own; they contain an internal dynamic that compels their extension to increasingly hazardous target systems, and that is what has happened in Vietnam.

Bombing the North has not, in my judgment, had much effect on the war in the South. It has not critically reduced the availability of supplies since

the logistic requirements of a army, fighting a small-arma living off the country, are surdly low in the terms in w are accustomed to think. (On pushing one bicycle can transp or five hundred pounds, as the found out in fighting the

and there is no shortage of c

I continue to believe, there bombing the North is not us it impedes negotiations, inve political costs and risks, and overriding military (or diplon vantage has not been adequa onstrated.

But there is a great diffe

STRIKE INCIDENT: A caseworker, entering the Melrose Welfare C Mayor Lindsay today thanked caseworkers who have stayed on

Of Our Time

Is the Hippy an Up

The Psychiatrists Delve, and Thor

By ALEXANDER PATERSON

Age: 18-20. Social status: middle class. Parents: Dominant mother, weak father.

These somewhat tentative characteristics are coming into focus as psychologists, sociologists and other scholarly youth-watchers begin to put genus hippy under the microscope. Hippies may not care about the findings, and many parents are probably past caring, but the new specialists find fertile soil for study in the family relationships that breed "flower power"—the potted plants of the East Village. One institution of higher learning—the New School for Social Research—has even elevated the hippy culture into a course taught this summer by Richard A. Koenigsberg, a lecturer in psychology at Manhattan Community College.

"Hippies are looking for involvement on a group level—to escape the dominant mother," said Mr. Koenigsberg. "If you love one person, there's a chance that person will bug

Continued on Page 18

00¢

McNamara Gets Plea for Troops

SAIGON, South Vietnam—Defense Secretary Robert S. McNamara, arriving in Vietnam today for his ninth visit, heard a request for more United States troops from his military commander, Gen. William C. Westmoreland.

Now is the moment, the general said after the meeting, "to step up the pressure on the enemy by reinforcing our mounting successes."

Ambassador Ellsworth Bunker's post-conference analysis was somewhat more qualified. "We have had a good measure of success," he said, "and I believe we are gradually achieving our aims in Vietnam. If we stick with it long enough—and this is not a short-term proposition—I am confident we will have reasonable success in achieving our objectives."

Similar request for more patience, more men and more time dominated today's comment, both public and private. General Westmoreland is reportedly asking for 100,000 to 200,000 additional troops to supplement the 485,000 troops scheduled for duty in Vietnam by the end of the year.

For Mr. McNamara, the question is not whether he will increase United States troop strength in Vietnam—some increase is considered inevitable—but how large it will be.

The Secretary arrived in Saigon prepared to hear General Westmoreland's case but it was reported here that he came with clear instructions from President Johnson to attempt to pare down the request, then ask the South Vietnamese and other Asian allies to share the added burden.

Administration officials fear that unless the general and the Secretary can reach a compromise, the military will argue that Mr. McNamara has tied their hands and attempt to deal directly with Congress for more troops. But they believe that an increase of 100,000 or more new troops would almost certainly require calling up some reservists in 1968, a politically disagreeable move in a Presidential election year.

Mr. McNamara spent more than 12 hours today reviewing military manpower and other problems with officials seated around a 30-foot oak table in the "High Noon Conference Room" at the Tansonhut Air Base. [The conference's code name was changed after television cameras caught the sign on the door.] The meeting was secret and reporters relied on an official spokesman for the mission, Barry Zorthian, for their information.

Mr. Zorthian described the discussion as "realistic and sober" and General Westmoreland told reporters: "The war is not a stalemate. We are winning slowly but steadily."

The rosiest picture of the day was given to the conference participants by Robert Komer, a former White House aide now responsible for bringing social and other reforms to the villages.

"Our main force military pressure on

Costs of War As Visit Begins

In lives, in lost equipment, in expense, in troop demands on the United States military, these were the costs of the war in Vietnam as Secretary of Defense Robert S. McNamara made his ninth visit there:

11,534 Dead
CASUALTIES: In the week that ended last Saturday, 161 Americans were killed in battle and 1,529 wounded, bringing the deaths to 11,534, wounded to 69,870.

600 Planes Lost
EQUIPMENT: Two United States jets were shot down Thursday during raids on a power plant north of Hanoi, making total air losses 600 planes.

Over $25-Billion in '67
COST: The Congressional Joint Economic Committee said yesterday that the Administration estimates of Vietnam expenses in the calendar year 1967 might have been understated by $4-billion to $6-billion. The committee said the annual cost "exceeds by an unknown margin the $25-billion figure we use as an identifiable estimate."

Forces at 466,000
TROOPS: When Mr. McNamara first visited Vietnam in May, 1962, there were 9,000 United States troops there, according to the current estimate is 466,000. Here are the dates of Mr. McNamara's visits and the Defense Department's estimates of troop levels at those times:

May, 1962	9,000
September, 1963	16,000
December, 1963	16,500
March, 1964	16,500
May, 1964	16,500
July, 1965	72,000
November, 1965	161,000
October, 1966	331,000
July, 1967	466,000

the enemy has permitted an increasing number of Vietnamese military units to be committed to pacification and has kept the Vietcong and North Vietnamese army from interfering," he told the meeting. This development has, however, taken a toll: as more and more Vietnamese troops are committed to the pacification program, United States troops are forced to assume an increasing share of the actual combat.

(From AP, UPI and Staff.)

Rossetti Named Tammany Chief

By SCOTT WILLIAMS

Old-line Manhattan Democratic leaders kept their firm grip on the New York County organization today when they easily elected Assemblyman Frank G. Rossetti as county leader.

Mr. Rossetti, acting leader since the resignation of J. Raymond Jones last March, won over Shanley N. Egeth, an East Side Reform leader, by a vote of 9 1/3 to 5 1/24.

In a speedy fence-mending move, Senator Robert F. Kennedy, who had been noticeably cool to Mr. Rossetti's candidacy, called the newly elected leader to congratulate him.

Mr. Rossetti promptly invited Mr. Kennedy to lunch.

Later, Mr. Rossetti said: "I am and will be a supporter of Senator Kennedy. I have not asked his support but would welcome it."

The husky 59-year-old Assemblyman also expressed relief that "despite rumors to the contrary," Senator Kennedy had not intervened in the contest for county leader.

It was not so much that Mr. Kennedy did not want to intervene as that the Reformers virtually made it impossible for him to do so.

Right up to the election they were split over whom to support for the county's top Democratic post. Four Reform leaders joined the old-timers and independents in backing Mr. Rossetti, and three other Reformers abstained.

Even if Mr. Kennedy had sought to intervene in support of a Reformer, a Democrat close to the Senator explained, he was blocked because the Reformers had "acted too late to win."

For a while before the election at the Commodore Hotel, there was a

Frank G. Rossetti

flurry of excitement over reports that Senator Kennedy had flown to New York from Montreal, where he was visiting Expo 67, to plump for Mrs. Ronnie Eldridge, a West Side Reform leader.

A Kennedy aide said the Senator had indeed cut short his visit to the fair, but only because he had learned that some Reformers wanted to confer with him.

After a series of cloakroom huddles

C mt

17

---

the earlier discussion, the incisive identification of the paper and the section in a box with a bold numeral, a theme echoed for every section.)

The innovating British journalist, Clive Irving, in a dummy **(16)** for a newspaper of the future, suggested a signal-and-text front page with capacity 'to make the best use of news interpretation methods as they are likely to be developed.'[1]

Here the symmetrical front page, tabloid on a four-column grid, is devoted entirely to reporting in depth on an American peace initiative in Vietnam, beginning with a summary set across two columns at the top and under the streamer. There is one element of a poster front page in a top-of-the-page 'contents' streamer which Irving envisaged as being in a second colour. Otherwise the rest of the news is not signalled and appears inside. The panel at the foot of the page is a solus advertising position—a clear rectangle leaving a clear rectangle for news.

The new concepts of the function of the front page should not be immune from criticism because they are brave experiments. Irving's risks losing some of the varied richness from the rest of the news; perhaps the back page of such an interpretative daily should be given up to a page of news capsules, registering and organising the events of the previous twenty-four hours. Palazzo's handsome pages risk an insufficient response to the exceptional; the semi-magazine format might be suitable for a Sunday paper, or a quality daily perhaps, but hardly for a rushed evening newspaper.

Of Palazzo's concept of the front page as a news-feature poster, one critic comments: 'My observation of that experiment was that the traditionally organised front page, that is, a page which weighs the news for the reader in order of importance, was a service which the poster approach eliminated and which readers of standard-sized newspapers would not forgo.'[2]

The demise of the *New York Herald Tribune* does not necessarily endorse this

---

(left margin fragments)

College today.

tnam

decision to begin bombing and on to stop it. The problem that is now relates to the consequences and implications of halting an effort that we have been conducting for over two years. I find it see how any United States government could unilaterally cease air attacks the North without some quid from the other side, so long as military leaders strongly assert these attacks protect American forces in the South and thus to save the lives of Americans, the exiguous logistic requirements the South, I think this thesis is based on fallacy, but it is a point almost uniformly put forward by military experts and on an issue, and it is their opinion and not that the American people will be so believe.

We, therefore, that we will go forward with the bombing, and hope that we will continue cautious in picking target systems, bombing of MiG bases could, judgment, create difficult problems, decision, since if successful it would most certainly lead to the basing of MiG's in South China, which could build up heavy domestic for an attack on Chinese aircraft.

ly, any order to mine Haiphong, or otherwise to interrupt of Soviet ships, would, it me, pose a direct challenge to own interests. If effective it would

on Page 9

morning, spits at pickets. 4).

lapper?

ares

By T. H. GARDINER

ade his observations of the literature, looks at the upkeep but with respect. "They 's risen again," he said last re also something new and

Town," Mr. Wilder shifted of coziness. He sat in the n from the Connecticut king as usual.

are always the same," he er. "You take that line of ne over 30. In 'Seven Ages s I am doing, there is one haracter says—'Don't make vs let you down.' "

rom youth, Mr. Wilder has

18

judgment. The new format was introduced only two years before the close of the *Tribune* and the forces which killed the paper had gone too far to be stopped. Certainly the new format initially increased advertising and circulation and, within the concept, the execution has a brilliance which remains a standard for journalists and designers.

The Sunday Times used to have a traditional eight-column front page of signal and text. The first change was the introduction in column one of a full column index to the news and feature contents of the newspaper. The feeling was that the reader, having paid his money, should not be left unaided and unaccompanied at the start of the seventy-two pages. That column was a colourful addition to the front page, but it pointed the way to a new development, and this was introduced at the same time as the page was redesigned in 1971 to accommodate wider text setting. The new development was the News Digest (18).

It differs from the summary index in that it is not a series of references to other pages. It is a complete self-contained digest of the main spot news of the day, all pulled together compactly in one regular space where the reader can quickly brief himself.

The Sunday Times devotes its main news space to exploring news in depth, and previously the simpler spot news had drifted all over the paper. For the reader wishing to pick his way through the paper, a short index was retained (column 8) concentrating on major features. The News Digest is in 8pt and aims at encapsulating all the important Saturday national and international news which can be told as briefly as a Sunday morning radio bulletin; it is not a column of fillers. Research shows that it is well read.

The News Digest is set at 15 picas; the other columns at 13 picas; and the index at 10 picas. The wider setting was introduced because of the findings of legibility surveys on ideal line-length for easy reading.

5 Page Layout

It is designed, that the country shall be furnished once a month (or if any Glut of Occurrences happen, oftener), with an Account of such considerable things as have arrived unto our Notice—BENJAMIN HARRIS, *Publick Occurrences*, Boston, 1690, the first colonial newspaper.

How should editorial space be designed so that the considerable things that have happened can be furnished to the country? There is an assumption in the question, and it is that the newspaper of today is primarily concerned with using type to communicate content to consistent standards—that it is more of a 'machine to think with,' as Professor I A Richards has described it, than a typographical entertainment.

There are other views. Allan Cohen and his staff of poets, artists, and prophets wanted to make the underground paper, the *San Francisco Oracle*, 'a graphic expression of man's highest ideals: music, art, ideas, prophesy, poetry and the expansion of consciousness through drugs.'[1] This book is nearer to Benjamin Harris than Allan Cohen while acknowledging, indeed advocating, the vivacity of modern graphics. Pages need not be grey and dull; they ought not to be if the flow of news and ideas, rich and unrelated, is effectively to be transmuted into print.

Reflecting News Priorities

But the translation of ideas into print must, I would argue, be in the manner most fitting for each message, it must be done with economy, and it must be received with comprehension. This requires decisions about type and about layout, but before we can embark on that, the first basic judgment is how ideas shall be sorted into boxes the reader can recognise and, if he wishes, open. What shall be the pattern within 'the mosaic image of the modern press'? The commonest is to divide page space according to a scale of values—the most considerable happening on the front page with the largest headline, the most trivial happening tucked far inside at the foot of a column under a small heading, and entertainment features presented in a more relaxed easy-going style. This is still probably the best way of organising newspaper content, and is what readers are used to, but the designer should recognise that there are others either for general or particular use. News pages could be divided, for instance, according to time, to place or subject. Everything that the newspaper heard about at, say 3 p.m., would be listed under a bold numeral. Or all the news from France or Yugoslavia could be listed under such place titles. Or all the fires, road accidents, speeches, natural deaths, government papers, and burglaries and so on, could be listed under such subject titles. An approach like this would suggest its own typographic and layout solutions. The weight of headline for each major category could be the same; it could appear in roughly the same place each day depending on events; there could be sub-headings under the major categories of time, or subject or place.

None of these categories provides a satisfactory general divider for the general newspaper, but calm subject and place categorisation has proved effective to the international news magazines like *Time* and *Newsweek*, and it has newspaper uses. All newspaper sport and financial news can

1

be sub-divided into subject categories, with simple indexing display—example **(1)** (the *Observer*) is a good example of the subject treatment for one sports feature.

A similar typographic style could be used by a weekly or regional newspaper for dividing news from different places. And many big events benefit by sub-division and display under equal-weight time or place headings. The big drawback with a newspaper divided wholly by event–time headings, is that news often overtakes itself, so a time-divided newspaper would risk repetition and waste: and for general news we are more interested as a rule in what happened rather than precisely when or even where. So there are good reasons for the survival of the traditional division of a news page by a scale of values, and it is to this type of page that most of what follows is addressed.

Communication at this stage is based on two elements: typographical style and the arrangement of type, illustrations and space on a page. The basic headline and text founts of the newspaper are relatively fixed factors, so much so that they are often discussed as being part of the format of a newspaper. I argue earlier in this series (*see* Book Three) that a newspaper requires a typographical style to maintain identity and that there

should be restraint in the deployment of display types. The communicating newspaper will use typography to establish the underlying unity between pages of common purpose, to sub-divide space coherently, and to maintain values. The values and sub-division are related, but whatever the basis of page sub-division, erratic typography imperceptibly but inevitably erodes the confidence of the reader in the standards of the newspaper. This is one of the first areas where a newspaper designed to reflect news priorities goes wrong. The display types are varied too much in size, style, and spread. The detailed typography differs between *The Bridgeport Post* here and *The Tampa Tribune*, but in both instances the variations produce giddiness **(2, 3)**.

Consistency in Signalling

The reader needs signals to indicate priorities —but look at the signals that are available:

Page—front or inside, etc.

Position on page

Length of text

Style of text setting

Size of headline

Weight of headline

Spread of headline

'Colour' elements, i.e. not in the chromatic sense but the contrast of blacks, greys and whites in type, reverse blocks, pictures.

It is wasteful and distracting for a designer to use all these signals. There should be economy and there should be consistency. Where varying values are indicated by varying display type-sizes and spreads, for instance, it should be done to a regular

pattern. There should be an observable proportion between the size of sheet, the range of headline sizes, the size of the biggest and smallest headlines, and between the headline sizing and the importance of the text.

The Basic Grid

We now come to the arrangement of type, illustrations and space on the page.

In the history of newspaper design nothing rivals the invention of the column. No modern newspaper can communicate coherently and economically without constructing its pages from a basic grid. Of course the column had been invented long before the *World* in 1898 ran its famous scoop across eight columns (*see* p. 24 earlier). The *World* stretched the type across the page for surprise effect, but even with modern types the page without a column grid must be regarded as the exceptional eccentricity which proves the rule. The *Daily Express* treatment of another earth-shattering event (4) is effectively within an eight-column grid, but the top of the page also shows that it can easily yield different permutations of text settings, all based on the standard measure. What the width of the standard columns should be is a matter for debate, but every criterion of efficiency and readability directs us to begin page design by deciding how the page shall divide vertically. Such is the restless urge for something new in newspaper design that designers are sometimes praised for breaking away from what is regarded as the tyranny of the column[2] and the column rule. Yet the two ways of approaching page layout both lead inevitably to the necessity of a column grid.

Column Widths

The first way is to begin with function and legibility. The function of the newspaper page is between those of the poster and the book. The poster has to attract attention or it fails. The book, once opened, does not have to compete for attention. The newspaper has to have its poster element, too, in attention devices, but their impact is subsidiary to the information whose promise, basically, has attracted the reader.

The only way to print sufficient information is by setting it in small type—and there are distinct conditions for the read-

5

6

7

ability of small type. It cannot be read comfortably except at certain confined widths. Unleaded text type as small as 7pt cannot be read comfortably if it is set across the width of tabloid or broadsheet page, and there are, as I have demonstrated in Book Two, upper and lower limits for the measure of text-type settings.

These are also the upper and lower limits of the optimum column grid for a newspaper. The limits depend on the x-height and colour of the type, and on the degree of interlinear white, but if we said that, roughly, in 9pt of most newspaper types the optimum line length should be 15 picas, then the optimum column width is 15 picas. The precise measure, give or take a pica or two, is less important at this stage than the principle that legibility dictates some form of setting so very much narrower than the full width of the tabloid or broadsheet news sheet that the page has to be divided vertically into a series of columns.

A newspaper which seeks to multiply display positions on a page can reduce the width of setting, to provide more vertical columns: or a newspaper may prefer the steadiness of wide-gauge text, but that does not in any way weaken the imperative that page layout must begin with legible divisions of text setting. Stanley Morison, as ever, has the right rebuke for anyone who finds this inhibiting.

'No printer in safeguarding himself from the charge of monotony in his compositions should admit, against his better judgment, any typographical instruction doing violence to logic and lucidity in the supposed interests of decoration. To twist his text into a triangle or squeeze it into a box, or torture it in the shape of an hour glass or a diamond is an offence requiring greater justification than the existence either of Italian and French precedents of the 15th and 16th centuries or an ambition to do something new in the Twentieth.'[3]

If we approach page design from the opposite direction we come up with the same necessity for the column. The page has to

arrange a variety of news stories in a distinct order. The column, whether it be 11 picas or 15 picas, is a prerequisite for legibility, but it is more than that. It is an indispensable aid for creating order, for enabling the priorities to be focused. In the phrase of the designer Peter Palazzo it is an 'automatic organiser.' It works best, too, when it is honestly valued: the most backward step, under the flag of freedom, has been the careless abandonment of column rule and cut-offs which so usefully define columns and separate stories. And there is a third reason for insisting on a basic grid for newspaper pages. It is faster to set type to a regular width and a great assistance in production if type or filmset strip can be moved between pages.

How Many Broadsheet Pages?

But what basic column grid should be adopted? The conclusion of the discussion on text typography in Book Two was that the general run of 11-pica columns in 8pt was too narrow for optimum legibility (and certainly the American abortion of 8-set 9pt). A few American and European newspapers have experimented with wide-measure columns of around 15 picas. The difficulties are mechanical rather than editorial: first, the American habit of actuating line-casting machines from agency tape standardised on 11 picas; second, the widespread acceptance in many parts of the world of an 11-pica measure for advertising. But here are sample pages of different column formats.

Nine and Ten columns

Nine- and ten-column papers (5, 6) are usually concerned to express a restless excitement rather than any consistent sense of news values. This format provides so many display positions that bustle is easily achieved, especially if, in addition, the text is relatively short. The scale is more than is needed for expressing a range of news values and, if the typography is not carefully controlled, the column, instead of ordering the

news, will begin to be a force for fragmentation. This is one reason why newspapers
presenting middlebrow-to-serious text of
more than a few paragraphs are ill advised
to flirt with nine- and ten-column format.
The other is that the readability of nine- and
ten-column setting on the average broadsheet page is poor, for reasons discussed in
Book Two.

Eight columns

Eight columns of 11 or 11½ picas each is the
standard for broadsheets—partly dictated
by national advertising standards of 11
picas, as mentioned. Of course layouts can
vary hugely between eight-column formats.
The eight-column format certainly creates
plenty of display positions—more than this
old *News Chronicle* page (**7**) handles satisfactorily, given the serious nature of the
newspaper.

7½ columns

The 7½-column format is sometimes called
W-format in the United States. The standard 11-pica measure is retained for six
columns. The seventh column is set about
1½ columns wide. The remaining half
column is distributed as white space in the
gutters. This has the production attractions
of retaining the standard advertising measure; of flexibility for copy in type; and of
being able to set by wire tape without being
forced by the rigidity of wire-tape setting
into a cramped page. So many of the North
American pages with only 3pt column white
would be better on W-format for that reason
alone. The 1½-column segment provides a
distinctive shape for special editorial effort
such as the *Knickerbocker News* Action Line
(**8**) or the summary index in *To-day*. It is
probably best anchored to the left, but the
Editor of the *Knickerbocker News* says that
they have found floating it has given them a
useful variant on the page: 'If you wanted
to place the 17·9 segment in the middle of
the page but wanted to avoid a vertical
appearance, you could place a 29·9 pica en-
graving (17·9 picas, plus 11 picas, plus the
one pica alley you would pick up) above it

and regular one column type next to it. Or,
if you wanted to place type rather than art
above the floated 17·9 pica you could set the
type 14½ picas and double it up.'[4]

Six columns

Six column (**9**) is generally called 'optimum
format' in the United States because it
begins by taking the optimum text line for
easy reading (about 15 picas) and divides
the page by that measure. This is a powerful
recommendation. There is a great gain, too,
in the small-type radio, TV and box scores
which in wider measure lose the absurd
abbreviations produced by 11-pica setting.
The number of obvious story positions is
less than in eight-column pages, and long
stories in the wide measure can look grey.

The managing editor of *The Courier-
Journal* (Louisville) (**10**) at the time of their
change[5] to wide measure observed that
bulky stories, if not skilfully handled, 'will
murder you.' In their experience six-column
broadsheet layout tends to be more horizontal than vertical. 'And if a story runs
much more than three inches deep under a
multi-column head you are in trouble.'
But these editorial problems can be overcome. The greyness of long slabs of optimum
measure can be overcome by sub-heads and
colour devices such as a well-placed half-
tone or reverse block or box or rules. *The
Courier-Journal* (Louisville) eliminated all
head shots in its new one-column measure
and sought to enliven the page by well-
cropped action pictures. There is less
flexibility in picture sizing, of course, because there are fewer column increments, but
the difficulties of optimum measure remain
mechanical not editorial. Where national
advertising is fixed at 11 picas the optimum
column cannot be used on mixed editorial-
advertising pages without the acceptance of
awkward holes. And type set specially for
page one cannot easily be transferred to a
conventional inside page. If advertising
can be squared off, if pages can be tailor-
made, if the works can reset, then these
problems diminish.

8

9

10

12

13

14

11

They do not exist, for instance, for the six-column *Frankfurter Allgemeine*, which rightly prefers horizontal ads—and has both elegance and flexibility (**11**).

The kind of ingenuity required has been demonstrated in Britain by the Welsh morning newspaper, the *Western Mail*, which in 1970 moved from an eight-column page of 10·8 picas to a six-column page of 14·9 (**12, 13**). The *Western Mail's* sister-paper, sharing the same plant, also changed —but to a nine-column page of 9·8 picas. To accommodate joint advertising, some of the *Western Mail's* pages carry both column measures. According to the Editor, John Giddings, this works much better than it deserves to. The difficulties are usually overcome by the strategic placement of a story set across 9·8 picas along side an advertisement set across 9·8 picas, thus converting three narrow (9·8) columns to two wide (14·9) columns so as to marry in with the rest of the 14·9 page. Sport, because it shares with the evening paper many services such as tables and cards, is on a basic nine-column page—but the *Western Mail* sets the main story of the night in a well-displayed bastard measure to keep continuity.

As with the Louisville *Courier-Journal* and other papers moving to wide measure,

the Editor reports favourable response from the readers. The Louisville *Courier-Journal* tried the format in a one-day experiment after the *Wall Street Journal* first made the move and got a vote of about 500–7 in favour.

Five Columns

The three papers illustrated (**14–16**) are *Die Zeit*, the Hamburg weekly, the *Christian Science Monitor* published daily in Boston, and the *Detroit News*. *Die Zeit* and the *Monitor* use five-column format for serious, analytical journalism requiring long text. The *Detroit News* is an attempt to use the same format for more general news journalism. Its columns are 14·6 picas, with wide column white (as much as $2\frac{1}{2}$ picas on the front page). The *Monitor* and *Die Zeit* are printed on similar broadsheet pages (slightly smaller than the *Detroit News*) and have similar text measures of about $15\frac{1}{2}$ picas. This five-column format clearly offers fewer display positions, other things being equal, than the conventional eight-column format. The length of text line, around the optimum for legibility, is ideal for newspapers offering text requiring concentrated reading—which *Die Zeit* and the *Monitor* do.

The *Monitor* changed in 1965 from eight columns to five in 9pt for this reason. It can continue the five-column format inside because it has been fairly successful in

15   **16**   **17**

18

grouping advertising in horizontal rectangles instead of the traditional American
pyramid; there are only a few awkward
holes which are generally left white. *Die Zeit*
succeeds more brilliantly with ads (mainly
horizontal rectangles) sized to its format.
The *Detroit News* is not able to continue five-
column format on more than a few key
pages because of the problems of the 11-
pica advertising standard. It manages on
page one to present a satisfactory range of
news values for a general newspaper, but
to do this it has to keep page one text relatively short or turn inside—four stories on this
front page are turned inside.

Five-column variants
The column grid need not be a strait-jacket.
Where the layout requires an extra column,
there are a number of ways it can be achieved.
The simplest is to continue basing the text
setting on the original grid. In **(17)** *Die Ziet*
gained an extra column by setting three
legs of text across the measure of two of the
standard columns. (Where this is done at
all frequently, the width of broken measures
should be agreed with the composing room
and laid down.) The other example of six-
column layout from a five-column page
requires rather more thought in layout and
text marking. The *Detroit News* has **(18)**
reduced column white from the 2½ picas on

the front page so that it can accommodate
four regular wide-measure columns and
two 9·6-pica columns—the standard on
those inside pages where it cannot set wide
measure because of advertising.

It is generally more convenient to fix
the five columns at the same standard
measure, but a further variant of the five-
column format is to set one of the columns
wider—as in the 7½-column W-format
referred to earlier. The *Lowell Sun*, Mas-
sachusetts, for instance, has one column of
19·6 picas, anchored at the left, and four at
16 picas.

Broadsheet Conclusions
Of the broadsheet column formats examined, the optimum or six-column format
has the most attractions. It gives better text
than ten, nine, eight or 7½ columns; it
survives the customary criticism that better
legibility is exchanged for less serviceable,
and duller, layouts. Papers like the *Monitor*
and *Die Zeit* (certainly) do well on five
columns and something like their format
would be ideal for, say, *Le Monde* and other
papers concerned to present fewer, longer
articles. But for the ordinary newspaper
attempting to present a spectrum of hard
news that extra column in the optimum,
six-column format, is worth having. It can
be exploited either for the popular or serious

19

20

21

22

newspaper, for the metropolitan or the country weekly. It is successfully managed by the *Wall Street Journal's* sister-weekly, the *National Observer,* for its mixture of analytical and descriptive journalism with a strong feature emphasis; by the Louisville *Courier-Journal* presenting general news; and by the *Western Mail* in Cardiff.

What has to be remembered by advocates of eight, nine and ten columns is that six columns still yield many, many possibilities of expressing values in page layout. It is like the billiard table, only three balls and six pockets but an infinity of possible plays. A headline can go across one, two, three, four, five or six units of a six-column grid, or appear at any vertical point in a single column. Text set the width of one column can double up across two columns and there can be the occasional variations of broken measure, such as three legs across two columns.

Tabloids

The tabloid has a smaller sheet for segmenting for editorial display. The general reaction is to try to maintain the multi-column flexibility of the broadsheet by reducing column width. This has adverse effects on the legibility and economy of setting, and it is questionable whether it is needed for display, especially since tabloid

layout is in practice as much concerned with the spread as the single page. The British popular tabloids such as the *Daily Mirror* **(19)** have been basically seven-column, at about 9 picas; the European and American tabloids generally have fewer columns. Possibly it may be argued that such a seven-column format is necessary for a paper presenting lots of short stories and wanting to give a visual impression of bustle, rich interest, and story value for money. But the multi-column format can hardly be defended for sustained reading.

Le Monde, at six-column **(20),** has a slightly bigger sheet and manages 11-pica setting, but there is no doubt it would be easier to read its longer articles in five-column format. And *Le Monde* certainly neither needs nor exploits the extra display possibilities created by its sixth column.

Five Columns

The three examples show how differently the five-column format can be deployed. The *New York Daily Mirror* **(21)** compares well in liveliness with the London *Daily Mirror* example, despite the absence of two columns. And it copes with a longish story, by tabloid standards, at the foot of the page. The basic column setting is $11\frac{1}{2}$ picas. The *Daily Nation* five-column **(23)** is a more routine news page in layout (basically double-column intros with single-column

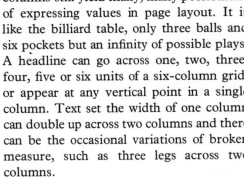

23 **24** **25**

£2,000 gift to Flying Doctors

Pro football gambling charge persists

Sports

Bulls beaten by Blazers 113-105

Dreary show by Chicago

Haywood gets 10 more days

Caray, new uniforms perk up Sox

heads in the shoulder corner), but it displays five headlines and a picture above the fold. The *Suddeutsche Zeitung* (**24**) has a slightly larger sheet than the other two tabloids. It is similar to *Le Monde* and demonstrates how longer articles can be presented with minimum headlines.

Four Columns

The text in four-column tabloids is around the optimum for text setting—14.6-pica setting in the *Chicago Sun-Times* (**25**) and *Washington Examiner* (**26**), and 14 picas in the *National Enquirer* (**22**). Layout tends to the horizontal. It is easier to read the text and easier to pick out the headlines, but the format does in practice produce pages with notably fewer display positions. Popular papers attempting four-column format would have to do better than the examples here; particular care has to be taken with cropping, sizing and placing of half-tones, with headlines (avoiding the *Chicago Sun-Times* back-page clash of oversized heads) and with colour elements such as graphics, rules, bold type and white space.

Varying Columns

Column format can be varied from page to page, of course. (It can hardly be called a format when it varies both from page to page and within a page without reference to a basic grid.) The varying format is most justified when it signals a distinct change of content, distinguishing, say, book reviews or editorial comment from general news, or when it is in response to content, such as when column setting is varied to suit a half-tone that needs a precise width. Long Island's *Newsday* and Australia's *National Times*, which favour fewer columns to a page, both vary column measure and column white. *Newsday's* standard $14\frac{1}{2}$-pica setting converts its page into four columns, and its standard 20-pica measure produces a three-column page.[6] The *National Times* is basically four-column, but it frequently mixes in a narrower column measure that would produce six columns.

Layout Analysis

I have been referring to the column grid as part of the basic format of the newspaper. The word format is borrowed from bibliography. Strictly speaking it means the shape and size of a newspaper but it is more sensibly thought of as referring to the more-or-less fixed elements in newspaper design. Allen Hutt, for instance[7], defines format as 'the shape and size of the page, expressed in the depth, number and measure of its columns.' Layout or make-up occurs within the fixed format (make-up is best reserved as a verb: we make up the page after we have laid it out on the design scheme).

Layout means the arrangement of head-

26

Virginia suburbs to drink

Cronkite wins election honors

Hobson only clear winner

27

28

lines, text, artwork, and white space on a page or sequence of pages. These definitions omit one element of newspaper design: the headline and text founts or typographical style of the newspaper. Since these are relatively fixed factors for the daily task of designing a page we can conveniently include them for this discussion as being part of the *format* of a newspaper. Layout, then, is the distribution of masses on a plan. All newspaper layouts can be categorised, and it will help the argument if the following analysis can be accepted.

   1 Layout is either static or dynamic.
   2 The static or dynamic layout must either be basically:
      (*a*) modular; or
      (*b*) irregular.

Static or Dynamic?

Layout can change while the format stays the same. The format of the London *Observer*, for instance, is a two-section newspaper printed in 11-pica columns on

broadsheet with Century Schoolbook headings. But within that format (**27, 28**) the arrangement of headlines, text, artwork and white space changes in response to what has to be communicated. This means that the layout of the *Observer*, as well as the format, is functional. The London *Daily Telegraph*, in contrast (**29, 30**), has evolved in layout terms in a way basically unresponsive to fluctuations in news. The layout as well as the format is fixed, so as to combine, oddly enough, a functionally designed format and a non-functional layout. Clearly it will be better if we can have a separate term to describe the layout which does not change. I propose to use the terms static and dynamic. The *Observer's* layout is dynamic, the *Telegraph's* static. The static layout fixes a pattern of headlines, text, and picture positions, and pours the news into the moulds each day.

Regularly in the *Telegraph* front-page layout there has been a lead headline across columns 1 and 2, regularly there has been a picture of three or four columns in the centre, regularly a double-column headline in the last two columns, and regularly there has been only one more double-column headline which has been placed underneath the picture. The inside news pages follow a similar pattern. Function is allowed to determine the run of text and hence to modify to some extent the daily positioning of other single-column headlines; and there are clearly times when the layout functions adequately for the day's news. This is another difficulty of using the term non-functional for such a layout. What it clearly does not do, however, is respond dynamically to the news. It is in a real sense a static layout. When on extraordinary occasions the lead headline is allowed to extend into a third column, the basic layout is not rearranged. The rest of the page is insulated from the change. Rather than move a picture in column 3 to make room for the intrusive lead headline a step will be cut in the picture.

With the *Observer*, on the other hand, nobody can predict what a layout will be. The lead may be on left or right, and if there is a striking picture the headlines will be submerged to make room for it. Within a fixed format the designer is attempting to respond dynamically to the news.

Which is better, dynamic or static layout? There is no immediate dogmatic answer. Function is again the test. Does the static layout work? Does it enable the messages to be communicated economically and effectively, given the readership? Superficially the static layout has the benefit of consistency. How much production help this is to editorial and printer depends on the simplicity of the static layout. The static layout can be an ingeniously complicated pattern of measured setting and interlocking units. Editorial and the printer may learn to produce this pattern daily more efficiently than they would be able to do spontaneously, but if it is really complicated it will remain a less efficient method of production than operating a dynamic layout which is based on simple principles. Most static layouts, in fact, have been simple. In so far as they are, they do make life easier for the production of the newspaper.

Once the static layout can be efficiently produced, the test becomes the viability of the fixed pattern for the varying events from day to day, and the degree to which the fixed pattern is rigidly imposed.

If the pattern is truly static it elevates form over function. The violence done to news values depends on the subtleties of the layout, but no layout designed *a priori* can genuinely reflect the news values of each and every day and their relationship to each other. The world does not order itself as conveniently as that. At the extreme the static layout produces newspapers which shout in the same tone every day, and newspapers which would treat the Second Coming as a routine event. Of course, a clever static layout, rich in news positions, may do rough justice from day to day and

29

30

the reader can grow accustomed to the formula. But it has other limitations. First, unless it already offers two positions of equal prominence and equal text-run, the paper can never suggest exquisite political balance (say, during an election or international dispute) by giving one position to one side's statement and the other to the opposing side. Secondly, a static layout positions is less flexible when a story breaks. If the layout pattern is to be preserved more work has to be done on the page because the repercussions of the rejig are wider (*see* pp. 144–152). Thirdly, static layout limits the possibility of expressing the text message in the most fitting selection and sequence of headline display words. Part of the skill of headline writing is overcoming such difficulties, but when the headline pattern can be met only at the expense of meaning it is the headline pattern which should be changed and not the meaning. The static layout does not permit this. The headline pattern is set before the text has been received. There is the negative risk of contorting language or meaning to make the headline fit—static layout daily breeds the worst headlinese gibberish; and there is the positive loss of the opportunity for marrying the text with the ideal headline words and letting these words dictate the shape of the display.

Fourthly, and most glaringly, is the corruption of picture journalism implicit in the imposition of an arbitrary shape on a fleeting image yet to be captured by the camera. The optimism that the world's best news photographs will all come in the shape, say, of a five-inch square to fit the preordained layout is appealing; it loses its charm when one sees what happens to the inconvenient picture. Equally, the static layout cannot effectively deploy the work of the graphic artist.

Some of the world's newspapers based on

a static layout implicitly recognise these handicaps, by breaking out of the pattern for big news. This has the desired effect of surprise emphasis, but the results are frequently unhappy. So unfamiliar are the editorial men to responding to news that the typographical forms chosen are invariably inefficient and clumsy pieces of private enterprise, inappropriate for the style of the newspaper. In the early days of the revised *Times*, while it was still on static layout, big news for page one was sometimes expressed by breaking out into a streamer— but a streamer in over-wordy Times Bold lower-case with insufficient white looked paltry by comparison with the streamers of the populars. The old *Yorkshire Post* made a similar mistake.

It does not follow that *any* dynamic layout is superior to any static layout. A layout which changes each day is not necessarily a layout which changes in the right

32

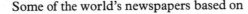

31

33

way. Change will add variety and surprise, but it must not do it at the expense of a continuity of news values or the identity of the newspaper. Some layout men get paranoid about this. They fear that someone out there (up there?) is watching them so that if ever the elements of a page arrange themselves in roughly the same way twice in a lifetime they will be struck down for un-originality. The fear is exaggerated. They are much more likely to be struck down for forcing a new pattern on a page when the text and artwork do not require it. Dynamic layout ought to be dynamic in response to news and readership, not to the layout man's itch for something new.

Modular or Irregular?

Modular layout breaks the page into a series of rectangles—headline and related text form a four-sided, rectangular unit. Irregular layout breaks the page into a series of interlocking shapes—the jigsaw. **(31),** Far left is a news page from the British *Guardian*; it is irregular. The *Guardian* feature page **(32)** is modular. If you cut out the headline and text of each of the *Guardian* feature stories you would have a series of neat cuttings, square or oblong. If you cut out a news story—say 'Powers over foreign tankers' in columns 4, 5, 6 and 7, you would have the shape of a pistol.

Compare the *Guardian* news page with modular news layout devised for *The Times* of London in its major redesign in 1970 (ignore the language—this is the paste-up lettering of the designer's original master dummy) **(33).**

The page from the *Sun* **(34)** is irregular. The page from *The Sunday Times* **(35)** is modular: the column measure changes for the rugby matches in the middle of the page, but the layout remains a series of rectangles. Both modular and irregular layout can either be static or dynamic. An irregular layout is more likely to be dynamic in our definition, because a real irregular jigsaw is unlikely to be practicable from day to day. But the *Daily Telegraph* has a static, though irregu-

lar, layout: there are degrees of irregular layout. An extremely irregular layout is distinguished by two features: (i) most or all of headline–text units on a page form irregular shapes and (ii) most or all of the headlines themselves are irregular in shape. In the *Sun* sports page, extremely irregular in layout, the main headline traverses five columns, then two. In the *Daily Telegraph's* mildly irregular layout the headlines are all modular.

Emphasis versus Organisation

What are the attractions and disadvantages of modular and irregular layout? The philosophy of functional newspaper design inevitably means that many of the detailed design solutions cannot be suggested in advance of the problem. It does not mean, however, that there are not principles to guide both layout policy and the inspiration of the moment. There are. They spring from the purpose of page design. What do we want from a page layout—the layout of any news page? Organisation is the first expectation. Nikolaus Pevsner has written of the 'rational co-ordination of heterogeneous functions that fascinates architects.'[8] Rational co-ordination of heterogeneous material fascinates page-planners, too.

There is no doubt that a modular layout organises the news into clear units. Peter Palazzo in his explanation of his redesign of the *New York Herald Tribune* perfectly caught the virtue of the modular system in a phrase. 'This modular system is very useful, it seems to me,' he said, 'because it acts as an automatic organiser for many news items on the page; I believe that much visual chaos has resulted from its abandonment.' Modular layout automatically organises the relationship of headline and text for the reader, and the run of the text so that there are no awkward jumps or turns which may lose or irritate a reader. Text, in a modular layout, is always under its related headline. It does not stray into another

34

35

column and, in a true modular layout, it is not continued to another page.

Modular layout is sometimes confused with quiet layout. It need not be. The headlines in modular layout can be as huge and as glaring and the text bedecked with decorations as in any other layout. A newspaper which adopts a modular layout does not thereby inhibit its wilder flamboyancies, nor need an irregular layout be raucous (see the *National Observer* (36) for instance). In five of the seven stories headline and text and illustration form rectangles. The lead story on Israel and the nerve gas story in the middle are the two which prevent this being described as a modular layout. There is only one qualification about the organising virtue of modular layout. It is that it sometimes leads a layout man to run a story shorter or longer than he would do on news values, simply to make a convenient rectangle. That is a danger in all layout, but modular layout imposes the extra restraint. The layout can almost always be reversed to avoid this kind of compromise with news values, but it may be a tricky job, and the temptation to cut two inches off one story and add two inches to another for the sake of a rectangle certainly exists. Modular layout, with this one proviso, has the edge over irregular layout for helping a newspaper, especially a broadsheet, to organise its news content. This is especially so when irregular layout is coupled with the indiscriminate abandonment of column rules and cut-offs between stories, a disease that has blighted readers of all too many American newspapers with bewilderment.

There is a second major principle in layout. The page has not merely to organise the news. It has to organise it to certain news values. It has to emphasise the important news to attract attention and to relegate the routine. So *emphasis* is a second value we expect from a layout. The organisation of news into a lot of neat equal and separate boxes would not be enough. Some of the boxes or shapes have to be bigger or gaudier

The scenario for escalation

36

THE NATIONAL OBSERVER

or quieter or smaller than others. And this is where many newspapers go wrong in a big way. They do not seem to appreciate that emphasis is a matter of relativity. The whisper in the quiet room is as emphatic as the shout in a hubbub. If every headline shouts there is no emphasis and that is what happens over and over again. It is this failure to realise that all display is no display that combines so frequently with severely irregular layout to transform a humble enough newspaper into a Kafkaesque confusion.

A layout can gain emphasis either by contrast or isolation. Peter Palazzo said that in converting the *Tribune* to a complete modular system he had attempted to create added readability 'through the judicious use of white space, good typography and a restrained use of pics and art work.'[9] We can, in fact, list seven ingredients of contrast:

37

type size, type design, type measure, rules, half-tones, line artwork, including reverse blocks and tints, and white space. Variation of type size and type design are overworked methods of contrast, and to an inflated scale because, I suspect, it is a clear verbal signal of contrast when written down on a layout. Instead, newspaper executives on layout should think much more *visually* in terms of the colour of the ingredients—to recognise that we are dealing with blacks, greys and whites. Consider the colour values in the spread here, on Vietnam **(37).**

Headlines and rules and the background of the reverse block are blacks, there is the greyness of text type, and the different shade of the light headline under the big black picture, and the different shade of the half-tone, and the white space of the inset and around the headline. Newspapers can gain emphasis much more effectively and eco-

nomically by colour changes than by inflating headline sizes. The student of newspaper design should try to look at a page as a black-and-white painting, and identify all the elements that change the colour. These are many and they are all tools of layout.

The illustration below **(38)** is a witty advertisement which demonstrates how emphasis can be created by blank space—perhaps the least-understood lesson in the whole of newspaper design.

Emphasis and organisation are the two basic elements but they are not a complete description. Organisation implies a sense of proportion in the weight or colour assigned to elements of a page, and balance in the distribution of the weight or colour. It implies text which is easy to follow, which does not jump away from its headline. It implies legibility and unity. Emphasis implies vigour, variety, contrast, movement. Clearly there can be conflict between the principles of organisation and emphasis, between unity and variety, and it is a satisfactory solution to this tension between them that is the test of a satisfactory page layout. The solution must depend on the newspaper and each particular message and series of messages. Entertainment newspapers or entertainment features may lean more to emphasis and variety than organisation and unity. But organisation can never be ignored; the wholly disorganised page cannot be read. And the fact that there has to be a reconciliation of the principles of emphasis and organisation should not obscure the fact that the two principles are in harmony. Emphasis must vary, and the principle of organisation means it should vary to a consistent, rational scale. Organisation means control, but control of the disparate elements of a newspaper implies the need for varying emphasis.

The arrangement of headline, text, art and white space in the grid can be guided by these principles. They are not a substitute for talent or judgment; they merely enable

38

39

40

41

judgment to be focused on what matters in a layout. And this is why it is worth examining some of the layout formulas that have been produced. Layout formulas stretch from one end of the United States to the other without reaching a conclusion.

It is imprudent, if not impossible, to devise in a vacuum a fixed layout pattern viable for all time. American textbooks often attempt this, producing half-a-dozen patterns. The newspaper, like the customer for a ready-made suit, is supposed to take one off the rack and make the body of news fit the pattern as best it can. Of course the news would suffer; it is as if the tailor says 'Sorry the trousers are too long, sir; you'll just have to shorten your legs.' Six basic layout formulas have been defined by American authorities such as Edmund Arnold and Bruce Westley,[10] roughly: Symmetrical, Informal Balance, Quadrant, Brace, Circus and Horizontal. Arnold in his latest work says he has lost his earlier enthusiasm for formulas because 'it is almost impossible to find a pure sample of a formal page layout.'[11] Westley says it is more useful to think of layout as based on four key elements (his are balance, contrast, focal points and motion) and 'three additional attributes, predictability, day-to-day contrast and the paper's over-all character.'[12]

But if layout formulas are misconceived, some do contain germs of truth, and a brief analysis of them should help to indicate some of the many structural possibilities within a column grid. We begin with the more limited geometric formulas suggesting layouts divided vertically, horizontally, diagonally and quadrilaterally; and we neglect, at the risk of incompleteness, the formula recommended in the Bulletin of the American Society of Newspaper Editors: 'Substitute a three-S make up formula (Sassy, Surprising and Satisfying) for the traditional three-D (Dignified, Dull and Disregarded).'[13]

Vertical Layout

Vertical layout gives the simplest page organisation. Headlines are set the width of the basic single-column grid and the text runs single-column. This is the oldest layout style (39). When headlines side by side are the same size and style it is called 'tombstoning' (40). As such it is extremely limited in the range of news values it can express, and it is visually depressing. But vertical layout today can have attractions. The vertical shape suggests energy,[14] which is appropriate for news, vertical layout gives the maximum number of stories above the fold, and the limitations of tombstoning can be overcome by a number of methods:

1 By alternation of colour along the horizontal line (colour being blacks, greys and whites). With modern display type, adjacent heads can be varied in weight to express different news values or tone; clashes can be avoided by setting the head in white, set left being the simplest form,

or by inserting a half-tone at the top of one of the columns.

2 By varying the width of the column grid, so that one wider setting is used to express, say, more important news. In the traditional vertical layout text is allowed to run around the top of the column and the next story starts where the previous text ends. Headlines fall haphazardly and the layout editor has no control of the colour on the page (41).

Horizontal Layout

Horizontal layout is another simple organisation but with more capacity for emphasis. The thoroughgoing horizontal layout is modular, with the text squared up under multi-column heads to create a horizontal unit. The page is then made up of a series of these units lying flat on top of each other. An extreme horizontal layout—such as (42), the *Chicago Sun-Times* in the Fifties— would have each headline set the width of the page with the text squared up.

There are four attractions in horizontal layout. The long story seems shorter; complete stories can be read with the page folded at the natural midpage fold and without the reader having to shuffle the paper up and down—quite an irritation in the bigger broadsheets; headlines are separated from each other by text, thus enabling each to retain emphasis; and unlike vertical layout, horizontal layout makes full use of the width of the page as a feature of display.

Against these four attractions there are two factors. The horizontal layout yields few stories above the fold and often only stories above the fold on page one are visible at the retail sales outlet. Secondly, a horizontal line suggests rest and repose. A page based on a series of horizontal lines may seem as monotonous as a prairie. The example (43) from the *Sun* of London, in its broadsheet days[15], is a horizontal variant: the second headline on the page and the leading article in the end columns break the rigour of the horizontal formula.

42

43

44

45

46

Quadrants and Diagonals

The quadrant formula envisages the page as four separate sections, divided by a line at the fold and again by a line down the middle of the page. Each of these four quarters is equally assigned, in Arnold's words, 'an attention compeller—a stopper,' which means a strong display unit consisting of either multi-column heads, pic or panel. The *Chicago Sun-Times* example (44) is an approximation.

This formula has the virtue of reminding the page designer that there is more to a page than the top. There are newspapers which could do worse than see that they have display or half-tone in the four corners, in what Kenneth C Reiley of Copley Newspapers, calls the hot spots.[16] The weakness of the formula, of course, is its geometric rigidity: first, the danger that there may be an inflation of news values artificially to provide 'stoppers' for the four corners; second, that the news may require the creation of a strong focal point in display type or half-tone.

A similar criticism applies to the injunction that there should be 'strength below the fold'—strong heads beneath the horizontal fold of the paper. Like the quadrant formula it omits any consideration of proportion. The unhappy result is plain in newspapers which have faithfully followed the formula, especially in Asia. Heads as strong as the lead appear beneath the fold on stories only a few paragraphs long.

Another variation of the quadrant formula is the diagonal, in which the designer is enjoined to place headings along two imaginary diagonal lines which divide the page and cross each other. The *Chicago Sun-Times* pages (45, 46) are rough approximations of diagonal layout. The formula has the small virtue of reminding us that headlines can be distributed anywhere on a page. But it gives no indication of the scale and spread of these heads. What such a rigid geometric formula does to text, news values and pictures can be left to the imagination.

Frame Layout

The frame layout is more of a gimmick than a complete formula. It offers little guidance on emphasis or organisation. The theory is that columns 1 and 8 on an eight-column page should be solid text, so that beneath the paper's title and eight-column banner heads, they frame the contents of the page. Why it should be thought necessary to frame the page like a picture is not explained; the white margins define the page area well enough, anyway. The absurdity of the frame make-up is that every day it insists on arbitrarily equal emphasis for two stories,

Brace Layout

In brace layout, headlines are arranged in steps so that the one higher in the page is supported by another running parallel. 'It gets its name from the triangular shape formed by wall, shelf, and brace when you shore up a shelf in your wife's pantry with a 2 × 2 or a metal wall-bracket. This make-up results from the very mechanics of newspaper make-up.'[17]

It results, one is tempted to say, from confusing a headline with a pantry shelf. A headline can stand by itself. A talented art director can produce a true brace layout of distinction, as Louis Silverstein of the *New York Times* has done in this experimental front page (47), but these are two disadvantages to bracing headlines one with another. The first is that each headline loses emphasis because the contiguous headlines compete for attention and deprive each other of contrast. The other is that brace layout forces the text away from its relevant headline. And, of course, brace layout cannot be modular.

The geometric patterns discussed so far may help either modular or irregular layout and do not take us anywhere in meeting the fundamental design problem of resolving the claims of organisation with those of emphasis. They indicate ways in which the grid can be sub-divided, but they give no indication whether horizontal units and so on should be combined to produce a page which is formally or informally balanced, or a page without any sign of order at all. These are, in fact, more fundamental matters than layout gimmicks. A choice has to be made, and it is a choice by no means unique to newspaper design. The history of any visual art is the history of a choice between symmetry, asymmetry, and anarchy.

Circus Layout

Circus layout (48) strives to emphasise. The term is an American one for the layout where everything seems to happen at once. 'It presents at least three rings under one tent and the reader is as confused as when he must shift his attention from the lion tamer to the juggler to the pretty gal in pink tights.'[18] In Britain we say the page is jazzy. The parallel in the underground press are those papers such as *EVO* and the *San Francisco Express Times*, which appeal to the visual senses, emphasising appearance over content (the 'head' papers). Circus, jazzy or head papers aim for layouts with variety, contrast and movement, and are happily prepared to let order and a scale of values go to the lions. The drama or comedy of the layout is as much a part of the message as the news. The reader is to be distracted, and entertained. This philosophy is helped by graphics and chromatic colour; in black-and-white papers it requires that every story is short—as many as forty to a broadsheet page and twenty to a tabloid.

Tabloid stories must be shortest of all because text soon runs to length in narrow columns. Anyone who has to produce a circus layout—and it has powered many a tabloid or metropolitan evening—should not make the mistake of assuming it means large headline type. On a tabloid, especially, that soon consumes the space. The successful circus layout needs, rather, lots of competing heads locked tightly into as intricate a pattern as possible.

Circus layout is regarded as suspect if the seams show. The layout man has to

keep breaking the column rules with horizontal headlines and make everything restive with bold text-type, sub-heads, borders, reverse blocks and underscoring. In the United States the paper's masthead is thrown into the melee, appearing in every conceivable position above the fold.

47

48

Symmetrical Layout

Here are three examples of symmetrical or balanced layout—the first **(49)** a balanced poster front page from the *Chicago Sun-Times* of 1959; the second **(50)** a classical page from the *New York Times* of 1948; and **(51)** a front page produced experimentally for *The Times* of London in 1966.

Symmetrical layout offers the designer the chance of clear organisation, but there are serious difficulties for functional emphasis. The layout attempts to produce an equal balance of weight around an axis, classically the optical centre of the page. Each side of the optical centre is a mirror reflection of the other. The headlines on one side are the same weight and form as on the other, and the run of text is the same on both sides. The optical centre is a pivotal point. The important point to note is that the optical centre of a page is in the mathematical centre of the page as a vertical unit, but is not in the mathematical centre of the page as a horizontal unit. It is a point one-third of the distance from the top. This is very curious, but the optical centre is the point at which the horizontal forces are in equilibrium with the vertical forces. It is the point of perfect balance.

Vincent Steer has described a useful test of this and readers might try it:

'On a card of rectangular proportions rule a vertical line from top to bottom the longest way of the card, dividing it into two equal halves. Then stick a pin into the mathematical centre of the vertical line and twirl the card in a circular motion. When the movement ceases the card will not hang in a vertical position, but will rather tend towards the oblique. Now stick a pin in the card at the optical centre of the vertical line, one-third the distance of its entire length from the top. Twirl it again and when the movement ceases the card will hang in a perfectly upright position.'[19]

To achieve a classically symmetrical layout you place the optical centre of the mass on the optical centre of the area. This is easy enough when you have only one mass or design element, such as a single set of headlines on a feature page.

The optical centre of the mass is determined in the same way as the optical centre of the area. It is a point at the centre of the width of the mass, but one-third the distance from the top of the mass.

Try out this idea of optical centre on a blank sheet of paper. Find and cut out a headline unit, say, 5in. wide by 3in. deep, or a block of half-tone cut from a newspaper will do. Bisect the blank sheet vertically. Place the display unit so that $2\frac{1}{2}$in. of its width falls one side of the line and $2\frac{1}{2}$in. the other side. Now move the unit up and down on the blank sheet until it seems to be in symmetrical balance. You should discover that at this point the optical centre of the headline unit (i.e. one inch from its top) coincides with the optical centre of the blank paper.

To achieve symmetrical layout when two design masses have to be disposed on a page, the larger or bolder of the two is placed at the centre of balance. The smaller is centred on the vertical dividing line at a point near the base. Naturally, the more display elements there are, the more judgment is required to produce a symmetrical layout. And the judgment is visual, not mechanical. That is the point of emphasising here the primacy of the optical centre; I do not recommend that deskmen who wish to get on should start sticking pins through layouts and twirling them in front of the managing editor. But, as in headline spacing (*see* Book Three), I do stress the importance of cultivating the eye's sense of balance.

The principle of symmetrical layout is often misunderstood. Symmetrical layout need not be static from day to day. Two single-column headlines can balance one day, two three-column headlines another. It need not be quiet, as the poster example shows. So long as there are two symmetrical halves, the composition of each statement is a matter for the designer. The balancing masses can be expressed in big or small headlines in modular or irregular units, though a symmetrical layout is easier to design in modular units.

The essence of axial symmetry is simply balance at the centre. The idea that symmetry stands for unchanging layout arose because many newspapers, once they had achieved a symmetrical layout, were reluctant to change it for another symmetrical layout and so they ended up squeezing the news into a predetermined shape.

Symmetrical layout has a powerful appeal for serious papers. It appears to satisfy the newspaper's need rationally to organise its heterogeneous content. It satisfies the mind's natural demand for balance. Conversely, symmetrical layout is no use for papers which thrive on excitement. The difficulty even for cool, serious papers is that the requirement of symmetrical balance will in practice restrict the requirement of emphasis to the point of distortion of news values. However much the symmetrical layout changes from day to day, it must still balance about an axis, and this inevitably means promoting or understating stories or pictures—changing their emphasis to make them fit a pattern. Anyone who has attempted to produce a wholly symmetrical page also knows that it is exceedingly difficult to achieve. It means the most careful casting-off, and agonies on the stone. For a serious, dignified newspaper, produced at leisure, or for features, these difficulties may not deter because of the attractions of symmetry in reducing the chaos of the world to a Palladian order.

The unanswered question is how strong is our natural desire for emphasis as well as balance, for movement and vigour as well as order. Perfect balance may produce a temporary satisfaction. It may even meet the requirements of the news. But it can also bore us to death. Asymmetrical layout, which follows, is an attempt to have both order and emphasis.

86

52

53

54

55

56

Asymmetrical Layout

Asymmetric layout can be modular or irregular. **(55, 56)** are two experimental pages from *Sunday Asia* (later successfully translated into production). They are asymmetric and modular.[20] Irving's front page (p. 62, **15**) is symmetrical; Palazzo's (p. 23) asymmetrical. The equilibrium provided by asymmetrical layout is dynamic. It excludes any *axial* symmetry, any predetermined point of balance. In symmetrical layout the elements are balanced above a strong central pivotal point. In asymmetrical layout there is a balance of unequal forces at unequal distances from the centre.

It is what the judges in the old N W Ayer design contest in the United States called 'artistic balance' and Edmund Arnold 'informal balance.' Vincent Steer has a vivid metaphor. It is the balance of a man walking a tightrope: 'It will vary in position according to the number of elements, their relative proportions to one another, and their value in colour or scale.'[21] In painting it is the equilibrium achieved by Piet Mondrian in matching big uncoloured areas against small coloured areas.

In newspaper layout terms, it is the equilibrium achieved by matching a large single headline on a page against the cumu-

lative effect of a multiplicity of smaller elements with strong colour.

The summary index in the end column of *Sunday Asia* is balanced dynamically against the colour of the lead headline and the single-column half-tone in column 2. In the second page the panel is off-centre, taking weight to the right, but the lead headline, the page logotype Trend, and the well-whited drawing of the shoe restore equilibrium.

White space is not part of the background, or a mere frame, as it is in symmetrical layout. It is an active part of the balancing force. 'Every element in the design sets up structural links between itself and the edges of the paper as well as with all other elements in the layout.'[22]

If the idea of asymmetric balance is hard to envisage in the abstract, it is easy to see in paint or print. The illustration **(52)** is a composition by Piet Mondrian whose art relied on a rectangular grid structure and an asymmetrical balance of primary colours and non-colours (grey, black and white). It could easily form the grid for an asymmetrical newspaper layout.

But have a look at the decimal currency advertisement **(53)** and the *Guardian* feature page. Here, too, there is the asymmetric balance of a Mondrian composition **(54)**.

THE TIMES

Dock strike threat over suspensions

Top bridge players in libel suit

Death fire company blamed

Employers' tough line against militants

LSE call for inquiry by outsiders

Nixon sets February 24 as date of London visit

Ex-nationalists to support O'Neill

57

Daily Mail

FIRST WORD TODAY

By J L MANNING

Stop this Soccer crowds scandal!

'Don't pay your bills' strike threat by MPs

Four escape from mid-air crash

Abominable snowmen?

Gina: I look better than ever at 40

WHAT was the answer

HOW

WHAT

Striped pants

End this stigma, says MP

Oil Central Heating
cheapest to run—now cheap to buy
£135 £185
£245
£325 £369
FREE

Three pay for their QE gold

Stunt students suspended

59

THE GUARDIAN

Cathy may come home to housing surplus in 1973

Unionist swing to Mr O'Neill

Guardian Northern editor

Scots Greys fight to last

3,000 dockers suspended for striking

More opposed to inquiry

THE WEATHER

STOP PRESS

Dysentry at nursery

61

THE TIMES

Dock strike threat over suspensions

Top bridge players in libel suit

Garrison outlines Kennedy 'plot'

Employers' tough line against militants

Privy Seal should make good impression

Bonn determined to go ahead with airbus

THE REST OF THE NEWS

London breathes more freely

Saigon may talk with Hanoi in secret

S Africans to float German loan—but gold clause likely

'Secret' engine seen in Russia

Mr's widow to 'go undecive'

58

Daily Mail

FIRST WORD TODAY

By J L MANNING

Stop this Soccer crowds scandal!

'Don't pay your bills' strike threat by MPs

Four escape from mid-air crash

Abominable snowmen?

Gina meets the Campbell clan

WHAT was Beatle Paul McCartney denying last night?

HOW

WHAT

Striped pants

The courage of a man

Russians 'quizzed by police'

Britain goes ahead

O'Neill calls an election

Three pay for their QE gold

Stunt students suspended

Oil Central Heating
cheapest to run—now cheap to buy
£135 £185
£245
£325 £369
FREE

60

THE GUARDIAN

Cathy may come home to housing surplus in 1973

Unionist swing

Guardian Northern editor

Scots Greys fight to last

3,000 dockers

Mr Callaghan ends fears

Police not to get riot gas grenades

Ferry plan for Isle of Skye

THE WEATHER

Shopping precinct for Labour MPs fear blunder

62

In the examples above I have taken a newspaper layout and spoiled it to demonstrate still further how asymmetric balance can·be achieved or destroyed.

The front page of *The Times* (57) is asymmetrical. I have converted it into more of a symmetrical layout (58). The original *Daily Mail* page (59) is asymmetrical. There is symmetry in those matching single-columns but the whole is not balanced on a central axis. I have then deliberately destroyed the balance by introducing (60) more horizontal headlines down page, which weaken the vertical force of the columns and half-tone against the strong horizontal lead.

My other example, a *Guardian* back page (61), has balance and movement. But the second version (62) again over-emphasises a down-page story, spoiling the lead and destroying the balance of the page as well.

There is no longer asymmetric balance: the page is bottom heavy. A real improvement for the page **(61)** would be to leave the layout alone but increase to 36pt the size of the double-column headline below the blocks, cols 4–5.

Achieving Asymmetry

If you go back to the *Sunday Asia* front page and copy it out on a layout pad you may sense how, given the scale of news values, the layout developed. Draw in first the four-column photograph and the lead summary index. If you are aiming at an asymmetrical layout, you will find yourself wanting first to introduce some compensating colour to the left-hand side of the page (the column 2 picture) and wanting to balance the lead with another strong horizontal at the fold (US Business), but since the weight of the lead is heavily to the left, the next horizontal headline must tend to the right. To have another three-column headline under the text of the lead would begin to give the page a static symmetry. So the US Business story asymmetrically set single-column against the lead's $1\frac{1}{2}$ columns, has headlines which break the column rule descending from the lead story. Once these stories are drawn in you are left with columns 6 and 7 under the picture story and the foot of the page.

Again, a three-column shape, this time of the US Business story, is not repeated. A headline goes across four columns, breaking the column 5 rule, and colour is required here to pull against the strong colour at the top of the page. The headline is therefore in bold to echo—in lower key—the bold of the lead headline and it is supported by a half-tone for colour.

Asymmetrical layouts have rhythm and momentum as well as a balance more subtle than symmetry. The attraction of asymmetry for newspaper design is that it enables the page to satisfy our natural desire for order, organisation and balance while also providing emphasis and movement. The eye is not brought to a point of rest as it is in symmetrical layout. It is drawn on throughout the page until the whole message has been comprehended. Balance is there but it is not mechanical. It resembles the balance of a Mozart symphony rather than the balance of a metronome. And the striking thing is that the layout does not force the news to conform to a set pattern.

Asymmetrical layout opens so many rational options that it assists, rather than handicaps, the overriding functional relationship of content and display. It can include elements which are symmetrically related, but it is not tied to a central pivotal point. If you think of the newspaper page as divided vertically and horizontally by a grid into a series of interlocking cells you have a permutation of strong and weak display positions which can be balanced with a permutation of strong and weak display elements. A weak display element like a light 24pt single-column headline in a strong position can balance, say, a bold panel or half-tone in a weak position— balancing by tonal colour rather than simply by geometric pattern.

There are an infinite number of these relationships. By their nature it is not possible to prescribe them in detail. The shape of the page changes as soon as you introduce the first dominant display. The shape of that will suggest a series of possible responses which, in turn, will be suggested by the nature of the message.

Conclusions

At the end of a chapter discussing design in the absence of a specific news stimulus, it may be necessary to say again what has been a theme of this book: that no aesthetic arrangement, no geometric delight, which fails to serve the message can be contemplated. It does not matter if the layout design has balance, order, movement, vitality, rhythm and is described as the layout of the twenty-first century; if the space it provides for a column story is only half a column then it has failed, utterly and irrevocably.

But certain principles do emerge with

sufficient force to enable us to elaborate the preliminary list suggested (p. 8) for assessing the functional efficiency of a traditional newspaper. For any newspaper, tabloid or broadsheet, in any situation with any kind of readership, the following principles apply for news-page format and layout:

Page Format

1 The first page of one or more sections must always identify the paper and signal its content.

2 The page format must be based on a column grid and the nearer to the optimum grid for readable text the better.

3 The format should be based on harmony in display faces for similar content, and the more reliance on one family the better.

4 The format should be capable of communicating any conceivable range of news while retaining a continuous sense of values.

Page Layout

1 The layout should have both organisation (balance, scale and coherence) and emphasis (vigour, movement and a focal point).

2 It should, therefore, arrange that predictable expected items are in predictable expected places. It should, therefore, also arrange that unpredictable, unexpected items should have the degree of emphasis they require. This requires dynamic, not static, layout.

3 The layout should be economical in space and in time of editorial and production.

4 Where editions change it should be flexible between editions to a consistent scale of values. This suggests dynamic, not static, layout.

5 Page layout ought to be immediately intelligible. What is related must be seen to be related. What is meant to be read, must be readable. This can be achieved either by irregular or modular layout but it is easier with modular layout.

6 Layout should choose changes of visual signal most appropriate for the message (headline display, colour graphics, positioning on a page).

7 Layout should exploit all the possibilities of a page and not merely part.

These are positive aims. What needs to be cleared away negatively has been well stated by judges in the British Newspaper Design Award.

'Muddled make-up and over-fussy presentation, embarked upon in a misguided effort to arouse, or maintain, interest; over-crowding main news pages with too many stories, so that the main stories lose impact and the reader is confused; allowing a main display heading and a dominant news half-tone to fight each other (to the disadvantage of both); paying insufficient attention to the detail of feature headings, including their subsidiary items—by-lines, tags, straplines and the like; ill-considered advertisement make-up (most noticeable in the weeklies) which sometimes completely subverts what editorial space is left; lack of any design standards in the typography and layout of house-set advertisements; indifference to the style of the title-piece, particularly in the sense of effective emphasis on its significant distinctive part.'[23]

And in 1966:

'In too many papers there appears to be a general lack of discipline or clear decision about the relative importance and therefore the varying typographical treatment of individual items of news or features.'[24]

Design standards have been improving in the British press, notably in the local papers, but too slowly. They have been improving more quickly in North America, but in the limited area of typography. Display standards are variable, the use of photographs lamentable, and hardly any newspapers have challenged their chaotic advertising sensibly. The underground press, in America and Britain, has nothing to teach on this, nor on typography, where it has a lot to learn from the traditional newspaper, but in graphics, artwork and the use of polychromatic colour in offset printing, the underground press has made many

63

traditional newspapers seem unimaginative. The judges in the N W Ayer contest in their final report said of American newspapers: 'A major development in recent years has been the abandonment by many newspapers of attempts to make every element on a page stand out and grab a reader's attention.'[25] That has been commendable, on the whole, but there is now too much anaemia in headline founts and illustration, too little use of graphic analysis and good artists (*see* Book Four) and of the colour elements possible even for a black-and-white paper; and some of the reaction against the crowding of the old-time circus layout has been excessive. For instance, those two distinguished American designers, Howard Copley and Ed Arnold, have been commending white space on a page in too indiscriminate a manner, with some awful results.

It is not right to say 'Fresh air is as pleasant in a newspaper as in a crowded room; so any way we can open up our pages is desirable.'[26] White space should not be squandered. It should be conserved and massed in those places where it throws light on in places where it throws light on display.

But one part of the American experiment —the trend to more readable columns— deserves the closest attention of newspaper people everywhere. Ed Arnold says with some justice that the 'optimum format' where body type is set at or near its optimum line length (*see* Book Two) is the most exciting layout development in the US.

It is tempting to speculate on the newspaper of the future. Of course there is no such single thing because there will be as many kinds of newspapers as there are news–audience relationships. To Clive Irving it will be hybrid, part newspaper, part magazine in format. To James Moran it will be like 'a marriage of *The Sunday Times* and *Daily Mirror*—lively but serious and educational and good to look at'[27] with web offset litho improving picture quality and facsimile transmission providing the means for local editions. But page design divorced from the pressure of news, as an experiment with front pages by advertising agency designers showed **(63),** will not take us very far beyond cosmetics.

My view is that the large tabloid format will gain favour, that circus layouts will give way to asymmetric, modular layouts. Body type will move to 9pt but still in serif letters. Variety and richness will be sought not in layout intricacy and headline inflation but in integrated editorial polychromatic colour (for offset papers) and in textural colour for black and white papers, and most of all in better artwork and graphics which will have to demonstrate analytical quality, wit and flavour.

But forecasters should have a sense of humility. When the perfect standard newspaper is produced it will be a very dull day for all of us.

6 The Tabloid Newspaper

*The allegation by the quality papers is that
while they are busy every day bringing down
ten more tablets from Mount Sinai, the popular
press is solely occupied with the diversions of
Sodom and Gomorrah. This is utter humbug.*

—HUGH CUDLIPP

A tabloid is not, in design, simply a broadsheet done on smaller pages. It has special opportunities and problems. Simply to shrink broadsheet layout and display sizes to fit tabloid dimensions produces the effect of looking at a broadsheet newspaper through the wrong end of a telescope. That was the mistake made in its very early days by Britain's *Daily Mail* when in the spring of 1971 it transformed itself into a 'compact' (of that description the Hon. Vere Harmsworth, chairman of Associated Newspapers said: 'We didn't want it confused with the term tabloid which has come to have a sensational image, so we had to invent a new word').[1]

The *Manchester Evening News* did it in reverse in 1950, turning itself from a tabloid to a broadsheet. At first the sizes and layout ideas of the tabloid were transferred to the broadsheet; and the pages were weak. More ideas and different headline sizes are needed to exploit the possibilities of a broadsheet. But the *Evening News* change was made to work, to the eventual extinction of its tabloid rival, when it had to respond to a series of big news events. Its booming classified advertisements worked better in a broadsheet since in a tabloid lots of classified (as in London's *Evening Standard*) produces so many pages that the back of the paper can be unmanageable: a pull-out centre section of classified, used by the *Wolverhampton Express and Star* and the *Manchester Evening News*, among others, is more convenient. Bulk of fifty pages and upwards can create a chore for tabloid

readers. Editorial pull-out sections can help but emphatic identification is required, as in this sectional front-page from the large tabloid *Times Educational Supplement* (**1**).

The unbulky *Daily Mail* was beginning to evolve more satisfactorily in page design when this book went to press, though lumbered with a pop seven-column format for an avowedly middlebrow paper. The possible column formats and front-page philosophies for tabloid have already been discussed; in this section we look at some of the other layout opportunities and problems.

I

The Centre Spread

These examples are all of failures to use the centre spread.

The broadsheet's most dramatic display area is the front page. In the tabloid the front page is rivalled by the centre spread. Type or pictures can be taken into and across the gutter to provide a large area going the full width of both pages. The paper can also be up-ended and a two-page vertical display area created across the gutter; clearly the vertical centre spread should be used only on those rare occasions when the words demand 22in. columns, say for some tabulation; or when a photograph or graphic art needs a huge vertical area, say for a detailed cut-away drawing of a moon rocket. British tabloids have used the centre spread

imaginatively. In North America and Europe it is a wasting asset, and the underground press, despite its yearning for graphic revolution, has by and large been cowed by the 2in. barricade of the centre gutter.

The first two (2, 3) from the *Cambridge Evening News* and a house paper, *Field Promotions*, both retain the gutter. The failure is aggravated in the *Cambridge Evening News* by the thin shape of the double-column headline on the right. If a newspaper is shy of attempting a centre spread (and it is easy to come a cropper), at least the gutter must be flanked by full lines or half-tone. As for the spread from *Field Promotions*, where is one supposed to travel on the left-hand page among the three headlines on the same story?

The examples (4-6) on the facing page are from Finland's *Suomenaa*, the *Philippines' Daily Star,* and the Stockholm *Expressen*. In all of them the gutter is used but the centre spread is being thought of as two pages rather than one. The seams show. The Finnish newspaper commits the sin of bringing text from the left page to the right page under an unrelated headline.

Above, four different treatments of the centre—of only varying success. First (7) is a picture spread from the *Daily Mirror* (New York). Curiously, considering its pedigree, the *Mirror* rarely pulls off a convincing centre spread. The 4in. wide picture of a model girl, with windy caption, seems merely to paper thinly over the gutter instead of treating the spread as a single unit. The picture is too small and its colour too concentrated in the middle; closer cropping producing a deeper picture would have helped the picture as a picture.

The *Rolling Stone* example (8) is a single-feature centre spread, but contrast the confident picture sizing and placing with the New York *Mirror's* diffidence. The *Rolling Stone* spread is pulled together inside Oxford rules.

The mixed *National Enquirer* spread (9) is effective enough. The weight and text run of the left-hand display is just right to provide asymmetric balance.

The *National Times* of Australia (10) gives us a centre spread by a serious tabloid. The spread has been treated as a single area. It is united by the thick rule running across and the horizontal headline enclosed in rules. The wide-measure text is easy to read and to follow. The weakness is in picture placing. The grey centre of the spread could do with the colour of the large half-tone which would make the text appear less dauntingly long to read; and in both half-tones the subjects are looking right away out of the page—apparently at something more interesting.

14 DAILY SKETCH, Friday, November 21, 1969

THE PINKVILLE MA

THE COMPLETE FILE OF EVIDENCE...IN THE WORDS OF THE M

WITNESS Do Chuc. Aged 48. A farmer. He survived because he fell at the first gun burst and was covered with a shield of his friends' bodies as the soldiers cut them down He says:

We were eating our breakfasts when our village was hit by artillery fire. The barrage went on for about 30 minutes. Suddenly there were eight American helicopters in the sky above us.

We had no reason to fear the Americans. They were our friends. The troops came from the helicopters and ordered us out of our homes. Everyone. Men, women and babies.

They marched us a few hundred yards and made us squat down. Still we had no reason to be afraid. The Americans are friends.

We were divided into three groups of about 200, 100 and 70.

They set up a gun on three legs and the people started crying and begging for their lives. A monk showed one soldier his identification papers, but the soldiers just said "Sorry."

Then the shooting started. I was wounded in the leg and other bodies just fell over me. There was machine-gun fire and rifle fire. I stayed still for about an hour and then it became quiet. When I got out from under the bodies, there were only about 80 of us who had survived.

WITNESS Ronald L. Haeberle. Aged 28. Former Army photographer who took pictures of the massacre. He says:

I couldn't believe what I was seeing. Off to the right, I noticed a woman appear from some cover and this GI fired first at her. Then they all started shooting at her. Aimed at her head.

The bones were flying in the air chip by chip. I'd never seen Americans shoot civilians like that.

WITNESS Michael Bernhardt. Sergeant in one of the three platoons which attacked My Lai. He says:

I walked up and saw these guys (soldiers) doing strange things. They were setting fire to hootches (huts) and waiting for people to come out. And then they shot them.

They were gathering others into groups and shooting them too. I saw them shoot an M79 grenade launcher into a group of people who were still alive. But it was mostly done with a machine gun. They were just shooting women and children like anybody else.

We met no resistance, and I only saw three captured weapons. It was just like any other Vietnamese village of old papas, and women and kids. As a matter of fact, I don't remember seeing one military-age male in the entire place, dead or alive.

THE INCIDENT at My Lai, known to American troops as Pinkville, took place 20 months ago. Reports have been buried in official files. Only now is America and the whole world able to piece together the facts of that morning of horror.

Charlie Company hit My Lai as the red sun was lancing through the smoke from breakfast fires, soon after dawn on March 16, 1968. Before it moved far across the sky, probably 400 South Vietnamese lay dead among the black ashes of the village huts.

It was a morning that stained the American purpose. A morning of incredible brutality and atrocities. Americans have been outraged.

A full military inquiry is investigating, and Lieutenant William L. Calley, aged 26, who was on the raid, is being charged with the murder of 109 civilians. His squad leader, Sergeant David Mitchell, aged 29, is being investigated for assault with intent to murder.

Few villagers survived the blazing guns. But those who did are recalling that bloody breakfast time. So are some of the soldiers who were there. This is their story.

WITNESS "Can"—a woman who, according to the North Vietnamese, escaped from My Lai and told in a letter of the atrocities:

From the moment the aggressors entered the village they fired on everything, sparing no one, destroying homes, killing the cattle.

The mother of one child, Mrs. Vo Thi Phu, was shot dead through the neck while nursing her baby. They covered them with lime and set fire to them.

The GIs went to the shelter of a Mrs. Mui. They forced her and another woman, Mrs. Mot, to emerge, raped them and then shot them dead, also their four children.

In another part of the village, a 60-year-old woman was raped and then a bayonet stuck through her throat. A pregnant woman had her abdomen slit open. Another soldier thrust his bayonet into a child's stomach. A man, aged 71, had his throat cut and his body thrown down a well.

A Mrs. Phung Thi Ly was killed with her two children by a burst of machine-

---

gun fire. Before she died she screamed to her mother: "I can't go on. Take care of the children in the trench."

WITNESS Michael Terry. Private in one of the platoons. He says:

They just marched through shooting everybody. Seems like no one said anything. They just started pulling people out and shooting them. At one point about 30 and 40 villagers were lined up in front of a ditch and shot, just like the Nazi thing.

One officer ordered a kid to machine-gun everybody down, but the kid just couldn't do it. He threw the machine gun down. I don't remember seeing any men in the ditch, mostly women and kids.

Later, when some of the platoon were taking a lunch break, I noticed some of the people in the ditch were still breathing. They were pretty badly shot up. They weren't going to get any medical help, so we shot maybe five of them.

Why did it happen? I think that probably the officers didn't really know if they were ordered to kill the villagers or

---

not. A lot of guys feel th[...] Vietnamese aren't human be[...] just treated them like animals.

WITNESS: an unidentifie[...] can soldier, who tells the tra[...] of a little boy. He says:

There was a small boy of th[...] standing by a trail with a gunsh[...] in the arm. He was clute[...] wounded arm with his other h[...]

11

At last, here are true tabloid centre spreads, conceived and executed as a unit.

The first **(11)** from the defunct *Daily Sketch* (Britain), is a simple but searing presentation of the evidence for the My Lai killings in Vietnam. The spread is held together by a deep white-on-tint reverse heading, with subsidiary line. Possibly the cartoon could have been moved leftwards one leg to provide a right-flanking column of text, but it would have meant shortening the introductory bold setting in columns 2,

3, 4. Colour is provided in the clean wide-measure text by a few lines of bold with a sans drop letter; the only pity is the frequency of that disconcerting W.

The *Sunday Mirror* **(12)** provides a brilliant example of what Harold Keble has called sophisticated sensationalism. Note especially the ingenious third-dimensional effect of angling the caged girl against the right-hand reversed panel. The headline stencil-lettering of course continues the spoof about the crated girl.

A picture spread from the British *Sun* (**13**), shows part of a feature reviewing the end of the decade. Both the pictures of the Kennedy brothers had been published before, but juxtaposed like this they made a powerful appeal. The spread is linked by a heavy rule across the top with reverse lettering and a pica panel rule. The separation of the pictures by a white band, providing space for two neat captions set left and set right, is a good touch.

Finally (**14**) a less startling but none the less sound use of a tabloid centre spread to provide an information feature, a second example taken from the *Sun*. This spread is part of a four page pull-out in the centre of the paper on the big race. The *Sun* uses the space to relax with 27-pica setting to provide a clear race card. It's all, except the winner, we could ask for.

15

18

16

17

Ad Shapes and Placings

The centre spread can carry display advertising, but the shape and placing of it, and of the related editorial is important. The editorial has the best chance when the display ad is a narrow solus running to the top of the page, leaving editorial with a clear rectangle; or alternatively a shallow (say 4in.) horizontal ad across one or both pages.

That is an unusual shape for an ad, but again it leaves editorial what it needs: a simple shape. The *Daily Mail* example **(18)** tries hard against the ad but does not really succeed, especially with the short top line of the heading. More successful is the spread on TV commercials **(15)**, where the *Daily Mirror* has the display ad to the top of the column, filling the bottom with one of its strip cartoons. The top of the spread then gets off to an unequivocal start.

It is possible in a tabloid to gain the effect of a spread even when the two pages are not in the centre. But the link must be more in the *Sun* **(17)** where the repetition of the overline display dress adds extra pressure to the glue of the heavy white-on-black reverse blocks.

The other attempt to link two pages, one with only a two-column editorial hole and huge bold display ad, defeats, not surprisingly, even the *Mirror* **(16)**. The layout man has correctly got Mr Wilson looking from one page to the other at the same depth as the headings on the second page, and there is a linking rule. But the connection, without headline, is not strong enough, especially since there is so much weight on the right-hand page. It exhibits all the wheezing congestion of a typographical patient who ought urgently to be admitted to our clinic (Chapter 9).

19

20

21

22

A Redesigned Tabloid

Fleet Street did not like the new *Evening Standard* when it first saw it in the autumn of 1969. Perhaps this was because an advertising agency had something to do with the new look or because familiar things were moved. Mistakes there certainly were, and they were remedied: the placing of the leading article in the end column of a double spread, as if it were a kind of afterthought; the excessive use of 12pt full face plus 3pt rules in various sections, sometimes broken into two or three bits with label words in 24pt in the breaks; the full-measure cut-off rules over shorts, which can create a ladder effect in a newspaper running to a lot of shorts. But the other major change of rules (the substitution of $1\frac{1}{2}$pt face rule for light rule) has rightly stayed, and so has the determination to set the paper exclusively in Century Schoolbook/Century Schoolbook Bold rather than the mixture of Century Bold in all styles, with Franklin and medium condensed grots for variety.

The new style **(22)** (though the rather inflated headlines could do with a shade more white) has vigour and style; the old one had merely bric-a-brac variety **(19)**.

The *Standard's* revamp gave it a centre spread for features which is useful for a busy evening paper. Feature plans can be devised in relative leisure to develop a consistently distinctive style. The spread consisting of Londoner's Diary (the old **(20)** and new **(21)** styles are illustrated), editorial, and feature is generally vivacious.

23 **24** **25**

Broadsheet into 'Compact'

The *Daily Mail* was the world's first popular newspaper, a mass circulation newspaper designed for a newly literate mass audience. On May 3, 1971, seventy-five years to the day after Lord Northcliffe launched the original *Mail*, the paper underwent a revolution itself. Vere Harmsworth, a descendant of Alfred Harmsworth (later Lord Northcliffe) turned the broadsheet *Mail* (see page 87) into a small tabloid (15in. × 12in.) and merged with it Associated Newspaper's tabloid *Daily Sketch*. Mr Harmsworth[2] said a tabloid had economic attractions: 'Although an 18-page *Mail* and a 36-page compact are equivalent in quantity of newsprint, the attraction to advertisers of a tabloid shape is well known. They have far greater impact, far greater page traffic, and they get it for less. From the point of view of the publisher he gets more per inch of his newsprint. We get a higher conversion factor on our newsprint.' As for the editorial, it would 'appeal to the existing enormous middle readership which doesn't want titillation—it is more intelligent than that—and at the same time finds the heavies not to its taste.'

The compact (23-25) opted for a signal-and-text front page with irregular layout changing dynamically day to day under a permanent full-measure title. Hermann Zapf's Melior Bold Condensed was chosen for the all-caps main headline. In the early days the news content, like the title, was boxed with rules with round corners, reminiscent of *Newsday*, Long Island, but this rule was later abandoned because it was rightly felt to appear too contrived.

A front page with a summary index as column 6 was considered at the dummy stage (23) but rejected. This was a pity, because it would have been a distinctive and useful feature in the *Mail* and it would automatically provide the colour and busyness the layout men have sought by getting three or more stories on to the front; the *Mail* has not followed the *Mirror* (New York or London) in having frequent single-subject front pages. When it does—with the Soyuz tragedy, at three-columns to the page—it looks much more convincing (25).

Given the aim of the *Daily Mail* compact of wanting to appeal to the middlebrow market, the design criticism must be that a seven-column tabloid format is a contradiction. It invites chopped-up short stories. The *Daily Mail* went for an $8\frac{1}{4}$-pica column, which is very narrow even for the relatively condensed Jubilee face transferred from the broadsheet. A second design criticism, given the planned appeal of the paper, is that the headlines take too much space—a common enough fault in tabloid—and they have been too fidgety in typography.

In the first example of an inside news page (26), the headline on the Essay Row story takes 10in. and the accompanying text

7in. That is not untypical. It is one of the consequences of seven-column format. In the second (TUC) example **(27)** the lead has text about equal in space with the headline and there is an awkward L-shaped advertisement which looks like editorial. Its projecting half-tone is separated from the news by too flimsy a fine rule.

The basic Century Schoolbook Bold works well enough, but there is restlessness in display dress. The neatly logotyped World Wide page **(28)** has no fewer than seven variations of headline style, down to a Franklin Bold caps with wavy underscore.

Where the new *Daily Mail* did succeed

at once was in its feature treatments—the editorial page **(29)**, the facing page **(30),** the letters **(31)** and Briefing **(32)** (and also the City page). All these, save Briefing, have been set wide-measure, usually 9pt, with up to 2 picas of column white. The editorial, which used to be on column 1 of the front page of the broadsheet, was moved to page 6 and separated from the features by a pica full-face vertical rule. The main headline dress has generally been simple—Schoolbook with perhaps a dash of Ludlow (or Cooper) Black. On Briefing, the idea of a quick compact up-dating has been sustained by graphics—the Cinderella of tabloids.

34

Newsday / 5 CENTS MONDAY JULY 8, 1968
THE LONG ISLAND NEWSPAPER

Cong: May Ask Outside Aid

National Liberation Front spokesman warns that the Viet Cong may ask for the aid of international 'volunteers' if the U.S. does not withdraw its troops from South Vietnam. Story on Page 3.

LBJ to Visit 4 More Latin Countries
The President says that he desires a 'new road of hope' for western countries. Story on Page 2.

HHH: Study Delegates
Vice president asks look at New York group's ethnic basis. Story on Page 5.

CORE Is Split On Black Power
Parley closes as 'rebels' quit. Story on Page 7.

SOUTHERN HOSPITALITY. An elderly woman greets President Johnson as he leaves a cathedral in San Salvador yesterday. At Johnson's side is his daughter, Mrs. Luci Nugent. The President was to leave El Salvador today on the return leg of his trip to Central America, stopping briefly in four countries to drop off their presidents, who attended joint meetings. Story, other photos on Page 2.

COPYRIGHT 1968, NEWSDAY INC. LONG ISLAND, NEW YORK, VOL. 28, NO. 239

35

Newsday / 5 CENTS FRIDAY DEC. 13, 1968
THE LONG ISLAND NEWSPAPER

Bridge Access: 3 More Choices

Story on Page 3

Pan-Am Jet Explodes; 51 Die in Crash

Caracas, Venezuela (AP)—A Pan Amm jet exploded over the Caribbean Sea and plunged into the water last night 16 miles from Venezuela's international airport north of Caracas.

Fifty-one persons were reported aboard, 42 passengers and a crew of nine, including a trainee stewardess. A search for survivors was continuing, but none was reported. Two Long Islanders, including the pilot, were among the crew members. Officials said it was possible not all the bodies would be recovered. Thirteen bodies have been recovered. "There are no signs of life," patrolmen said after a 12-hour search. The Boeing 707 was Pan American's flight 217, non-stop from New York to Caracas. Most of the passengers apparently were Latin Americans but some were U.S. citizens or residents.

Mosquito control tower said that it lost radio contact with the jet six minutes before it went due to land. At the time, the plane was 16 miles from the airport and approaching at 1,000 feet. Pan American spokesmen in New York said that the jet sent no message that it was in trouble.

Pan American said that the jet's captain was Sidney E. Stillwaugh of West Islip, L.I. The co-pilot was William J. Canoll of Upper Saddle River, N.J.; the engineer, Richard H. Titus of Ridgewood, N.J.; pursers, Alfred C. Perez of Valley Stream, L.I., and Mrs. Heidrun M. Coplan of New York City, and stewardesses, Francisko C. —Continued on Page 2

UNCLE AGAIN. Sen. Edward M. Kennedy smiles as he gets into his car yesterday at Georgetown University Hospital in Washington after visiting his sister-in-law Mrs. Ethel Kennedy, who gave birth yesterday to the 11th child of the late Sen. Robert F. Kennedy, a little more than six months after his death. (Story on Page 6.)

COPYRIGHT 1968 NEWSDAY INC. LONG ISLAND, NEW YORK, VOL. 29, NO. 87

36

Newsday / 5 CENTS WEDNESDAY DEC. 18, 1968
THE LONG ISLAND NEWSPAPER

LAUGH-UP. Astronaut James Lovell, right, cracks up over joke by fellow Apollo 8 astronaut Bill Anders during break in training yesterday at Cape Kennedy. The astronauts were in a mission simulator practicing for their moon mission scheduled to lift off Saturday. (Stories, other photos on Pages 2, 10-11.)

Grumman in the Running For Major Jet Contract

The Navy narrows the field for a jet fighter contract that could amount to $25 billion for Grumman. It could be a boon to the state's economy, possibly offsetting losses forecast by Gov. Rockefeller's planners after the Vietnam war ends. Stories on Page 3, Back Page.

COPYRIGHT 1968 NEWSDAY INC. LONG ISLAND, NEW YORK, VOL. 29, NO. 91

Newsday
5 CENTS · PUBLISHED FOR LONG ISLAND BY LONG ISLANDERS · SAT., JUNE 29, 1968

McCARTHY DEMS BOLT NY CAUCUS

88 Killed in VC Raid on Village
Story on Page 3

DAY IN COURT.

LBJ Signs Law Hiking Income Tax
Stories on Page 3

33

An American Tabloid

Newsday is America's seventh largest evening newspaper (1969 circulation 428,484). For nearly twenty-eight years after its founding in 1940 *Newsday* adhered to the classic tabloid pattern of bold Gothic headlines on the front, almost always with a single large news picture **(33)**. Headlines inside were Tempo on a magazine-style format with wide columns and no vertical rules. In July, 1968, the entire paper was redesigned. Paul Back, art director of *Newsday*, has said 'I redesigned *Newsday* to desensationalise it.'[3] And it is an advanced example of what a serious tabloid might be.

The first lesson, especially for North American newspapers, is that display advertising need not wreak havoc with editorial design. Not a single page of *Newsday*'s vast number (200 to 300) is marred by the grotesque shapes produced by intrusive display advertising. *Newsday*'s ads are in whole pages; or where they share space with editorial, in a clear rectangle, usually a vertical half of the page.

Any newspaper with as many pages as a book faces a major problem of guiding the reader through the paper and identifying the sections quickly. A man *may* turn over 299 pages once to find the item he wants, but there are no records of survivors doing it twice. *Newsday* separates its sections, usually three, by thumb tabs.

The thought which has gone into the organisation of the content is evident, too, in the detailing. The logotype and poster-style front pages **(34–36)** are neatly enclosed in ruled boxes with rounded corners; so are the similar logotypes of other sections. Century has replaced Gothic (though unfortunately the style of initial capitalisation has been retained). The lighter Century Modern was abandoned as altogether too quiet for page one, though Light and Bold Century are mixed inside. The new front pages are cleaner and more flexible: where the news does not require a raucous shout it does not get it.

But perhaps the most admirable feature of *Newsday* is the relatively undramatic matter of text type **(37–39)**. Inside, the 9pt Electra has been replaced by 9 on 10pt Century Schoolbook, and it is very inviting to read. The text modules are wide but vary:

37

38

39

sometimes two modules at 23 picas, sometimes three of 19 ems; sometimes four of 14 ems. The four-column module provides a livlier news page. Typographical gimmicks are eschewed. There are no drop letters, no bold, no stars. The words, organised in clear units, are allowed to speak for themselves.

The basic design weaknesses of *Newsday* are two. Firstly, pictures: the poster-style front page with picture which *Newsday* has adopted requires a photograph with instant impact. The photographs on *Newsday's* front page are too often unmemorable or fussy in their detail. So they are inside, too, but it matters more on the front. Secondly, the paper makes little use of explanatory graphics (*see* Book Four) or drawings. They would help communication and give extra bite to pages that are sometimes too bland.

40

Tabloid at its Best

Finally two examples of popular tabloid display at its best. The Prime Minister and his Foreign Secretary (41) were waiting ceremoniously at London's Victoria Station for the arrival of the President of Turkey.

41

The then Foreign Secretary, Mr George Brown, had been in a spot of bother the night before. The picture captures a moment of silent admonition and apparent repentance. It is splendidly sized the full length of the page.

This page design began with that decision: once the picture had been given its best size, irrespective of column measures, the remaining space was devoted to typography in bastard measure, which would match the bold simplicity of the picture. The wording is just right and the white space helps the eye to cope with picture and headline in one glance.

Big pictures call for caption type to scale. Only one quibble: does the headline underscoring add anything?

The *Daily Mirror's* Mirrorscope (40), now sadly infrequent, was a brave and successful attempt to provide serious news analysis within the gay confines of tabloid journalism. Here text is organised in rectangles under full-measure reverse blocks and condensed sans headings; spreads were frequently distinguished by compact graphic units and specially commissioned artwork.

7 International Design

There is no virtue in the type of newspaper chauvinism which regards anything done by 'the foreigners' as grotesque or suspect.
—ALLEN HUTT

Mutual incomprehension would seem to be guaranteed, so different appear their newspapers, from a meeting between Japanese, English and Bengali newspaper designers. But when such a meeting took place at a seminar in Seoul in 1965 under the auspices of the International Press Institute, the designers were delighted to find they clung to many of the same principles. Agreement, for instance, on the amount of white space required around display type underlay the differences in language and national culture reflected in the newspapers. The influence of 'national temperament' on newspaper design has certainly been exaggerated. The national influences relevant to design are not the alleged national discipline of the Germans, or the cunning of the Chinese, or the passivity of the Dutch. They are real factors such as the level of literacy, the style of the language, the absence or presence of radio and television competing with hot news, the sophistication of readers, the speed and mechanics of printing.

These factors *ought to* affect the design. In India for many years the newspapers continued to follow the style of the London *Times* of Queen Victoria (long paragraphs, limited illustration, and classical symmetry in headline decks) despite India's low literacy and shortage of newsprint. Imitation, in a vacuum, is never going to produce good design (and was one reason for low circulations in India). But it is equally foolish to presume that every vagary of national newspaper style is due to real factors. What we have to do is be clear about the real, and justifiable, differences which influence newspaper design—and the imagined differences of national temperament.

These are so often offered as an alternative to analysis or an excuse for some horror. This is pernicious because it has stifled the exchange of ideas, the rational discussion about how design should respond to real differences so that we can borrow what is good and bury what is bad.

As a beginning to this process, here is a selection of international pages. It is followed (p. 109) by an analysis of twenty-six leading papers, with uninhibited Anglo-Saxon comments.

Germany (Bild Zeitung)

The poster page one at its most strident (the big panelled headlines all tempting the reader to text inside). But note, despite the inflation of type, the restraint in choice of faces—a contrast to most French and Latin American poster pages.

104

Japan (Asahi Shimbun)
Japan's largest selling newspaper (5.4 million each morning, plus another 3 million in the evening). The columns run horizontally, 8–12 to a page. The lead intro here (at the top right) extends to five of the horizontal columns. This *Asahi*

Shimbun page is based on the traditional Japanese pattern of vertical headlines, though there is one strong horizontal tinted headline at the top. Typographical colour is provided by headlines and tints; photographs in Japanese newspapers tend to be small and unimpressive.

Malawi (Malawi News)
British-style African daily, mixing several display faces (Bodoni/sans) but minimising harsh effect by plenty of white space and exploiting top of the page well.

Brazil (Jornal do Brasil, Rio de Janeiro)
Poster page one in restrained style with all the headlines in Bodoni, and clear rectangles for well-whited text. Classified advertising in column 1 and across the foot of the page.

Turkey (Hurriyet)
Powerful but not overpowering. The big headlines are simple, but cleanly set and well separated, the cut-out head is neat as is the front page, and the text type is notably clear. No advertising.

Australia (Daily Mirror, Sydney)
Poster page one, blazoning three stories which are told inside. The page gains from the standardisation of display type and judicious white, but the title area is cluttered.

105

Chile (La Nacion, Santiago de Chile)

Poster page one exploiting panels, reverse blocks and type changes, subjugating the title to no fewer than eight display elements. No advertising.

Cyprus (Agon)

Self-contained page, asymmetrical. Nine-column module, with several variations on the basic setting style. There are thirteen items but an uncrowded feeling because the headlines are well dispersed. No advertising.

United States (Miami Herald)

Clean, eight-column self-contained page of modified symmetry contrasting horizontal lead with strong vertical emphasis in matching heads in restrained Bodoni Bold. The *Miami Herald* has since dropped column rules and (somewhat unhappily) increased the size of headlines. No advertising.

Lebanon (The Daily Star, Beirut)

Eight-column, self-contained asymmetrical page, with handsome white between columns and attractive display type.

United States (Morgantown Post)

Six-column self-contained page, admirably organised in clear news units. No advertising.

Thailand (Thai Daily News)

Poster page one, heavy on half-tone and headline with the paper's reverse-block title submerged beneath reverse-block news headlines.

Nicaragua (La Prensa, Managua)
Moderately restrained poster page one, using text and half-tone as a sandwich between the headlines from various families.

France (France Soir)
Poster-style, with the Russian invasion of Czechoslovakia dominant. Made readable and effective, despite the type variations, by reasonable white and the other stories separated in panels.

Greece (Athlitiki Icho)
Horizontal sports poster page with a minimum of text on a sheet 24 in. deep. Even this does not fully convey the impact, since the printing is in four colours, but of course display like this is voracious on space.

Italy (Il Giorno)
New Italian daily, dramatically asymmetrical, in eight columns (against the usual Italian nine) aiming for ten stories on the front (with turns to the back) plus editorial in column 1. Heavy on headline decks in mixed families.

Zambia (Times of Zambia)
Self-contained front page in nine columns, standardised on Bodoni, with sans kickers in well-controlled asymmetrical layout on British pattern.

Switzerland (La Tribune de Genève)
Orderly poster page with emphasis on large half-tones and captions to lead the reader to the fuller text inside. Headlines are strictly limited and are well whited.

India (Ananda Bazar Patrika, Calcutta)

Splash full-page treatment for the death of Prime Minister Nehru (from the first newspaper with the vision and courage to write simple spoken Bengali instead of the conventional Sanskritised form; it also pushed the development of the Bengali keyboard for line-casting). Because of the language, headline and body type inevitably consumed a great deal of space. No advertising on the page on this day as a special mark of esteem for Nehru.

Japan (Yomiri Shimbun)

Vertical display, with only one horizontal headline (white on tint at top right).

South Africa (Rand Daily Mail, Johannesburg)

Wide sheet (17 in.) with nine columns, the redesigned *Rand Daily Mail* is based on Century Bold with Gothic Sans for emphasis and variety. Column 1 provides a summary of inside news.

Spain (El Correo Catalan)

Front page in picture-poster style with a minimum of headline and text. No advertising.

Peru (Expreso, Lima)

Strong poster page, using panels, reverse blocks, bold sans headlines and half-tones to highlight three stories. The title is a third of the way down the page beneath a dominant news display.

India (The Inquilab)

Urdu newspaper, heavy with calligraphic headlines in several decks. Orderly, despite absence of column rules. The half-tones in the centre relieve the page enormously.

Turkey (Yeni Gazete)

Crisp poster page highlighting no fewer than twenty stories (which are told fully inside). Despite this and the profusion of second decks, the page looks clean because of the use of white space around the Bodoni headlines and the well-mitred panels. No advertising.

India (Malayala Manorama)

Economical display in single-deck headlines, judiciously deployed and well whited, but weak on colour because of the nature of the display type and the limitations of the half-tone used.

Nigeria (Daily Times)

Three stories on a simple page. No halftones but plenty of colour from big text type wide-set, and bold Gothic headlines reasonably well apart.

The Same Day's News in 26 Front Pages

The twenty-six pages analysed in the following section were all published on the same day (February 1, 1968, the day of the Vietcong raid on the US Embassy in Saigon).

Christian Science Monitor

The *Christian Science Monitor* is a serious newspaper emphasising analysis and news-in-depth. It does not attempt to present a range of world news on the front page, nor to bait the diet with human-interest sugar or fillers. The page is meant for sustained reading, and the new design therefore correctly emphasises coherence and quiet readability. The eight-column format in $7\frac{1}{2}$pt, more suited to a paper projecting a profusion of telegraphic news events, has been abandoned in favour of a five-column paper with legible line of 16·9 pica ems set in 9pt Excelsior. This format limits the layout possibilities, but the *Monitor* is right in claiming that layout is still responding dynamically to content. Despite devoting column one each day to Focus, a news analysis, the *Monitor* has shown itself able to change emphasis in the remaining four columns, though of course it has to restrict its display to three or four items. Here there are three (Vietnam, Rockefeller, and world poverty, and all these are forced to turn), but variety is introduced by good graphics and the poster-type panel Inside Today which summarises stories inside the paper and provides colour with a tint block, bold type, and half-tones.

The *Monitor* says that the five-column format has produced complexities on its inside pages, principally with the advertising layout. It preferred not to risk loss of advertising by shifting advertisements from an eight-column to a five-column format, so the 16·9-pica text column has to be somehow fitted in smoothly with advertisements built on an 11-em module. Where the advertisements can be grouped in squares of three or eight column blocks, there is no

problem, but otherwise spaces have to be filled with odd-measure setting. Some advertisers grumbled at first about their advertisements being in horizontal rather than pyramidal configuration, but these complaints have died away, and the remaining difficulty now is the loss of production time in setting inside text to odd measure. This has been somewhat offset by increased productivity from longer typelines, but, like the *Courier-Journal*, the *Monitor* has noticed no space gains from the economy of longer lines: 'Writers and editors can't resist the temptation to fill any slack by adding still more background details to stories.'[1]

In moving to five-column format, the *Monitor* also opted for the all-down style of lower-case headline, which is unusual in America, but perhaps its single most distinctive design feature is the use of maps and diagrams. The labelled map of North Vietnam perfectly complemented the text: many other newspapers on this day left the reader struggling to visualise for himself.

Mainichi Shimbun

Japanese newspapers are published round-the-clock: the *Mainichi Shimbun,* for instance, has an 8–10 page evening edition in which 4–6 pages are changed over four editions. The morning edition of 16–20 pages has 8–12 news pages being changed through six editions. Many Japanese papers are now using page one as a summary guide to the range of news, with details and analysis-in-depth inside—Japanese journalists are very conscious of television being first with the news.

The layout is functional: it changes to project the changing value of news constituents. Design is greatly influenced by language. Written Japanese requires a newspaper to use something like 2,400 separate Chinese, Japanese, and Roman characters (compared with the mere 44 keys of a Western typewriter). The large newspaper publishers have their own typefaces, but because of the profusion of required symbols, headlines in line blocks are increasing. A wide range of decorative tints is added to these for variety. A second consequence of the language is that, since the characters and ideographs are more easily read when set vertically there is a vertical emphasis in layout. The text runs vertically, of course, but there has also been a predominance of vertical headlines in Japanese newspapers.

Lately there have been attempts, for variety, at more horizontal display stress in the pages—hence the introduction of horizontal headlines such as the white-on-tint block across the top of this page. Where horizontal headlines are used, it is good practice in Japanese to give them plenty of white to eliminate 'optical' obstructions in reading the symbols.

The *Mainichi* page one here is admirably clear in its headline distribution. Variety is achieved by mixing light Mincho and bold Gothic type, by tints, and by horizontal and vertical headlines on the same story (though the page would function more economically with fewer decks of headline). The sequence of text is clear—with the help of horizontal column rules. One of the weaknesses of Japanese and other Oriental newspapers, though not of the *Mainichi,* is allowing the text type to wander confusingly over the page.

Japanese journalists are advised[2] to adopt four rules in layout:

(i) Not to arrange top and bottom headlines in a straight row.

(ii) Not to put headlines of the same size side by side.

(iii) Not to bring the bottom of headlines flush with each other.

(iv) Not to allow rules to extend across the upper part of the page.

The basis for these rules is not peculiarly Japanese. It is to limit the illegibilities produced by headline clashes and the deadness possible in a rigorously squared-off page. Similarly, with the occasional horizontal text setting, a limit of 20–25 words is set because the longer line is difficult to read, just as in Western languages.

Izvestia

Izvestia is the official paper of the Supreme Soviet and is probably the liveliest in layout of the leading Soviet newspapers. The layout is functional, responding to the news. It is in eight columns (in contrast to the six-column *Pravda*) with mixtures of bold headline type, sans and serifed, roman and italic, and reverse blocks, and an interesting juxtaposition of horizontal and vertical layout. The general pattern in the Soviet Union is horizontal make-up with the type squared up underneath, as in columns 1 to 5 here, but columns 6–8 present a strong vertical contrast. The page is basically self-contained (with only one continuation), but there is a curious hint of the poster technique in the box with blobs at the top of column 1. The lines here read:

> May the friendship between the USSR and India be strengthened!
> The mother country joyfully greeted the sailors of the heroic steamer.
> Successful operation of South Vietnamese patriots.

The first two headlines are slogans for news which appears on the front page, but the third on Vietnam refers to a story inside the paper. No cross-reference is given. Four of the headlines on this front page are on the same story of the official visit of Kosygin to India: the lead story economically headlined in columns 1 to 5, which continues on page 2; and three of the other headlines below. The bastard-set panel in columns 3–5 is an account of an annual leaders' council, identified by a rather clumsily designed symbol block.

The second lead is the italic headline at the top of columns 6–8, distinguished by having two decks (Full Unity of Views—The Visit of Comrade Dubcek to Moscow). Underneath the second lead is a standing reverse block introducing a tersely edited black-bordered panel of foreign news briefs, set double-column with occasional paragraphs in bold.

The distinctive feature of *Izvestia's*

text layout is the rectangular unity within clear panels. Five weights of panel rule are used on this page, including the double fine rule round the picture, but except for the badly-mitred corner at the top of the foreign news panel the presswork is good and the effect one of calm and order. The headlines are simple and carry good white, and with the possible exception of the 6pt picture caption, the text type is admirably clear.

Globe and Mail

Canadian newspapers, like their American counterparts, prefer the lead on the right. Here are nine 11-em columns, without column rules, the heads set left, strong horizontal emphasis and no multi-column intros. The main weakness is the profuse heading count of the light italic sans: the smaller multi-column sizes (column 5, Ministers Council) are hard to read. Individual letters in this fount are ambiguous —see the j in junta, column 2—and not at all as distinctly formed as the letters in the roman sans: compare the letter a. The italic is particularly anaemic as the (undersized) second deck of the lead. The bold sans of the lead is a welcome bit of news punch on an over-reticent page.

The good points are the simplicity, especially of the text. The 9pt type is easy to read and there are no awkward turns. There are no cross-heads, which chills a cool page further, but with 9pt this is tolerable. The nine-column panel at the foot of the page,

bastard set with two half-tones, brings much-needed warmth and the subsidiary information with the title is neatly continued within two thin rules.

The leader page speaks in a quiet, civilised voice. The text is mainly the serious and informed comment of a distinguished Canadian daily and the restraint in display and headlines properly focuses attention on the text, which is a delight to read in wide measure. The similar treatment for letters acts as an encouragement to readers.

Le Figaro

There is a broad theoretical distinction in France between the front pages of the 'news' paper (*journal d'information*) and the 'opinion' paper (*journal d'opinion*). The opinion paper—*Le Monde* is the classic example— uses page one to project text, and this text is a mixture of news, analysis and comment. The articles may continue to another page, but there is a solid beginning of text on the front. The 'news' paper on the other hand treats the front page as a poster for head-lines and photographs with the text to support them relegated to another page.

The poster style began in the late 1930s, influenced by the bold splashes of the London *Daily Express*. (Today a classic poster page is *Le Parisien Libéré*.) The newspapers which were strong on textual analysis and comment did not feel they could adopt the poster style without losing their essential identities. Even today *Le Monde* forswears illustration. Some of them, however—like *Le Figaro*—compromised by dividing the page betwen dramatic news presentation and textual opinion. *Le Figaro* combines what the French call the traditional and the modern style. The top is a modern poster, with photographs and the news summarised in headlines. But there are also complete signed articles in columns 1–2, 6, and 7–8.

In considering the design effectiveness of *Le Figaro* and other papers in the international section, it is important to distinguish between the means and the end. The effectiveness of the poster style is a separate question from the type anarchy by which the idea is executed. Raymond Manevy in his study of the evolution of French layout defends the poster style as enabling the French papers to present on one page 'a summarised but suggestive picture of the main and unusual events of a day all over the world.'[3] So it does—but need the typography be what it is? *Le Figaro* at the top is a razzle-dazzle of founts and sizes without sufficient white for legibility. (Note how much easier it is to read the uncrowded heads on the signed articles at the bottom of the page.) This type mix has also been defended as freeing the journalist from the tyranny of metal. On many popular French newspapers, though not *Le Figaro*, the overall content of the headline is decided first and then it is left to the printer to find a type which will make it fit. The emphasis on the primacy of words is surely right, but it must be carried through. The words must be right but they must also be legible: and the confusion of

hectic and overcrowded type defeats this philosophy. It may express Gallic verve and the excitement of news, but it could all be more immediately comprehensible.

Le Figaro, like most French papers of its size, has eight columns. The smaller-size sheets like *Le Monde* are in five broad-gauge columns. *Le Figaro's* Egyptian slab serif logotype is a splendidly bold survivor from the paper's birth in 1856 and deserves a cleaner title area.

Indian Express

Lively Indian daily with dynamic asymmetrical layout. The headlines, in the all-lower-case style, are well distributed through the page, and so are the half-tones and text colour. It is a pity the *Express* has followed the American pattern of dispensing with column rules, a habit generally producing cleanliness with confusion. It does here. Some story cut-offs have been retained but there is no consistency in their use. The column 3 panel, 'The doctor plays it safe,' is rightly cut off from the lead, but the bottom-of-the-page story, 'Early M.P. Government fall predicted,' is tied on to unrelated stories above. The UNCTAD story begins with a four-column map, leading into a story in column 8 (which turns) and then there is a panel (Thant) in column 7. The multi-line headlines are effectively simple in Century Bold (though the lead headline is curiously changed to the bolder Bodoni and is too close to the page folio).

The main difficulties in design are in the detailing. The $6\frac{3}{4}$ on 7pt body type is rather small, but where a larger type is sensibly used for intros it is used only for two or three lines before dropping into unleaded body type (*see* column 1, Chavan); the transition is too sudden. And the descent from a three-column introduction to two lines of single-column in the Kosygin story is unhappy; it would have been better if the half-tone had been allowed to come fully into the shoulder, taking the type into the middle leg. The captions and turn lines are refreshingly bold and clear, but the four-column map lettering is a shade too small for comfort.

Clarin

A South American example of the poster style. The *Clarin* from Buenos Aires exploits the idea at two levels—several main stories are summaries in big headlines and pictures, which is the French style, but then a two-column panel is taken (columns 1 and 2) to cross-refer in text type to another dozen national stories. In this way the page gives a wider range of news than if the whole space has been taken with big headlines. The heads are all sans-serif with contrast provided by variations in light, bold and outline letters. The white space provided by the outline type in centred short lines is a great help. Given the style, there are two outstanding weaknesses to the design of the *Clarin*: the failure to relate captions directly to pictures, and the weakness of the title itself. A white-on-tint title would be more distinctive and would discreetly support the clash of heads in the overcrowded top-left corner.

The leader page is in three legs of wide-measure type, clear and restrained, and without ads.

Dagens Nyheter

In Scandinavian style, this Swedish daily uses page one mainly for a headline-and-text summary of news more fully dealt with inside. There is no doubt that the sandwiching of the text summary between the display type decks relieves the page of the razzle-dazzle of the pure poster style seen in French popular papers. The inset panel, used as an axis to the page is another very effective typographical expression of the poster page. As with the *Clarin* panel its restraint relieves the page of the thud of headlines, but the *Dagens Nyheter* panel is even more successful because it adds warmth and colour to the page by the subtle use of blacks, whites and greys in half-tone, bold type, bold rule, and white-on-black reverse block. The *Dagens Nyheter*, of course, sensibly achieves its headline variations wholly within Bodoni lower-case, ringing the changes from roman and italic, bold and light, and lines centres and stepped.

This variation is sometimes achieved unhappily at the expense of forcing white between the letters of words (*see* the lead headline and Bitterhet i USA in columns 1–3), a deplorable practice which destroys the recognition of words as integral units. The layout style is horizontal, but not to extreme: note how the design separates headlines in the right-hand bottom half of the page by refusing to square off the text.

Aftenposten

Another poster: there are twelve main stories, similar to *Le Figaro*, but *Aftenposten* is somewhat easier to read than the French populars such as *Le Parision Libéré*, because the text helps to cushion the heads, there is reasonable white in the Bodoni lower-case and some attempt is made to avoid too many juxtapositions. The layout is only moderately successful here. The short legs of text type, as in column 5, Stor Norsk Orde, are uninviting, and the headline juxtapositions that do occur are uneasily related (especially the cramped single-column heads against the double-columns).

The consequence of this, and of the inflated sizing of the horizontal heads, is that few stories are clearly signalled. The lead story suffers by having two separate sets of second deck in bewildering competition for attention. But the biggest handicap of all in the design of the *Aftenposten* is the intrusion of so many display ads in display type. The long double-column intros in bold are made tolerable by ample leading: note the leading through the eight-column text. The main display types are Bodoni roman and italic.

The leader page is in eight columns; all in roman without bold, and all in simple shapes, with minimum display. The effect is clean and orderly, helped by the absence of strong display ads.

The Hindu

India's prestige newspaper has been re-designed over the last few years. It was previously a classical all-caps and decks paper modelled on the old London *Times*. It was excessively formal and paid little attention to points of detail such as the lengths of intros and paragraphs. The new style is economical in space, having substituted restrained multi-line heads for multi-decks, and offers a variety of positions for news display for a self-contained front page. The heads are legible, in reasonable white and set in lower-case: they would be even better if the style of initial capitalisation of every letter were abandoned.

There are, however, certain inconsistencies. First, typography: the Tempo Heavy italic panel in column 1 is not a considered type mix (as in the *Berlingske Tidende*), but an intrusion. So are the diamond-studded cut-off rules. The cut-offs on the page are puzzling: some stories are cut off with a half thick-and-thin, others with a fine rule. A standard cut-off of a thick-and-thin would be a usefully decisive separator in a page questionably without column rules; for panels a double-fine would match the austere clarity of the general design. Second, layout: the weight of the heads for the lead

and second lead is commendably restrained, but the third and fourth positions on the page have, in proportion, been scaled down too much. And why are some heads set left and others centred?

The redesigned leader page of *The Hindu* is admirably clean, but the use of a display ad in the leader-column position over the paper's title-piece detracts from its dignity.

Corriere della Sera

Italian dailies have the lowest readership in the whole of Europe. The dominant feature of Italy's biggest-selling daily paper (462,000 in 1968) is the text setting. There are nine columns set close up to the column rules with a minimum of vertical white. The paragraphs are literary, rather than typographical, with long chunks of bold and one whole story in italic, and the cross-heads are written excessively to full measure.

The initial effect is forbidding, especially with each line of head written full-measure. The design has more subtlety than at first appears. The body type is a handsome 9pt; the heads are always properly whited top and bottom, which makes them legible when not juxtaposed; and the squared-off heads are usually always clearly related to their text (there is admittedly some am-

biguity in this issue where the text leads begin in both column 1 and column 3).

The horizontal layout style is common in Italian papers. *Corriere della Sera* design responds to the day's news: here the top of the page is dominated by two four-column heads. On another day a trio of stories, each with three-column heads, may share the top. The horizontal style is not pressed to its extreme: note the way the lead text is run so that the heads on subsidiary stories in columns 2–4 and columns 6–8 are forced up the page. If this careful distribution of heads down page were also followed at the top the *Corriere della Sera* would be much more quickly legible.

The style must consume a great deal of editorial and setting time—but note how finely proportioned to each other are the main deck and its subsidiary blurb. The shading down is just right.

Berlingske Tidende

The *Berlingske Tidende* does not manage to present a summary of world news on its front page, but its design succeeds brilliantly in giving maximum prominence each day to three or four main stories. What it

loses in range, it gains in coherent impact. The horizontal heads are well distributed through the page and each can be seen as a clear signal related to its text. This is because the headlines are usually simple units and well whited. Note the use of the five-column half-tone strip at the top of the page to avoid the clash of the lead and second-lead heads.

The *Berlingske Tidende* design responds dynamically to the news of the day—sometimes there is a banner across seven columns, sometimes the lead is in three columns. There is a risky but successful mix of Bodoni and two weights of sans.

Where the Bodoni and sans are used in the same headline unit (columns 3–7) the sans is a gentle light face that serves as a monotone foil for the Bodoni's dazzling contrasts. This light sans is also well used with the bold: as an overline it does not compete with the main deck in bold, and it provides a welcome change of colour.

The page is helped a great deal by the absence of display ads, especially next to the title which is sensibly centred on its white. Given the style, the main criticism is that the headline sizing is wasteful and imprecise as an indication of priorities.

Eleftheros Kosmos

Greek papers tend to be rigorously horizontal in layout so that headlines, squared off in caps, run into each other all over the place. That there is nothing inevitably Greek about this is demonstrated by the *Eleftheros Kosmos* (rough translation: *Free World*). Though caps headlines have been the style on Greek papers because of the difficulties said to occur from the many accents of lower-case, the *Eleftheros Kosmos* has most of its heads in lower-case and they are separated most convincingly by wide-measure setting of intros and single-column setting for the caption. There is good colour contrast in the main story typography of light and well-whited bold and indeed all the headlines carry adequate white. The half-tone colour is well distributed and the page is effectively anchored with a colourful five-column story under milled rule, reverse block and caps heading. There are points of difficulty for the reader in wide measure, notably in the main story intro which should have been leaded more to aid eye-transfer; and the second decks on the single-column heads in columns 4 and 6 are unnecessary. But altogether the *Eleftheros Kosmos* is much more inviting to read than the traditional Greek design.

Die Welt

German design emphasis is on coherence and the most economical use of the space possible, consistent with legibility. There is no doubt that the wide-measure column produced by scheduling six columns to a page is easier to read, and like *Die Welt* most German papers choose six-column format. The layout style is symmetrical and horizontal, stories are generally boxed off in modular rectangles to produce an inescapably clear relationship between text and headline. The lead treatment here lacks this logic in the unhappy separation of the Vietnam picture in columns 5 and 6 from the other Vietnam material in columns 1–4.

The page would have been better if the picture had been moved in two columns and the panel on the paper's writer moved down page. This would have created a two-column top for other news and also some useful colour in the centre of a rather cold page. But the formal horizontal style does normally produce closely related text and display. The disadvantage is that in squaring off, several heads have to run side by side. The potentially disagreeable effects of such juxtaposition can be limited, however, and it is worth noting how *Die Welt* does it.

The successfully juxtaposed heads are

always in the same fount (Bodoni is used throughout); they are always in the same style (centred lower-case against centred lower-case); they are well separated by white or column rules (by both here); and they are almost always in the same size. These four features distinguish the juxtaposed heads at the foot of columns 4 and 5. The Brandt head in column 3 is lost because it has not been made to match in size with the FDP head in the next two columns. Some of the detailing under main headings is fussy and might be abandoned in the interest of economy.

German newspapers have a wide choice of display type: in addition to the famous type foundries, special matrices are offered by the slug-machine companies. One wonders how long *Die Welt* will resist the appeal of a warmer display signal. But note the rich clarity of its title letter.

New York Herald Tribune

The international edition of the *Herald Tribune*, published with the *New York Times* and the *Washington Post*, is distinctly easier to read than the domestic *New York Times*. Apart from the American predilection for initial caps, which is an incidental hurdle in scanning a headline, the *Herald Tribune*

makes the best possible use of Bodoni. The horizontal heads are restricted to one or two lines; they are in lower-case with a minimum of words; they are in clear and simple relationship with the text and almost always have the white space focused in the right place—not between decks or letters, but illuminating the headline as a unit.

The symmetrical, informally horizontal layout provides adequate positions for news priorities and the effect of juxtaposed headlines in columns 1–4 is softened by white produced by the set-left head in column 1 and the indentions on the other heads.

The page of the *Herald Tribune* displayed here uses design to communicate some comprehension of the reality in Saigon by combining the general and the particular. In the panel in columns 1–4, the reader is given a general view of the battle at the US Embassy by the use of type superimposed on the air view, and then, in counterpoint in columns 6–8 there is a close-up of the men in the fighting at the Embassy. The graphic analysis in the picture is fairly elementary, and so is the matching of the two pictures, but hardly any newspapers anywhere in the world attempted to communicate as the *Herald Tribune* did in this simple but telling fashion.

Chicago Tribune

The most striking impression from the *Tribune's* page is how much news impact most of the other papers gained by exploiting a news photograph. There may be good reasons for the light-hearted artwork here (a Zodiac calendar), but even in colour it is noticeable how anaemic is a front news page that does not focus on a dramatic news picture. The *Tribune's* gothic banner headline is emphatic and clear—the type is sufficiently condensed to make for sensible wording and the headline is given enough white space. Below this banner there is confusion from a crowding of heads of mixed founts and especially from the six-column Bodoni italic head which leads into a single-column story in column 8. This horizontal head leads into a second deck at the end of its run; with the lead the reader has to come back to the beginning. It is preferable for long horizontal heads always to have a consistent relationship to the start of the text.

In addition it is hard to see why the *Tribune* divides the main deck from its subsidiary deck with a half-rule, a fussy vestigial remnant of the days of multi-decks. There would be an immediate gain in clarity by dropping these rules and also those enclosing the title Zodiac Calendar, which produce an irritating tramline.

Both of the third decks in the first and second lead are equally superfluous. Certainly some of the space saved by limiting the headline display here could be used in columns 4–7 to support the four-column artwork. The line-up of heads of different sizes and founts is messy. It is a pity, because The Editor's Digest of the News is a useful summary, combined with a detailed index The stories all turn, but to early pages.

Much could be gained from simplification (e.g. a reverse block with the single word 'Digest'). The aligned crossheads in cols 1 and 2 (which read 'Seeking Out Enemy' and 'Seek Out Enemy') show the value of sharp-eyed stone editing.

The Courier-Journal (Louisville)

The *Courier-Journal* (and its evening associate the *Louisville Times*) switched in 1965 from eight 11-em columns to six 14-pica columns with a pica of column white in place of column rules. This is one of the widest measures of American papers in six-column formats. In 8 on 8½pt Corona it is eminently readable and helpfully story cut-offs have been retained.

The Louisville newspapers changed to six-column format to produce more legible lines and to make headlines easier to write. They say[4] that in addition it has enabled them to abandon awkward abbreviations in radio programmes and box scores, and that reduced hyphenation in the longer text line has also helped to offset the space losses produced by longer headlines and bigger pictures. The number of stories that can be accommodated on page one has shrunk to six-to-eight display stories. One of the problems is that stories seem to run longer, and bulky stories in six-column format have created layout difficulties for them. Accommodating advertising to the new format has been achieved by abandoning the differential rate structure between retail and national advertising. The national advertiser producing display to an 11-pica format had the choice of resizing his ad or floating it in the added white space at the old advertising rate. General advertisement lineage increased 30 per cent in the first twelve months of six columns, and despite a reduction in general rates of between 25 and 41 per cent general revenue ended up practically even with the preceding twelve months.

The layout is asymmetrical with horizontal emphasis. Unlike most American dailies the *Courier-Journal* places the lead story on the left ('We think it makes sense to put the main page story where the eye naturally goes first.') The lead headline gains by having no competition from other display type, though the awkwardness of the long descenders of Bodoni Bold is all

too apparent. The *Courier-Journal* is flexible and dynamic, responding with different layouts to changing news. The basic style is horizontal, though it is usually carried out more neatly than here. The clear rectangles which are the basis of the page layout are broken by the irregular way the column 2–3 picture and text type are related in the lead. The set-left upper-and-lower heads all benefit by reasonable white space, but the white around the side-heads in the text is misused. There is too much of it and the side-head is floated midway, instead of being set closer to the text to which it relates.

All the main stories here are turned, but sensibly to the back page of the first section. The *Journal* regularly uses the earpiece positions for two cross-references to stories inside the paper. The weather and the small down-page index are allowed to float into varying filler positions, which must be a nuisance to the reader.

Denver Post

This Colorado daily is two stages removed from its old razzle-dazzle circus make-up when about half of page one was devoted to horizontal display elements in garish competition.[5]

In 1963 the *Post* went to 9 on 10pt Corona text, set unjustified in an 11-pica column. Now it appears in a six-column format, justified. The horizontal headline display has been considerably simplified in Tempo Heavy, but has to be carried further for full effect. The amount of display type around the lead headline defeats the purpose of trying to give it prominence. There is no need for the five-column second deck, nor for the single-column third deck. But which third deck? The difficulties encountered simply by abandoning rules is well demonstrated here. The story in column 2 headed Westmoreland Expects is the one the reader is supposed to go to after the main deck: there are three white directing arrows between the second deck and the single-column, and there are three arrows in the white between columns 5 and 6 directing the reader from the picture to the text in column 8. Column rules would organise these relationships more neatly and surely. The omission of cut-offs is also questionable: the cut-off rule is a good device for indicating the end of a story and its omission a good device for relating two stories.

The cut-off is especially useful when by accident or design a horizontal headline is less than perfectly matched with rectangular text units. Filler pars can meet the gap but may introduce a note of bizarre irrelevance. The filler par, Fare Protest Halts Traffic, used at the end of the story in column 6 is about traffic conditions in Kiel, Germany. Typographically the *Denver Post* is single fount, giving unity, but two points of detail require comment. The Tempo Heavy does not knit well together when letter-spaced (compare the spaced Wage–Price head in column 3 with the compact italic above it). And the cross-heads in column 1 need an extra 2 points of white above to do what they are intended to do. In layout, the most debatable elements are the tint block across the top (it just about works), the finger-tip of text type at the top of columns 2 and 3, and the strong picture well sized and placed (compare this page with the *Chicago Tribune* p. 120). This is surely not strong enough in the first three columns of the paper adjacent to lead and to the title.

Some American states do not allow the title to float in this way, but where they do the newspapers exploiting short floating title-blocks need to give earnest thought to what they do with the space left at the top of the page. If it is not to be used for the most logical purpose of beginning the lead, it should be used for a self-contained unit—a head and text story, or perhaps a news summary or index—which should match the depth of the floating title. The present *Denver Post* title is so shallow and wide that the hole it creates in columns 1–3 is hard to use for a self-contained matching story. For the *Post* one way to make this space more viable would be to redesign the title-block so that it is narrower and deeper. (When the old *Daily Herald* in Britain was re-born as the broadsheet *Sun*, the title was not merely allowed to float but assumed a different shape according to the requirements of each day's page.)

The Times

The Times has changed its layout style since this page (*see* pp. 34-35) but this front is the best single reply to American feelings that the retention of rules and cut-offs means a retention of fuddy-duddy greyness. This *Times* page is admirably lucid and not a whit grey or fuddy-duddy. A hairline rule is insignificant greyness in a pica of column white and, page design apart, is welcome for the local tension it produces within the column, directing the eye where it ought to go. *The Times* page sensibly concentrates its white space where it is needed, around the splendid Times Bold, the crisp, colourful

display type with a large x-height specially designed for the paper.

Each story on the page is clearly signalled with simple headlines in restrained sizes. There is a satisfying porportion between length of text and weight of heading, and the sizing and spacing of such details as cross-heads and by-lines is above reproach.

Of course it is possible to see refinements: the column 6 headline on the breath test would be better without the third line, and the picture choice, sizing, and cropping is questionable (the three-column block has too much extraneous detail, while the dramatic column 1 block reduces the figures too much).

But in general typography, page layout, and printing, this *Times* page one is a re-markable example of the sane intelligibility a leading serious newspaper with a static format can bring to a day's disordered events around the world. Comparing American contemporaries, it is worth noting that not a single story turns to another page.

The Hartford Times

The strongest element in the page is the column 1 wide-measure summary-index. This is impressively executed, with space reserved for news not lavished on unnecessary display. It is clear and distinctive because of its use of small amounts of white space and the decisive subject dividers. The rest of the page is divided into six 11-em columns with rather more than a pica of column white in place of rules. The typography is commendably simple—one or two lines of the same fount (Record) and except for the head '2 College Boys,' which is too small, maintaining a proper proportion between headline, text, and position in the page. Cut-offs have been omitted but chaos avoided by not using irrelevant filler paragraphs. The layout style is horizontal, with heads cleverly separated and distributed—the map helps as a divider—but something has gone wrong in column 2, where the pimple of a paragraph Hippie

New York Times

American newspapermen refer to the 'good grey *New York Times*.' It is indeed both good, editorially, and grey in appearance. The news section has changed little in forty years, though there are signs it is now prepared to adapt the design expression of the Twenties so that justice is done to the content of the Seventies. By custom the *New York Times* places the most important news on the right in column 8, but the three-column caps head in three lines is more weighty than usual. The second most important piece of news is placed in column 1 'unless it is in some way related to the leading item or falls into the same broad category of subject matter.'[6]

Thereafter the presentation of the news content is deliberately organised to a sense of priorities, and the layout, no longer rigidly symmetrical, succeeds in providing a variety of viable page positions. The difficulty with the *New York Times* is not, however, in the layout. It is in the typography. It is, undeniably, just not inviting to read. It no longer conveys authority, merely a sense of the antique. The text typography is not too bad. On page one it is a readable $8\frac{1}{2}$ on 10pt, in eight 11-em columns ($8\frac{1}{2}$ on $8\frac{1}{2}$ elsewhere), though most of the time it is allowed to run too close to the column rule: 3pt is not enough column white.

The headlines are at fault. They mumble. They are barely discernible because of the choice and use of types (Latin Antique Condensed, Bookman, Cheltenham Bold Condensed and Extra Condensed, and some Century Bold). First, the condensed types are hard to read at the best of times, especially the Cheltenham Extra Condensed. Second, they are even harder on the eye when displayed with minimum white, as in the *New York Times*. The words are allowed to melt into each other producing conglomerates (INCINERATORPLAN in col. 1). Third, the condensed sans used as a second deck produces too many letters for easy scanning at the size used.

Fourth, four decks of headline with these faults is overwhelming: see column 1 again, where there are something like 200 letters to discern and put together in word units.

Fifth, the lower-case heads continue the American liking for Initial Capitalisation of Each Main Word Which Erects an Optical Hurdle at the Beginning of Each Word.

Sixth, arrangement of the single-column staggered decks in rigorous symmetry is monotonous and contrived.

The possible typographic reforms for the *New York Times* are apparent even within this page and even accepting the basic fount. For instance, the four-column anchor at the foot of the page is readable because the text is indented with one headline reasonably spaced. So is the single-column head continuing the lead in column 8 (HUE IS EMBATTLED), thanks to the spacing.

Continuations are a problem. Every story turns, and the eleven stories here turn to eight different pages.

Australian Papers

The Australian preference for narrow columns and lots of them to a text-size page is seen at its extreme in the Brisbane evening which has eleven 9-pica columns separated by minimum white. This gives the *Courier Mail's* text a character count of around twenty to a column, similar to the eleven-column *Age*, Adelaide. The *Sydney Morning Herald*, the *Melbourne Herald*, and the *Age*, Melbourne, are ten columns to a page, but the new national *The Australian* has moved to eight and is all the more legible for that. The excessively narrow columns, set in 8pt or 9pt, mean more eye-transfers per column for the reader. In turn they produce longer runs of grey text, which means more frequent paragraphing, or more cross-heads (in the *Courier Mail* the frequent large cross-heads have inadequate white). Mechanically, narrow columns are slower to set, and mean more hyphens and letter-spacing (*see* Book Two).

The editorial argument for the narrow-gauge setting is that it produces more news positions. This is certainly a good argument for a popular tabloid which, if it is to create a sense of busyness on its small sheet, is forced to narrow measure. But it is a doubtful argument for a broadsheet,' and demands extreme care in the distribution of display type if the reader is to be able to see the messages for the mess.

The *Courier Mail* mixes Bodoni Black, Cooper Black, Franklin Gothic Bold, Cheltenham, and Placard, and though an attempt is made to keep heads away from each other the effect is still of being beaten by a blunt instrument. Two points are worth noting: the freedom the *Courier Mail* gains at the top of the page by a small title (the blackletter survives in many Australian papers), and the vigorous use of two well-placed pictures.

The Australian is notable for its attractive title, well spaced with the symbol at the left, and typographically for the Century and Century Bold Extended. (The lines in the second deck of the lead could, however, be pulled closer together.) Note also the striking cross-reference panel at the foot of the page.

Cape Argus

South Africa's English dailies reflect English patterns—Bodoni, Century Bold, and Gothic Condensed are the display founts for self-contained news pages. The *Cape Argus* has nine complete stories and only one turn of text to another page. This is convenient for the reader (contrast the *Los Angeles Times*) and there are, in addition, summary cross-references in columns 4 and 5. The design expression of the editorial concept is erratic. First, typography: the Bodoni headlines, if inflated, are varied effectively, but the Vietcong caps head in columns 4 and 5 is oversized and shouts down the three-column headline on the Carrier story above (caps, being blacker than lower-case, should be sized down one size from the comparable lower-case head). The light sans at the top of column 1 is far too weak for its position and contrasts badly with the Bodoni (a much better face is used on the index panel in column 5).

Layout: The design distributes the heads quite well in the nine-column $11\frac{1}{2}$-pica page so that each can make its signal clearly, but there are glaring faults. The aircraft-carrier picture in the end columns has a story—in columns 3, 4, 5. There is no attempt to relate the two units. The treatment of the lead story is also unsatisfactory. The main headline straddles two pictures but only the picture on the left is relevant. Of course the irrelevant picture is set apart by a hairline rule, but there is no justification for the confusing and straggly shape of the lead, which produces as an incidental irritation the column 1 picture title whose typography is so weak.

Compare the effectiveness of this lead treatment with the excellent anchor provided by Zambia Petrol Queues. Here the headline is a simple shape clearly tied to its text, and there is ideal proportion between headline size and length and position of text. The text type of the page in nine $11\frac{1}{2}$-em columns is well edited in reasonable paragraph lengths with clear cross-heads.

The leader page of the *Cape Argus* (like the *Rand Daily Mail*) is a mish-mash of ads and comment, its editorial a poorly displayed three-column after thought.

Los Angeles Times

One of the better examples of the US trend to wider setting, fewer columns and with white column space. Here the design is comprehensible and clean; except for the lead story, heads and text are in clear self-contained rectangles, and the white space is distributed to a consistent idea—to illuminate heads, and to separate columns and stories. The coherence of the *Los Angeles Times* is an example to many American dailies which have simply dropped column rules and scattered white through the page without doing it to a consistent pattern for a consistent purpose (*see Illinois State Register*). At best this is wasteful and it is often confusing, leaving the reader to guess what relates to what. The *Los Angeles Times* also demonstrates that it is possible to achieve varied display without wide variations in headline size.

There are several minor criticisms, and one major. The minor ones are the angularity of the main headline fount; the retention of initial caps which are harder to read and remove the benefit of caps for indicating proper nouns; the irritation of the two broken rules in columns 4 and 5—the Priest and Professor story would have been better enclosed in a full panel; and the line-up of headlines at the top of columns 4, 5 and 6. Abandoning the second deck on the lead would have pointed the reader more quickly to the relevant text. (The story with the picture is also easily missed in columns 2 and 3.) The major criticism is the number of text turns. Every story on this page is continued elsewhere, sometimes a long way back in the paper.

The *Los Angeles Times* has a five-column leader page in a light Bodoni and no ads—a lesson for the *Cape Argus* opposite.

Straits Times

This Malayan morning paper used to be modelled on the London *Daily Express*, with even bigger banner headlines. It has now gone into lower-case, gaining emphasis for the lead by bringing the weight down the page. The lead headline is immediately readable. This is true of the headline treatment throughout; it is bold and simple— Century and Century Extended in lower-case, with an occasional head in Franklin Bold Condensed. The only elaborations are the underscoring of the column 7 head (excessive for a light head), the lead overline (just right in weight and length), and the light rule border round the Envoy Bunker head. The text typography, too, is designed for ease of reading—frequent paragraph breaks and good column white in an eight-column 11-em page. The broad criticism is the waste of space, especially in the lead. The antique title does not match the rest of the page and is overcrowded.

Winnipeg Free Press

Eight-column page at 11 picas to a column with head in Bodoni Bold and Bodoni Black, emphasis and lead on the right. Though a serious paper with heads, in one family, seldom exceeding three columns, the *Free Press* veers to circus layout in the multiplicity and disposition of headlines. There is nothing wrong with the policy of squeezing more stories to the page. The fundamental difficulty with the page lies in the headlines. Bodoni Bold glitters. Bodoni Bold with stars and lots of Bodoni Bold with lots of stars glitters too much. The result is that the middle of the page carries too many signals. The second decks in columns 1 and columns 2 and 3 are unnecessary and their small size is out of proportion to the main head. All this is aggravated by the style of initial capitalisation, the inconsistent whiting of the decks, the erratic shapes, and the inflation of display sizes (*see* for instance Chrysler Accord in column 7, headline equal to the text on the page).

8 Mechanics of Newspaper Design

Type must be arranged by a typographer to a purpose (the author's purpose), but also to a convenience (the reader's convenience).
—SIR FRANCIS MEYNELL

Once upon a time the printer made up the newspaper. When it was time to go to press, he would take the metal available, advertisements and editorial, and fit them into the forme. The metal was all the same measure so there were few practical difficulties for the printer, though there were some for the reader. Ads and editorial were mixed up. A report which did not finish in one column might turn up in the next column or the one after that.

Important news might appear anywhere in the page; or not at all if someone overlooked a galley of type. The finest examples of this cheerful anarchy may have disappeared but the malady lingers. The leading Colombian daily, *El Tiempo*, with a circulation of 300,000 over a vast area from Bogota, had, until recently, no headline designations, no headline sizes, no specified typefaces, no dummies.[1] Twenty long stories, all with multi-column heads, might be scheduled for page one and, come press time, were sorted out in bedlam with stories jumping perhaps to five or six pages inside. Ads could float to the top of a page and there was no shortage of over-set matter.

There are many newspapers in the world which prepare plans for page one and all the advertisements, but leave the inside pages to chance. The pages are put together on the stone, perhaps with a spattering of multi-column headlines, and certainly with a prayer that there is enough metal around to fill the holes.

The design of an effective newspaper begins earlier than this. Flinging the paper together on the stone may be exciting but it is erratic in its expression of news values,

and it inevitably wastes time. Columns of over-set are the usual memorial to brilliant improvisation.

Dummies

The first step is to pin together a rough dummy of the newspaper to be published, identical in the number of pages but reduced in size for easy handling. A half-size dummy works well ($8\frac{1}{2}$ by 11 in. for a broadsheet paper). There is no need for this preliminary dummy to be as detailed as a dummy used in page layout. As a minimum it should be scored with column rules.

The purpose of this first dummy is to enable the editor to see how the total space and the sequence of pages can be matched to the day's schedule of news and features. Since the number of pages is normally set by cost criteria, and essentially by the amount of advertising, the advertising department prepares the initial dummy indicating in it the spaces it requires for classified and display ads within agreed limits. This is presented to the editor with the proposed total of advertising columns and the total of editorial columns written on each page and totalled on the front. Once the space totals have been agreed, the real work of newspaper design can begin. The editor assigns pages to the various editorial departments (features, news, women, sport, etc.) and, in liaison with the advertising department, arranges the best sequence and shape of the advertising.

Placing the Ads

It is not wise for any newspaper executive to move advertising around without consulting the advertising department. An advertiser may have paid for a special position at a special rate—and that is only one of the inhibitions. Advertisers do not like appearing on the same page or double spread as competitors; women's advertisers have no enthusiasm for appearing on the sports pages; and advertisers who include a coupon for the reader to complete should never be placed where their ad falls on the back of another coupon advertiser.

The objectives in shuffling the ad around in the dummy will vary with the demands of the news. For a picture pull-out section the aim would be to create a series of half-pages, beginning on a right-hand page, with eight columns open at the top and advertising mostly confined to the lower half. Whatever the daily requirements the dummy is the key. And there are general long-term objectives whose accomplishment begins with the dummy, essentially the creation of a sound framework for coherent editorial sequence and viable page layout. These are the general aims:

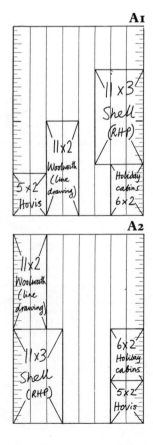

1 The first page of any paper should be almost wholly free of advertising: for a broadsheet paper a column is a maximum and for a tabloid half that.

2 The basic groupings of editorial matter must be maintained. Classified advertising, for instance, might acceptably fall between news and sport, but it would confuse the reader to have news on pages 2, 3, 4, classified on 5 and 6, and news on 7.

3 Within the paper right-hand pages should be kept open at the top for editorial. Left-hand pages can carry more advertising. Where there is also heavy advertising for the right it should be discouraged from taking more than two legs in the top right corner. There is more reader traffic for right-hand pages and advertisers are prepared to pay extra for these positions. There should none the less be a limit to the sale of top right-hand positions.

4 As many simple rectangles as possible should be created for editorial. Classified is clearly more malleable for this pur-

pose than display—but care must be taken not to split classified advertising sections because it can cut the response rate. There should be a ban on absurd spaces for editorial filling such as a 2 in. gap at the top of a page, the blight of American newspapers.

5 The advertising sequence should be spaced to limit the effects of crowding. Avoid having two crowded pages in succession, especially facing each other. Where there is a full-page ad on one side of the spread, limit the ads on the other side, especially at the top of the page.

6 Where editorial plans an early press time for page, make sure the advertising content, too, can arrive early.

7 Editorial should insist that the rough dummy for editorial contains all relevant information on the nature of the ads schemed. If the ad is a half-tone, editorial will want to avoid scheming a large editorial half-tone on the same page. If it to be solid grey text (classified), editorial will want to scheme some offsetting illustration; and so on. The nature of the ads can be indicated on the dummy even before the ads are set. Later when the editorial man is planning page layout he should have a proof of the ads on his pages. This should be easy to organise since proofs of set matter go to the clients and it is simple to pull an extra proof. Ad blocks brought into the paper should also be proofed.

Here, finally, are examples of badly disposed advertisements and how they should be corrected.

A1 The ad layout in A1 would be perpetrated infrequently today. It breaks the fundamental rule that the reader should have an orderly presentation of news and of ads. The two should be separate and seen to be separate, and where possible the editorial shapes should be clear rectangles at the top.

A2 The A2 diagram shows the regrouping required.

B1 A more typical bad grouping of display ads, creating an awkward space at the top right hand.

B2 is the correct disposition.

Notice that the ads are marked on the dummy to scale, and with the size and spread written in as an additional check. The other information is the name of the advertiser, a rough indication of the typographical nature of the advertisement, and the advertising department's reminder of specific injunctions relating to the position of the ad. 'Solus' or SP written here would mean that the advertiser has been promised he will be the only advertiser on the page. The letters 'RH' and 'LH' mean right-hand or left-hand page. 'Bar sport' means the advertiser does not want to be on a sports page. 'Outside cols' means the left side of a left-hand page, the right of a right-hand.

Editorial Sequence

Marking the editorial content of the pages of a dummy is the final step at this stage. A newspaper which has accepted the virtue of organising the content in clean sections can usefully carry out a colour analysis. Draw a series of equal rectangles to represent each page of the newspaper in sequence.

Assign a colour to each main category of editorial content: green, say, for home news, red for foreign, blue for local, yellow for business, pink for industry, orange for job advertising and so on. Now take a typical issue of the paper and colour the columns of the linear dummy according to the content of pages they represent. In the end one can see at a glance how effectively the paper is sectionalising the news, and what other possible permutations there are.

You can make up a newspaper or magazine by pasting proofs on to a full-size sheet. If this is done to a preconceived design—as it is in most magazines—it is accurate to a line, and helpful visually. A magazine can do this because it has time. A paste-up to a preconceived design is too slow for newspapers, and it is unnecessary: it is simpler and

quicker to put the type into the page and pull a page proof. A paste-up without a preconceived design is futile. The design of a page cannot be left this late. The design must take place before type is set. Design should define metal.

The tools you need are layout sheets; soft black pencils; one red pencil; an eraser; 24 in ruler; scissors; paste; adequate working space, preferably a drawing board.

A layout sheet is more detailed than an advertising dummy. It is marked with column rules and scaled in inches at both margins. Since the advertising department sells space at the bottom of the paper, it prefers to work in inches measured upwards from the bottom; editorial works from the top and prefers the inches to be scaled from the top.

Two scales running in opposite directions to meet the needs of both departments are a useful check against inaccurate transfer of advertising sizes from the master dummy to the page layout. In addition, each column rule should be marked at every inch: alternatively lines can be drawn across the sheet at each inch to complete the grid. The layout sheet should have ample margins for special instructions to the printer.

The purpose of the layout sheet is to organise the content of the page. It goes to the printer so that the stonehand can place the metal and illustrations where you have planned them. The first decision is whether to use full- or half-scale layout sheets. The full-scale layout sheet has the advantage that it makes visualising easier. Every headline can be sketched in at size—especially easy when the full-scale sheet is semi-transparent; pictures can be schemed at size; a long run of type looks a long run of type. The full-scale sheet is also more accurate: an inch is an inch and there is plenty of space to write in clear instructions to the printer. The disadvantages of the full sheet for broadsheet papers (but not tabloid) are that it is cumbersome on the stone, it is harder to organise carbon copies of the full

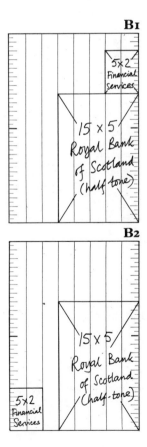

B1

5×2 Financial Services

15 × 5 Royal Bank of Scotland (half-tone)

B2

15 × 5 Royal Bank of Scotland (half-tone)

5×2 Financial Services

designed half-scale sheet is best for news layouts on busy newspapers, especially where there are a lot of pages and a crowded stone. The full-scale sheets handicap the stonehand, who needs clear space around him for galleys, rules, spaces, late corrections. (Feature layouts are different, *see* pp. 139-140.)

There should always be at least two copies of a layout: one for the printer, one to be retained in editorial. When there is a development which means changing the page you can see immediately, on your own copy of the layout, what the possibilities are. It is easy to take carbon copies with a half-scale layout sheet; with a full-scale sheet, make the copy on a half-scale sheet. There is no need for second full-scale sheets.

Experiment and Practice

The beginner at layout should practise assiduously before he tries the real thing. Take several newspapers and translate the finished pages back into layout diagrams. A way to check progress is to take one of the printed newspaper pages, preferably one of the earlier ones copied, so that memory is not too much help. Cut this page with scissors into its basic constituents of headlines, text and illustrations. Using the layout, reassemble the page by pasting headings, text, and so on, on to a full-scale sheet. Does it look right? Or did the diagram omit some essential instruction which has handicapped reconstruction?

Here are **(3)** a completed page and **(4)** the layout from which it was produced, shown at the same size. The layout sheet does not attempt to give all the information there is on the printed page. It provides a clear, simple map. The compositor making up the page on the stone does not want to have to read excess information. It is confusing. But he cannot make up a news page quickly and accurately without eight essentials:

1 The page number, edition and appropriate ad spaces.

sheet, and it takes marginally more time to draw up a full sheet than a half-scale sheet.

There is a further point. The editorial executive should feel free to experiment with alternative layouts. Always getting it right first time is an attribute of the complacent. It is more economical in paper and time to try rough sketches on a half-scale sheet. Preference and particular circumstances must come into this. In my own view, a properly

2 The size and measure of all headlines.

3 The measure and run of all text type.

4 The position of 1 and 2 on the page.

5 Positive identification of every story.

6 The measure and depth of blocks and their captions.

7 Positive identification of blocks.

8 Instructions on spacing and column rules where these depart from the style of the paper.

There is no need to indicate the point size of the text type, indentions in the text type, ordinary by-lines (except where these help identification), paragraph openings, nor to write in the exact wording of the headlines.

Picture and Story Identification

It helps *picture* identification if you can rough sketch an outline of the picture content, but it is no substitute for positive identification in words. Where the layout sheet says 'Marine at window' the back of the picture print sent to process should carry the same wording, 'Marine at window, page one.'

Headlines and stories are identified by subject—Russian space man, spy, art ring deal. These should pick up key words in heads and/or intros. Such identification is preferable to relying on catchlines taken from the text folios. There is the risk of confusing two stories which attract similar catchlines, and in the rush of production catchlines are sometimes dropped from the top of galleys of type. What can usefully be added to the layout sheet, when available, is the number assigned by the printer to a galley of type already set and proofed.

Headlines on this full-scale sheet take approximately as much space on the layout as they will in the printed page. Work for news pages should be accurate but there is no need to fuss trying to measure to within a few points: in practice an eighth-of-an-inch tolerance either way will work very well. Where the headline type is a variation from style this should be indicated, because it is an additional help to the comp in identifying

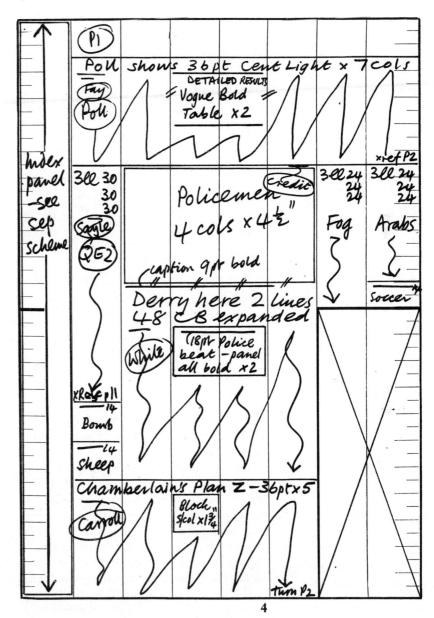

4

the right headline. The full wording of the heading is not necessary, nor is it necessary to repeat the type marks for every line of headline, provided the spread and size are clear. As for elaborate sketching in of the serifs and weight of the headline type, on news pages it is merely an indication to the comp that the layout man has nothing better to do: since comps know type rather well, they may also be critical of the artwork.

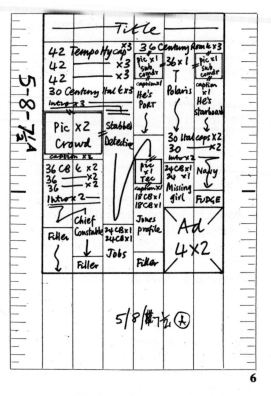

The run of the *text* type is indicated by straight lines and arrows: sketching in lines of single-column type is another futile occupation on news pages.

The column rules and cut-off rules separating stories are all indicated in this layout. Practice will vary from office to office: in some the layout assumes the insertion of column rules and indicates their omission by writing across the column rule. Office styles do not matter here, only that layout men should know and follow theirs.

Having seen how a layout should be done, let us see how it is done by a typical beginner.

The beginner drafted the layout sheet (5) for a tabloid page. What he was really trying to present is shown in the revised layout (6). The beginner here was a fully trained reporter attending a course organised by the National Council for the Training of Journalists in Britain.

The layout springs from a set of actual news material supplied to the course. It is not the most disorganised layout, and it drama-

tises typical faults. Putting aside the quality of the make-up, the layout sheet is a masterpiece of confusion:

1 There is nowhere a single indication of headline size measure. The comp could not blank for the main headlines. The whole page would have to wait until they arrived.

2 The four pictures are marked for column width but not for depth.

3 The two single-column portrait blocks of the submarine commanders are not identified. Which block goes where?

4 No captions are marked for these two blocks.

5 It is not clearly indicated that the material underneath ties on to these two blocks. The way this should be done is shown in the layout on the right.

6 Is the double-column block connected to the lead or the story below?

7 The ad size is not given.

8 The Polaris headline appears to be ruled off from its story.

9 The intro for the Navy story, column 6, is marked, murkily, as a 10pt bold × 1, but the lines suggest it is meant to be across two columns.

10 What happens in column 4 is anybody's guess. Is the single-column block part of the lead story which turns very awkwardly into column 4? Could D/S be short for Detective-Sergeant?

11 The layout is barely legible with so many crossings out. These were apparently the result of trying, needlessly, to write in the exact headline wording. Crossings out can be eliminated if you use a pencil, and rub out errors. Another way to correct errors, especially useful if the error occurs near the end of a layout, is to paste a small piece of paper over the error and redraw that particular part of the scheme.

Laying out a Page

Planning a page for a newspaper with a fixed layout style (of which the London *Daily Telegraph* and *The Hindu* are classic examples) is not really a design exercise. The design has been set already. The page planner here has his task reduced to two judgments: filling the most important holes with the most important stories, and estimating the length of text accurately. But how does planning begin for a functional page where the aim is to make the design respond dynamically to content?

Let us assume that we have, unset, all the material we have to present, and also have the context to the newspaper's customary format.

Begin by drawing the ad(s) in the correct columns at the correct depth. Double-check that these instructions have been transferred accurately from the master dummy because an error here will throw out all the planning and wreck a tight production schedule. Professionals make errors at this stage surprisingly often. Double-check. Now note down on a separate pad the other physical variables for the page:

(i) A catchline for each story followed by its length in column-inches, e.g. Fire 20; Taxes 12, and so on.

(ii) The best headline wording for the main story, e.g. Fireman rescues his own wife.

(iii) The number and size of all potential illustrations e.g. Fireman rescue preferably 5-col. at 4 in. deep, plus portrait head shot of wife 3 in. deep single-col. and so on.

The totals for text and picture space, plus a reasoned guess at display space, may well exceed the total space on the page. If the excess is small, say no more than half-a-column on a text paper, the layout should be worked out in detail. Once display space has been allocated and this shows that the excess is greater than supposed, there is a set of choices:

(i)   Reduce the length of every story.

(ii) Reduce the length of some stories.

(iii) Reduce or omit illustrations.

(iv) Transfer less important stories to another page or omit.

(v)   Turn viable lengths of text of one or possibly two longer stories to another page.

A practical layout man can estimate how realistic a list of stories for a particular page is, without adding up totals.

The basic projection decision made now affects the whole shape of the page: what are the most important, one, two or three ideas the page is to communicate? Every news-page design should begin with this question, and it should be answered after a series of quick rough sketches on a layout sheet. There is, say, a memorable news picture which needs to be six columns wide, 5in. deep. This size has limited mobility on an eight-column page, but all the possible positions should be sketched in on different layout sheets. The purpose is to see how the shape dictates the remainder of the page. How does it affect the display of the best wording for the main headline? Are the positions remaining appropriately bold or subdued for the second priority item?

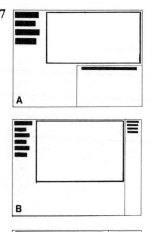

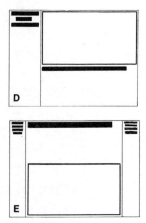

The picture may be so important that it is worth amending the wording of the main headline. Or one may have to start experimenting with the picture as a four or $5\frac{1}{2}$-column. There will generally be two or three items which make conflicting claims top of the page on space, and the only way to assess the possibilities is to sketch them. The series of sketches in (7) shows the method.

When the picture is not decisive, planning begins with the strongest text item, say a long story (25in. of text). This requires careful headline wording. Write the head, choose the type—and let the words determine the shape. Again there is a choice of positions for both head and text, each to be rough-sketched. How do they fit in with the illustrations planned? Is there enough space for them to work satisfactorily? Do they modify the prominence of the lead?

There are a surprising number of permutations of text and headline: (8), for instance, shows nine possibilities, involving a four-column headline. Theoretically they are not all equally desirable. **a** pushes the other headlines or pictures down page. **e**, production irritations apart, steps the text too dramatically for comfort. **d** produces three good shoulder positions. **g** risks a clash of headlines. Intro setting can vary: ×1 (a,b,c); ×2 (b,g); ×3 (h); ×4 (f); ×4×3×2 (e); ×4×2 (d,i).

A Sunday Times Front Page

Let us take for a practical exercise in the mechanics of make-up an actual *Sunday Times* list (October 27, 1969) for page one:

(a) Lead: preparations for London demo: 34in. text; 4-col pic $4\frac{3}{4}$in. deep.

(b) Paper's own blurb for Robert Kennedy's diary of Cuba Missile crisis: prepared panel (text and half-tone) 2 col × 5in. deep.
    News story on general's criticism of the Kennedy diary: 6in.

(c) Russian in space—practice for moon

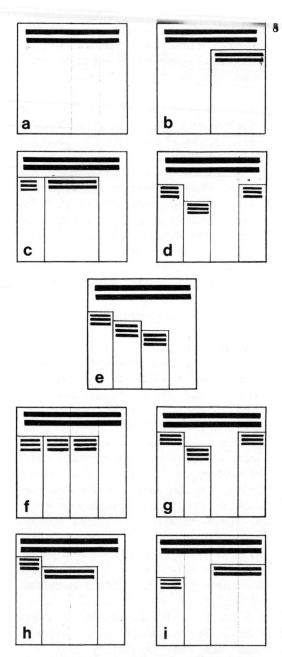

attempt: 15in. including $2\frac{1}{2}$in. tabulation on US/Russian achievements. Possible portrait pic of Russian.

(d) Exclusive on a £150,000 art ring deal: text (including set of Parliamentary questions), 50in. Headline wording must be 'MPs question £150,000 Art Ring deal' because of legal implica-

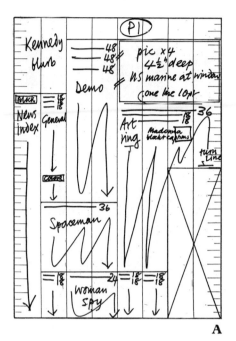

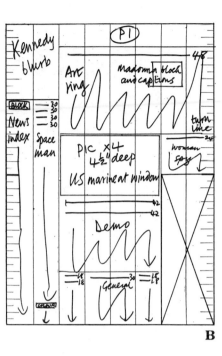

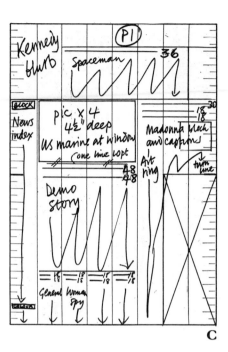

A   B   C

tions of the story. Small picture of painting. Small portrait of a key person in the story.

(e) German spy story: 9in.

(f) Several short news items.

(g) The paper's fixed column-one summary of the rest of the news.

(h) An 11 × 2in. advertisement in cols 7 and 8.

The first problem is space. There is too much text for the space on page one. The first decision is whether to move anything from page one or to start everything on page one and continue some stories inside the paper. It is judged that all the stories are sufficiently important to start on page one. The two longest—the demonstration and the art ring—will have to turn to page two. About 45in. (just over two columns) of text has to be turned. It is decided to turn 20in. of the lead (leaving 14in. for page one) and 25in. of the art ring story (leaving 25in. for page one). More of the art story could be turned on to page two only by making it wholly a page of turn stories and this is judged inadvisable. So we now have the

constituents for page one. Next come the basic projection decisions.

The editor wants the Kennedy block to be visible when the newspaper lies folded at the retail sales outlets. It therefore has to be above the fold, and there are only two practical positions: intruding over the folio in columns 1 and 2 or in columns 7 and 8. Here are rough sketches trying to solve the page layout problems with the Kennedy poster in columns 1 and 2, with comments on each rough sketch.

Scheme A: Rejected. Gives too much prominence at the top to one story. For Saturday hard news the moon story seems lost with a three-column headline down page.

Scheme B: Rejected at once. As soon as the art story or any other is placed here it is impossible to place the four-column picture above the fold.

Scheme C: Rejected. The space problems are all solved and several of the problems of prominence, but in sketching a top-page position for the art ring and moon stories the demo story has been squashed down too much.

D

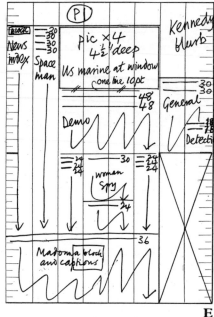

E

F

Scheme D: Accepted for one edition. The column 1 summary has been turned into two in a panel with the General's story. This is not wholly satisfactory but it enables the anchoring of the lengthy art story at the foot of the page. The multi-column spread there with short legs enables the slabbishness of the long text to be broken up. The five Parliamentary questions which begin the story and delay it too much are also conveniently split off to be read in a panel within the story with a detail of the painting.

This scheme was printed, but was rejected later. It was ambiguous about what the newspaper judged the most important story. And it was recognised that the Kennedy brothers block in columns 1 and 2 had them both looking the wrong way, directing the reader's eye out of the page.

Scheme E: The Kennedy poster moved to cols 7 and 8, accepting the slight illogicality in announcing the contents of the paper in two different places: the news summary stays in column 1.

Rejected because of the Russian moon story. The prominence of a single-column top is just right, but there is not enough room for the text (a turn is rejected because there are already two turns and they are always to be regretted).

Scheme F: Accepted and printed. The Russian space story, moved to column 6, gets the length it needs. The excellent news picture justifies its prominence in cols 2–3.

The scheme works better—and looks better. It is not perfect. Papers with different personalities and format and readers would express the same news in different ways. But the important lesson in the mechanics of design is the variety of answers, and that they require an open mind. The first layout idea may make the best of a lot of the material, but where time allows, there may always still be a better way. Respect the material: it would have been disastrous for that *Sunday Times* page to cut good stories, or reduce the picture to a three-column, or acquiesce in a shape for the art story which interfered with the headline wording.

Designing as You Go
The ideal is to have all the material before rough-sketching begins, or, at the very least, the main picture and story. On an evening

newspaper this may often not be possible. Layouts have to carry some headline shapes and sizes for stories that have not yet materialised: this is to save time. The composing room can cut its rules and dummy the page ready for the type; the foundry can make a casting for a theoretical block. There are times on evening papers when most of the page will have to be planned in advance. It is undeniably bad. It means forcing the content into predetermined shapes. Wherever it is the practice, it should be examined to see just how essential it is to do things this way.

There is a middle way when the wait is for the main story or picture. This is to have clearly subsidiary stories edited into single-column text, with the deskmen marking their copy 'headline to come.' There must be a log of these stories and their length: as soon as the main story and picture arrive, the stories already set can be schemed into the page with the freedom to choose the headline shapes most appropriate.

The log really is essential, and it should be more than just a list of catchlines. It should carry in a column on the left the total space, in descending order (in half-columns here). As the log grows the numbers on the left are marked to show space still available. On the right you note how the space was allocated, and how much to each story.

Features Layout

A full-scale semi-transparent sheet should be used for layouts for features and magazines. Have to hand type-charts of the available display type,[2] and if possible photostats, at the required scale, of probable illustrations. (Alternatively, in a well-endowed office the effect of reducing or enlarging an illustration can be viewed on a Grant projector or a Copy Scanner.)

Begin by reading the copy and studying the illustrations. If text is not available, talk to the News Editor to establish what the article is trying to say and the mood it is trying to establish. Rough out possibilities

		Space available
100	Cols	Moon shot (40″)
99½		,,
99		,,
98½		,,
98		Jail escape (12″)
97½		,,
97		Honeymoon (10″)
96½		,,
96		

for marrying headline, text, white space and illustrations. In particular, work out the wording for the display type. These preliminary doodles can be on small pieces of blank paper or a half-scaled dummy. When a satisfactory scheme emerges, soft pencil it on the full layout sheet. Draw the display wording space without bothering to specify a typeface, and rough check the space open for text against the length of the article.

Now it is possible to experiment at full scale. Put the illustration, or preferably scaled photostat under the semi-transparent layout sheet and view it in position and in alternative positions. Do the same for the display type by tracing the words required from a type chart on to separate small strips of paper, one piece for each word, and manoeuvre them on the layout sheet. (Some designers prefer to place both illustration and type beneath the sheet, so that it is easier to visualise the roughened effect of a printed page.)

In choosing the type from your established range select a face and style that fit the wording as well as the theme. The evocative qualities of a face are a matter of judgment in the light of the current aesthetic. It seems to me as foolish to deny that type carries mysterious flavours of elegance, practicality, romance, and so on, as it is to say there is a typeface uniquely suited for each message. Beginners, of course, should mix typefaces at their peril; there must be some sympathy between them (*see* Book Three). Avoid, for instance, mixing a Modern-face roman like Bodoni with an old face like Caslon.

Only when the relationship of display type, illustration, and white space is satisfactory can the layout be finished for the printer. Paste up the photostat—and advertisement proof if available—and clearly mark instructions for areas of type, illustrations and white space. The display type itself should be traced on to the full-scale sheet either direct from the type chart, or from the trial slips of headline wording.

The strips themselves should never be pasted on to the full-scale sheet. The optical effect of their edges is to suggest that there is less space between the lines than there is, and there is a danger of ending up with too much white on the page itself. Always specify the typeface with its name, series number, and size in points (even in photo-composition, in which point sizes are irrelevant: many printers using filmsetters still describe their various sizes by the metal equivalent for convenience). Indicate whether the text type is solid or whether it should be leaded and specify its width in ems. It is not enough for these instructions to be on the copy. In features they should be on the layout as well. The style for instructions is like this:

> Text: Set in 9pt Helvetica (Linotype G58) 1pt leaded throughout across $17\frac{1}{2}$ ems.

With filmsetting it is possible to make up the material oneself. A reproduction proof (Ozalux) of the filmset type is pasted up as artwork for photographing as a whole. There is some slight loss of quality because the image goes through three extra photographic processes.

Try to have the page proof supplied with the advertisements, if any, in position, or anything else—such as a title block which will be on the published page—that affects the appearance. Trimming the proof, so that the margins are what they will be when published, also helps in assessing the look of a page. Check the proofs against the layout and make corrections on the proofs cleanly: a messy page only confuses the printer.

How Others Do It

Layout, as I said in the preface, has always been treated as something of a mystery. The newcomer can watch the high priest perform and he can learn the jargon, but he must not ask what the secrets are and the reasoning behind it all. He must learn, he will be told, as others learned, from imitation and from the shaft of lightning that will illuminate the sky when he transgresses one of the unwritten and unexplainable rules of the creed. As a contribution to the exorcism required, I asked three leading British newspaper layout men if they would come clean and set out for others the principles which guide them when they come to design a page. Here are their replies.

MIKE RANDALL

As Editor of the *Daily Mail*, was Journalist of the Year and responsible for the restyling of the newspaper which won a Newspaper Design Award.

He is now Managing Editor, News, of *The Sunday Times*.

I take the sheet of layout paper. It is $15\frac{3}{8}$ in. wide and 22 in. deep. I pencil in the ads. I read the copy. I am hoping for two things. I am hoping to capture the writer's mood, to be certain about his emphasis, to be in tune with his copy. And I am looking for a headline.

When you are lucky, when mood and headline come together in exciting conjunction, your enthusiasm rises and your creative instincts get the necessary adrenalin. I look at the pictures. I see the headline visually. It may be a running headline. It may be a stark, big, three-word headline. Whatever it is, I make the type fit the headline and not the headline the type. Now it begins to take the shape that I dictate and not the shape which is sometimes dictated by a list of contents which have to be accommodated without sufficient consideration of the why and how.

In brief, if the words are good, I am moulded by them. I feel I must care for them, nurse them, protect them, and then give them the presentation they deserve.

If the words are bad, good presentation can make them look a little better. You may thus fool yourself and your colleagues. But you will not fool the reader.   *MR*

COLIN G VALDAR

Former Editor of the *Sunday Pictorial* and *Daily Sketch,* and former Director of the Daily Mirror Group.

Now Chairman of Bouverie Publishing Co. Ltd.

Layout *must* arise out of the copy, so I read the copy first. As I do, I pencil possible headlines—which, in features, are seldom inspired by anything before the third paragraph—and assess the prominence and space value of each item. The shortest item may merit greatest prominence; the longest may need to be insinuated into the layout in a way which does not deaden the page with unrelieved acres of type.

Two conventions now take over. The first is that advertisements have to go in. The position and weight of their illustrations and text must be known before layout can start; so I get a proof or risk a clash. If an advertisement is pleasing I exploit it, rather than fight it. To the reader this is all part of the page.

The second convention is on type. On news pages the style of the paper will dominate, but even for features I believe one sans heading in a page of Caslon faces is likely to

work better than an even mixture of the two.

I use a layout sheet which is the actual size of the page; layouts on miniature pads preclude the excellence which is seen only in pages which have been designed every pica of the way from head to foot.

A page is not a solus poster; it is part of a complete newspaper, so I need to know the position of the page in the newspaper (and particularly the make-up of its facing page). In this respect alone, the layout man on the front page has an easier task; he has nothing to fight or to complement. His special burden is that he must 'sell' his page and hint at the variety of his choicest wares in the top five inches; that is all that will show on a newsagent's rack or counter.

Having decided the headline weight and text space for the principal item, where do I put the impact on the page? A reader's eyes looking at a double spread fall first towards the top right-hand quarter of the right-hand page, next they travel to the bottom centre between the two pages (so I keep pillar ads away from the centre if I can), then up to near the centre top of the left-hand page.

So the bull's-eye position for picture or typographical impact is, I believe, towards top right, probably ending in column 7 of an eight-column page. This helps to break the ugly vertical rule which so often splits a page by being continued beyond the top of a double-column pillar ad to the head of the page. That empty column 8, if used for a modestly displayed item, will prevent a clash if a layout devised for a right-hand page (particularly in tabloid) is later moved to the left-hand.

I always try to interrupt every top-to-bottom rule. This is not only because they rob a page of integration, but also because full-length columns of text are almost impossible to read on crowded buses and trains. Horizontal make-ups are one answer; they enable the hemmed-in commuter to read several complete stories without refolding his paper.

When pencilling in the heads and text

areas, I try to remember that relevant pictures (caption underneath, please) need to be integrated and not stuck on like outhouses.

When the page layout is completed, I ask myself: (1) Does the reader know where to start and where to go next? (2) Are the white spaces as functional as the text, or does the page look like a stuffed matchbox? (3) Is there room in the acres of 7pt to weave in a small double-column item in 10pt or pica? I may have nothing on hand to fill it, but I believe in accepting the challenge and finding something—a letter, a paragraph from a book, or a quote. A reader who might otherwise turn the page often finds his gaze pulled towards such an oasis.

Eye-pleasing newspapers alternate elegantly packed news pages with their more open feature pages; this is a relief to the reader's eye and explains why telephone directories are dull to look at even though they may be full of good names.   *CGV*

CLIVE IRVING

Formerly Features Editor of the *Daily Express*, redesigned *The Observer*, Managing Editor of *The Sunday Times*, Deputy Editor of the *Sunday Times Colour Magazine*, Magazine Executive for the International Publishing Corporation, Executive Director of London Weekend Television, and now a freelance consultant in Britain and the US.

Good newspaper layout is an expression of values—the relationship between each item on a page ought to show the value that the paper places on those items. For this reason editorial judgment is an intrinsic part of layout. Values, of course, alter from paper to paper. This is less true than it used to be, to the extent that whereas at one time it was thought vulgar for 'quality' newspapers to use large photographs, this silliness has now disappeared. But the priorities between say, the *Daily Mirror* and *The Guardian* on what constitute important values are very different. I am saying this because it seems

to me vital that whoever produces a paper's layouts must have a deep, instinctive understanding of that paper's values, and newspaper design cannot in any sense run independently of content.

Thus, for me, the look of a page is, and should be, influenced more by an estimate of relative values than by anything else. I can illustrate this best with two 1959 examples from my own files.

They are two *Daily Express* leader pages which I designed as features editor. One of them Lord Beaverbrook liked very much, the other one provoked a violent reaction. Lord Beaverbrook kept a close watch on his leader page. And on everything else.

The page had a number of standing elements, some of them a curse when flexibility was essential. There was the leader column in column 1, the cartoon which usually, though not exclusively, went at the top of the page, the Beachcomber column, Rupert, television and radio, and two double-column ad positions. The cartoon, in particular, cuts the number of options available for fresh layout solutions. The 'Murder in Paradise' page **(9)** was an absolutely conventional page (lacking the Beachcomber column for some reason) and produced an absolutely conventional solution. The main feature was a late one, earlier editions carried something else, and the page was designed and sent to press between 10 and 11 p.m. It made a nice combination of detail: photographs, headline writing and typography.

The other page **(10)** is a more unusual animal. It was a Saturday, and there was no cartoon. The previous day we had reported the death of the racing driver, Mike Hawthorn. It happened that the current issue of the magazine *Esquire* was running a remarkable 'stream of consciousness' interview with Stirling Moss, which revealed more of the psychology of Moss and his contemporaries than anything I had seen.

There was no standing rule on the *Express* about the length of leader-page articles, but we all knew that Beaverbrook thought 800 words enough for anything, and he was fond of quoting Biblical precedents for the combination of economy and revelation. The Moss article ran to about 4,000 words in *Esquire*. I got it down to about 1,800, beyond which it seemed to me that its value would be destroyed. So I ran it at that length. One other vital thing happened before I designed the page. What would normally have been the 'standfirst'—the hyperbolic introductory paragraph—flowed so freely from my pen that I decided to turn it into the headline. This became known as the Irving laxative style of headline. I was fond, and still am of the *Express* case-room's 'square Gothic' face, the standard *Sunday Express* display face, which works particularly well with a 'long read' display, and I used it here against a light tone background, with a halftone of Moss and his wife in one corner. The rest of the layout then simply required running text, one more half-tone and some

10

bold paragraphs. By normal *Express* standards it was sacrilege. But everybody agreed that the piece was outstanding, and it ran.

Beaverbrook exploded. There was a *diktat*, not defied again for many months, that leader-page articles of more than 800 words should never appear. The page became a prison. But it had been worth it, and the Moss page illustrates how a completely fresh layout can evolve solely because of an unusually good piece of writing. All layout should be as flexible as that. News pages, I feel, should occasionally drastically alter their values when, on similar occasions, an event or a piece of reporting justify it. I recall the issue of *The Observer* devoted entirely to Kruschev's denunciation of Stalin, which was brilliantly designed by Kenneth Obank, as an example of classic layout resulting from powerful content and an outstanding value judgment.   *CI*

Rejigs
Page one is made up and proofed. Soon the presses will be running. Then there is a piece of big late news which makes the page obsolete. What we would all like to do, I imagine, is imitate the dramatic Northcliffe act of pushing the whole forme off the stone on to the floor while we dictate new headlines, issue instructions all round and marry everything magically to produce a new page. In reality we have to study how to do a 'rejig,' which means the reorganisation of the page with minimum delay and maximum effect. It is an essential skill for anyone who hopes to have anything to do with production, especially on an evening newspaper where replates are like reflex actions.

Newspapers luxuriating in a local monopoly should not relax; they will be judged by the competition of radio and TV; and they have a duty to their readers.

The basic design problem is to de-emphasise the old lead and to gain prominence for the new story. First, an analysis of the main ways of rejigging, followed by practical examples.

1. Simple Substitution
Substitute the new lead in the same text and headline shape as the existing lead. This has been the classic reaction of newspapers with fixed formats expressing a carefully scaled sense of news values (the English *Daily Telegraph* or the *New York Times*). Simple substitution means that the basic plan of the page is retained: column rules, blocks, and story patterns are not changed, and nothing is cut. Of course something has to go. At an extreme, where the page is carefully scaled in its news expressions, the second lead takes the position of the existing third lead and the third lead is downgraded to the fourth, until a story drops off at the end.

There are two limitations to this process: the downgrading process can be eliminated if two pages are open. The old second lead can then be transferred inside as a lead. But this facility is rarely available for a quick replate.

The downgrading process can also be simplified if the page is largely made up of single-column stories of the same weight of heading, i.e. if there are many stories judged to be of the same value, then you will not be involved in having every headline on the page downgraded.

The advantage of rejig by substitution is that it preserves the scale of values in the existing format. It is attractive to newspapers which set a high value on the continuity of their news assessment. But, for a quick replate of one page, simple substitution has disadvantages. If the existing lead shape is in complicated text or heading setting, editorial and production time are lost. Second, still more time is taken if the downgrading process involves rewriting and resetting several other heads or intros. Third, a story is lost from the page which was previously judged good enough to be in the paper and in page one.

2. Substitution and Cutting
The same procedure, but rather than lose a story from the page, create space equal to the amount taken by the new lead by cutting back on existing stories. The preference for this method depends on the length of the new lead; the ease with which existing stories can be cut (some may have the inhibiting complication of turning to another page); and the value of the story thereby retained on page one.

11A

11B

3. Superimposition

Run the lead in a new shape superimposed on the old page in such a way that it affects only an isolated section of the page. The part of the page affected will need stories or pictures cut to accommodate the superimposed new lead. The speed of rejig by superimposition depends on the success in limiting these changes. This rejig can be exceptionally quick, and is well suited to newspapers seeking to respond dynamically to the news.

4. Omission

If there is a large picture, leave it out and run the new headline and story there.

Any of these main ways of rejigging a page can, of course, be combined.

Daily Telegraph Rejig (Simple Substitution)

The **(11B)** story of the raid on the US Embassy is substituted in the exact position and shape of the old lead **(11A)**. This is made second lead; the second lead is moved into third position. Here the downgrading stops with the movement of the old railways strike to another page. This is all right when two pages can be replated. On a quick replate of page one only it would not be acceptable because it would mean losing an important story. This rejig has the advantage of retaining the subtle scale of news values and the continuation to another page of the insurance story text is neatly preserved at the same point.

But the headline setting is an element of delay in the work involved in effecting this rejig:

Write and set thirteen lines of headline in nine decks.

Set the new lead in double- and single-column.

Reset three paragraphs of the old lead.

Reset two paragraphs of the old second lead.

Recut column rule, column 2.

Shorten the China story.

146

12A

12B

Northern Echo Rejig (Substitution and Cutting)

The US Embassy story is substituted (**12A, 12B**) in the head and text shape of the old China lead. The old lead is well accommodated by giving it prominence in column 1 with a 36pt heading (compared with a 30pt for the old Aden story). The Aden story displaced from column 1 is moved down page to columns 4, 5, 6. Here it occupies the identical space taken by the displaced baby story. As the page works out, the Aden story has been devalued too much: what was worth column 1 before has been down graded to eighth position. On a previous scale of news values, the Aden story would have merited the position of a column-8 top or the Nigeria story. But against the damage to the scale of news values we have to consider the time saved in the avoidance of head and text resetting and the recutting of rules. The Aden story, set single-column, moved very easily into the single position tripled up at the bottom of the page.

The major criticism is the devaluing of Aden and the loss of the baby story, but the rejig is relatively quick. There is no rule recutting. The work involved is:

Write and set ten lines of head.

Set new lead with three-col intro.
Reset three pars of old China lead and transpose the five column-one stories to column three under the new lead.

Daily Mail Rejig (Substitution and Cutting)

The (**13A, 13B**) new lead is substituted in the same position as the A34 story—but with a different text shape. The old A34 lead with bastard setting has been reset and updated and the matching picture remade so that the A34 story becomes a simple double-column in the shoulder of the new lead. The means-test story has been displaced. The substantive changes are confined to a three-column area of the page (the transfer of the bees story, col 5, to a col-8 top, is an independent reassessment of news values). But this is a relatively slow rejig. The work involved:

Write and set nine lines of headline.
Set new lead, with boxed by-line and 3-col intro.
Reset all bastard measure of old lead.
Make block of policeman.
Remake block of girl.
Recut column rules in column 3.

13A

13B

14A

14B

14C

14D

columns and devote them to a head, picture, and text on the late news. The China story switches to the back page **(D)**, and the murder hunt is cut by 7in. to go under the panel. The *Mirror* has not attempted to preserve its original scale of values, but it has dramatically exploited the late news. This is not a quick rejig, but the new page one is intrinsically better in its bold simplicity. The work:

Write and set ten lines of headline.
Reset five paragraphs of murder hunt.
Shorten murder hunt.
Cut five column rules on page one.
Make new block.
Set new lead.

Daily Mirror Rejig (Substitution)

A tabloid like the *Daily Mirror* cannot do much downgrading on a small page one. It has to make bold decisions **(14A—D)**.

The *Mirror* response to the late news of the Embassy raid is to clear the first $5\frac{1}{2}$

THE GUARDIAN
Monday August 21 1967

China issues ultimatum on Hongkong

15A

THE GUARDIAN
Monday August 21 1967

China issues ultimatum on Hongkong

Gunmen strafe US Embassy in London

15B

16A

Belfast Telegraph

Faulkner spells it out—to Derry, SDLP and Lynch

THE CHOICE YOU MUST MAKE

IRA charge: housewife stays silent

Riot victim's widow gets £11,500 award

16B

Belfast Telegraph

BIG NEW BANNER ACROSS 7 COLS

Old lead head rewritten across here

Second deck here

new lead

17A   **17B**   **17C**

Guardian Rejig (Superimposition)

The four-column block (**15A**) is cut to three, releasing the top of column 7 for a double-column headline on the Embassy (**15B**). The displaced story on the murder hunt is neatly moved down to the shoulder of the new second lead. Here the murder story retains its relative prominence. The Court Lees story displaced from column 7 by the US Embassy text is transposed to the shoulder position in column 6, and the German refugee story is moved downpage.

The *Guardian* rejig preserves its scale of news values. Cutting the block is a quick solution (much quicker, of course, than the *Mail's* remaking of a block). The work involves little resetting:

Cut the old block.
Reset the old caption—with fewer words so that the column rules in columns 4, 5 and 6, need not be shortened.
Set seven lines of head.
Cut two column rules.
Shorten three stories (murder hunt, Court Lees, and German refugees).

Rejig Variants

So much for the way different newspapers treated one late story. Those examples by no means exhaust the possibilities. First let us look at a more dramatic rejig by superimposition and then at two permutations.

Superimposition

The lead (**17A**) retains its headline wording and text setting—but it is moved lower down the page. The new lead head (**17B**) is superimposed in the space vacated, first with text single-column and then wider setting in a later edition (**17C**). The first rejig involves: set eight new lines of headlines, and one intro × 2 (Novarro), cut two column rules.

Superimposition and Substitution

A quick way of combining rejig by substitution and superimposition is open to papers in a banner headline (**16 A, B**).

The old text has been kept in its exact shape and position. It is not forced down the page (as it is in rejig by superimposition). It is cut off from its old banner with a rule. A new smaller head takes the place of the old second deck.

The skill in rejig by this method is to find the best slot for beginning the new lead text under the newly worded banner. A single-column opening will do, though a double is better: a single-column relies too much on the directional effect of the rules. The skill is in creating an opening which involves little resetting: slicing a column off a block is often the best way out. Setting up the body size of the new lead also helps the eye: with a short new lead, the whole text should be run in 10pt.

18A

18B

Substitution and Omission

The London *Evening News* was leading on an Olympic Games picture story (**18A**) on an afternoon when three policemen were shot dead in London. The policemen died at 3.19; the new page (**18B**) was off the stone twenty minutes later. This is an impressive performance. The tip-off on the story reached the *News* at 3.22; it was confirmed at 3.27, so the whole rejig was accomplished seventeen minutes after the *News* first heard and twelve minutes after the confirmation. In between, the story and headlines had to be written and set and the page redesigned and made up. The *News* made two bold decisions. First to write the most natural headline wording—3 Policemen Shot Dead —and then set it in suitable type size. That wording needed two decks (at increased size), hence it meant saving space across eight columns.

The second bold decision was to find the space by omitting two stories altogether for one edition—George Brown and the Weather story (columns 4 and 5). The rejig then proceeded as follows: The old lead headlines were dropped. The pictures and captions of the old lead were moved two

columns to the right, to create an opening in columns 1 and 2 for the text of the new lead.

Of course there are other ways to rejig this page. Here are two:

Alternative 1; This would not be in the style of the *Evening News*, but it would be brutally simple for maximum speed in a newspaper without the setting capacities or stone skill of the *Evening News*.

(i) Drop banner and all type above it.

(ii) Rule off Games story second deck (Official in Scuffle).

(iii) Use eight-column top of the page space for new lead banner and bold-type bastard set in six legs across eight columns.

Alternative 2; This would be in the *Evening News* style.

(i) Drop the Games banner.

(ii) Substitute new banner in same shape and position (the wording would have to be the inferior '3 Policemen Killed').

(iii) Rule off new banner from Games second-deck headline, which would be retained.

(iv) Hold out stories at foot of columns 4 and 5, cut George Brown and Choc Ice stories and force both down column,

18C

18D

losing lines 4 and 5 of the George Brown headline, and line 4 of the Choc Ice head. (v) Run text of new lead double-column in space created at the top of columns 4 and 5.

This would almost certainly be slightly quicker than the *Evening News* rejig. It would, however, lack the punch of the *News* rejig, carried on in further editions (**18C, D**).

Summary

The route to a quick rejig should now be clear. Make the best use of existing metal or photostrip material. Avoid discarding work already done. All resetting or re-photographing of headlines and text, all new cutting of rules, and all block remaking, is work repeated and time lost. It is creating nothing new. There are implications, too, for original page design. Immobile shapes put a page in splints. It is much more flexible when it is built up on single-column text setting of one size and face, when there are no drop letters, fancy indentions, or boxed credits, when the heads are simple multi-lines set by machine, and the shapes of head

and story are simple rectangles. Some resetting will be unavoidable in any rejig, but the task is to do only that which is strictly necessary to achieve prominence for the new lead. Here flexible and dynamic page planning scores, since it can cut resetting and re-editing and achieve prominence by superimposition—by creating new positions of prominence from a combination of bolder headlining in the right place, bigger body type and possibly bastard measure—but still one that can be set readily at speed.

Speed in a rejig can also be improved by

following a routine in which the priorities are right. The steps to take are, in order:

1 Assign the copy to a deskman to read.

2 Tell the printer there is urgent work on a page so he can assign a man to do the work and give setting priority to material for that page.

3 Think out where the rejig will go. Don't try to do this in five seconds flat. Take ten: an extra few moments' thought can save time all down the line, as well as allow a clearer idea to form of the length of the new lead and its potential developments.

4 Rough-crayon the position of the rejig on a page or page proof so that it will certainly work. If there is a big simple element in the plan on which the printer can begin work, send him a message. (For instance, if copy is going into the page in four legs to a depth of 4in. the comp can begin moving type down the page.) Of course, postpone any other complicating instructions to the printer for the moment.

5 Give instructions for any new block-making required.

6 Give instructions for resetting existing metal. If a complex story needs shortening, give the instructions to the deskman who handled the story. Simple cuts can be done on the stone. Deskmen must avoid writing the word 'rejig' on the copy or anything else which will lead the printer to take the existing metal out of the forme. Reset intro paragraphs should be marked: Reset as substitute intro.

7 Give instructions for the new lead. Ask for the headline to be finished first if it is a wholly new shape. The early arrival of the headline in metal or photostrip helps the comp making up the page.

8 Give instructions for any block cutting (quicker than remaking, of course) or any use of stock library blocks.

9 Plot the rejig for the make-up man. In a quick rejig, direct personal instructions on the stone (or at the assembly desk in photo-composition) are desirable, supplemented by a written plan. At a pinch an experienced executive can dispense with a new plan, but it is in fact safer to give a written guide. If the editorial man is called away the make-up man can continue working without delay. The rejig plan need not be elaborate. It is a waste of time writing a whole new layout if only part of the page is affected. Take the carbon copy of the old layout and write in the position of the new material and the transposition of the old. Paste strips of blank white paper over the old layout's discarded shapes and write the new instructions boldly on top. Another method is to take a page proof or published page and mark in the new shapes with crayon or felt-tip pen. (Cutting stories on the stone is dealt with in Book Two.)

There is one other possibility for improving a rejig: the use of a stock block, mentioned in item 8. If a famous person is involved, the library may be able to produce the metal of a stock single-column head shot. It is a matter of moments in letterpress to have this mounted and sent to the printer. It pulls its own weight and it can be a useful filler in an emergency.

A more difficult decision is when only part of the story is immediately available, or the story without an accompanying news photograph. This is a matter of judgment in each case, partly governed by the nature of the story—is the detail all that important? —and partly by the peculiarities of any individual newspaper's editionising and circulation policy.

Clearly there is a conflict of desirable objectives in any rejig—between speed and aesthetic principle, between speed and the fullest treatment. Given a late news break, there is no doubt of the fundamental criterion of an efficient rejig. It is the ruthless elimination of everything which adds time, even if it means incidental violence to a scale of news values or to appearance, and even if it means missing some of the detail. Imagine the effects of your rejig and reduce the work of all departments to the irreducible.

9 Design Clinic

*The art (of architecture) is impracticable
without its craftsmen.*

SACHEVERELL SITWELL

Bad design can spring from a basic misconception or from a multiplication of faulty detail. Nobody in newspaper design should ever underestimate the cumulative affect of bad detailing. It is the same in architecture. Much imitation Georgian architecture follows the general proportions of original Georgian but fails because the details of brick, window and door fail to follow the original exquisite style and proportion.

We need in newspaper design to be able to spot the minor symptoms of disorder and know what to do about them; the uneasy feeling that 'something' is wrong is not enough. What follows is a clinic where sick pages or parts of pages are diagnosed. Some of the inmates are chronic invalids, representatives of an international epidemic; some are ambulatory; and some are already fit and well after drastic treatment.

Page Organisation

(1) Abuse of white space. White space is not a virtue if it is scattered indiscriminately through the page. To be effective it should, like colour, be conserved and massed to illuminate a headline or to separate one feature from another. In detail, there should be a lot (i.e. 12 to 24 points) of white around the title; around the illustrations; over advertisement cut-offs and above headlines. There should be a little (i.e. 6 to 12 points) between head and by-line and first line of text.

The *Illinois State Register* has been commended for its use of white, but it is hard to see what purpose is served by the huge white indentions on some columns, with the head protruding into the gutter. The white on this page is wasted space, and in some instances works against an effective page. The caption to the middle picture of the crashed car is set, without headline, just below the paper's title. With 4 ems of white each side it is related to nothing, certainly not to the picture it is supposed to serve. There is still nothing to beat the old rule of putting captions beneath the pictures, irritatingly simple for the *avant-garde* but damned helpful to the reader who just wants to know.

2

Vary the subjects

(2) The headlines ringed on this *Guardian* page are all on the church and religion. It gives the impression of a confined range of subjects and reduces the appeal of the page. If, in scheming a page, the layout man discovers he has same-subject stories, which are in danger of yielding similar headlines, the choices are clear. Instruct the headline writers to avoid certain words, then vet the heads to make sure they avoid distorting the news; make a virtue of the profusion by pulling all the religious stories together; or see to it that the similar stories go to other pages.

3

Bad marriages

(3) Getting three families to live together is difficult for any typographer. Doing it in as crowded a space as in this title is likely to produce schizophrenia in the best of us. The slab serif clobbers the other two faces, and especially the Bodoni Bold Condensed.

The Bodoni Bold is forced into more bad marriages in the page, first with the antique face for Worksop's Royal Day. The lead type is as suggestive of regal grace and gaiety as knife-hewn initials on a tree trunk. The MP headline in sans is awkwardly shaped and heightens the effect of mean cramming. All three headline decks are jammed too close to each other to be easily readable. Body type intrudes too high in column 5, with a pimple of a crosshead to juxtapose badly with the lead second deck.

The picture carries too much distracting detail. The Queen looks well in it and if that section alone had been enlarged and the rest discarded, the whole page would have gained.

4

Playing jigsaws

(4) Typically unhelpful sports page (produced in this instance by photo-composition and web offset). Cricket and soccer are mixed up without much of a clue even from the headlines. The layout emphasises horizontal heads, but their relationship to text is muddled. Some sit on top of all their text; some obtrude over unrelated columns. Quite a jigsaw. The detailed typography is similarly erratic: nine changes of character in headline style. The heads down page are too big in proportion to their stories and in proportion to what is considered the lead headline.

5

6

Typography

(5, 6) Type cocktails deter. Compare the heady brew of the *Barnsley Chronicle* with the simple *Times Herald*. Which is easier to read? Which gives a clearer view of the news? The *Times Herald* does it by unifying the page in two faces, simple and extremely economical shapes, just sufficient white space to illuminate the display lines, and a well-behaved title. This page is helped a great deal by having the halftone to separate the title from the sans lead head. Note how the bastard-set panel in 9pt leads the page: the change in measure, in plain roman text without bold or caps distinguishes the lead.

The *Barnsley Chronicle* has six typefaces, text in bold, and in bold caps, and in italic, but it does not carry the same conviction. The inset headline Silent Protest would be all right down page, or inside, but is thin at the top and allows the Miner's Son to steal the page.

The panel itself is not distinctive enough for its position. The lead type is small, and the measure cramped. Note the difference in the column white between this panel and that in the *Times Herald*'s.

As you can see, the Barnsley page is weighed down by its elephantine title. There is nothing wrong with the choice of face for title; it is the clutter that weakens it.

Strength below the fold

(7) The *Bridgeport Post* (Connecticut) does a fair job of reporting the news, but a poor job of displaying it. The most obvious weakness is the positioning of the half-tones. The useful colour provided by the half-tones is not used to most effect because it is all concentrated in the upper half-page and the rest of the page collapses. The middle and bottom of this page cry out for colour. Nor are the shapes of the half-tones interesting in themselves. And indeed the main half-tone of two buffaloes rubbing noses has been reduced too much to do justice to the image.

The second major flaw with the page is the absence of any strength below the fold. We are confronted with a monotonous display of two-line headings, single-column. Near the top of the page in column 4 we have a watery sans heading. As well as repositioning the half-tones, we ought on this page to have one or two headlines below the fold which break the column rule in either double- or triple-column display.

The third difficulty with the page is the reader's in finding what he is looking for from page one. Most of the text on the page comes from continuation stories. Each has the words 'Continued from Page One,' and each picks up the flavour of the page one wording—sometimes with odd effects: 'He Also Vows to Push Curb on Inflation.'

But the continuation stories are scattered over the page and the continuation line in bold body type does not stand out enough for the reader easily to find the story he is looking for. The fourth and fifth flaws are details. Firstly, there is the continuation of the Asian story from the bottom of column 6 to the top of column 7. It turns under an unrelated joke paragraph, whereas it ought to turn under the story's own heading, which should thus be double-column. Secondly, the cut-off rules which sandwich the headlines add bittiness to the page without any purpose.

Importance of ruling

(8) La *Tribune de Genève* produces some attractive pages on a six-column grid, but this is not one of them. It illustrates the importance of coherent ruling and the proper placing of a half-tone. There is no logic apparent to the average reader in the bitty column rules here. The stories pulled together by column rules just above the fold under the heading about the Thirteen Arab Ministers would, one assumes, be related, but aren't. Stories concerning the same part of the world are not pulled together by column rule or cut-off. It foxes the reader when so many of the rules are badly mitred or run for erratic lengths, leaving odd bits of white. As for the half-tone of Cassius Clay, it is obvious what a major improvement it would make to the page if it could be moved to the centre to lessen the monotony of the Egyptian headings floating in white.

7

8

9

What FUTURE FOR THE CHURCH OF ENGLAND ?

The image of the Anglican Church carried by most people is out of date. The Church is changing, experiment is in the air, a commission has even proposed a revolution in organisation. This article is the first of two which look closely into the way the 'Sixties are influencing the clergy and the million or so who will go to church today

by ALLEN ANDREWS

"FALL out the Roman Catholics and the Jews!" The warrant officer screamed get us through the Mersey Tunnel"—and going on their way to Liverpool rejoicing. listen through amplifiers in the adjoining hall—" whose faces," says a cool observer, " come

Staying in tune
(9) Choosing type to evoke a mood is a subtle affair. The effect is lost if the reader/viewer is conscious only of the fact that the designer has been trying to be clever: 'Look no hands.' The Church of England headline begins with a black letter, to suggest old-fashioned habits in the Church, and then picks up computer-type, presumably to emphasise the more modern organisation the writer feels the Church needs. This is far too clumsy. Beginners should keep both hands on the bars and not attempt to change moods within one small typographical unit.

10

CARPET WEEK Special Offer BROADLOOMS
Whitby C OLIVER & Son Ltd
MICKLEGATE SHOWROOMS, Tel. 55106 WHIP-MA-WHOP-MA-GATE. Tel. 23152

The Yorkshire Evening Press
No. 27,427
FINAL
WEDNESDAY, SEPTEMBER 6, 1967 ★ PRICE 4d.

JOIN THE LEGGY GIRL MOVEMENT IN BERKSHIRE PANTIE STOCKINGS BERKSHIRE

'Govt. should review price increases'

THE Government should review the "severe increases" in electricity prices announced last week, the TUC General Council said in a statement issued at Brighton today.

The statement and the council believed that the interests of maintaining price stability, the Government should have relieved the electricity industry of the obligation to make such severe increases in prices.

If necessary, this could have been done by reducing temporarily the industry's overall financial target.

The council considered that, even at this stage, the Government should review the decision and should consider what action was needed to avoid any other comparable increases under consideration in the public sector.

The view was put that the proposed increase should be referred to the National Board for Prices and Incomes.

"Second the situation in the electricity industry reflects the effects of deflation on the cost and price structure of highly capitalised industries, and is an added argument for action to stimulate economic activity.

"Third, the decision illustrates the need for a thorough-going re-appraisal of the principles on which the pricing policies of the nationalised industries are based, a re-appraisal which is the responsibility not of the Prices and Incomes Board but of the Government itself, in consultation with the major interests concerned.

SLAP IN FACE FOR GOVT. BY VOTE AT T.U.C.

From our industrial correspondent

THE Trade Union Congress, at Brighton today, gave a slap in the face to the Government for its failure to manage the economy better.

By a majority of 1,381,000, Congress passed a motion condemning the use of deflationary measures which, while creating unemployment, had not improved Britain's competitive trading position.

This was a substantial victory for the militant unions.

TAKE-OVER BID FOR YORKS. INSURANCE

TWO of Britain's leading insurance companies — the Yorkshire Insurance Co., Ltd., with head offices in York, and the General Accident Fire and Life Assurance Corporation, Ltd. — are likely to join forces.

News of the recommended merger came in an announcement today from the boards of the two companies.

£375,745 will

This said that, following an initial approach made by General Accident in March, and "an examination of the benefits to be obtained from a joint operation of their businesses" they had decided to recom-

SIR ALGAR de CLIFFORD

ARSON: OFFER OF £50 REWARD BY PROFESSOR

PROFESSOR GERALD AYMLER, head of York University's History Department, today offered a £50 reward in anyone giving information leading to the arrest of the fire-raiser who set fire to his Margate home on September

Railmen to see Gunter

Voting figures

Matching text to position
(10) Top-of-the-page positions are for top stories. That is the convention and it is correct. Here the paper seems not to have made up its mind. The panel on price increases at the top of the page is squashed in 8pt body type. The paper seems to be saying with one breath that it is important (because of its position) and with the other (because of its text-size type in that position) that it is a normal news story. The form is not expressing the function. The corrective is to set the body type of the panel into 9 or 10pt, and possibly in four legs across five columns to emphasise the special nature of the story. The tie-on with the other TUC story is not happy, but more offensive is the abrasiveness of the Tempo Heavy Sans against the Century Bold.

11

Weigh In
News and views of angling activities in South Lancashire

By TOD SLOAN

BLUE WINDERMERE

NEARLY every angler who has tried fishing Lake Windermere this year has noticed a vast difference in the standard of fishing, and all of the local club secretaries report they cannot recall when it has ever been so poor.

There have been the isolated good catches made usually during mid-week, but many anglers have been to the lakes a dozen times and have still to roughly the same distance to the North and South of Windermere and have just as variable weather conditions.

Trout fishing on most other waters has been reported as being from average to very good for the time of the should take hold of the whole of Ireland for the next three weeks.

Sea angling off the Irish coast has been relatively poor for the past month, although what has been caught would make anglers from other

Lack of line-up
(11) An attractive idea, boldly set in white space, but spoiled by allowing the lines to wander. There is no line-up on the left or the right, so the unit loses its unity.

Tell a mother that her son takes drugs and a horrific picture will leap to her mind : a haggard figure with dead eyes and wild hair, unrecognizable, unapproachable, irredeemably embarked upon a life of living hell. But to the boy himself, the pathetic wreck of hooked humanity may have as little connexion with his idea of drugs as a shambling alcoholic with a bottle of vin rosé. The older generation and very many of the younger tend to react violently against the drug phenomenon. But an increasing number of today's youth are tolerant of, intrigued by, or involved in the drug scene. Suzy Menkes reports on the prevailing attitudes towards drugs among young people

12 "The greatest mistake the anti-drug campaigners ever made was to tar all drug takers with the

It is perfectly easy to imagine the "swingers" still using marijuana at the age of 40, although

torian idea of self betterment seems to have been replaced by a desire to worsen yourself. This

Misused Bodoni

(12) The fat letter of Bodoni Black (or Ultra Bodoni) makes a colourful change, but it is a display letter and not for text. It can be read comfortably only in short doses. The first of these examples shows the abuse of Bodoni Black as a long over-line. Eye-transfer from line to line is difficult; there is just too much of it.

(13) Bodoni Black abused again—and with two additional sins. The top overline in italic is far too wide to be read from line to line. The type is too small for that and the space between the glittering lines of Bodoni Black too little. Secondly, instead of each picture caption being related to its picture, which would be helpful, the captions are all run together in another solid mass of Bodoni Black. This means a great deal of eye-transfer from caption to picture and back again, a task which is rendered even more difficult by the failure of the designer even to begin each separate caption on a new line.

This is a classic example of a page designed for the designer and not for the reader. It looks exciting but it cannot be read.

13

by Hilary Gelson

HOLIDAY TOYS *Although eight million British school children may regard the annual summer holiday escape from school bells, examinations and form reports with a heady sense of freedom, end of term implies a strict return to duty for all mothers. Apart from having to prepare three meals a day, there will be expeditions to plan and games to organize. Here are some ideas on planning a successful school holiday this summer.*

Above left: Red Indian wigwam—in two sizes. 5ft. £2 8s. 6d. and 6ft. £2 18s. carriage 7s. 6d. Feathered head-dress. 6s. 11d., postage 3s. At John Dobbie, 79, Wimbledon High Street, London, S.W.19. Above : Nylon rope ladder with wooden rungs, in three sizes. 6ft., 12ft. and 15ft. from £1 12s. at Heal and Son, Tottenham Court Road, W.1. Far left: All that is necessary for digging up a field of broad beans—strong wooden wheel barrow, price £2 17s.6d. Professional gardening tools scaled down—spade 30in. long 19s. 6d., hoe 3ft. 6in. 19s. 9d, and rake 3ft. 17s.9d. From Paul and Marjorie Abbatt, 94 Wimpole St., London, W.1. Left : Trackster car propelled by strong wooden handles and fitted with brakes and an adjustable seat. Price £17 5s. from Paul and Marjorie Abbatt.

158

Legibility

(14) Two blunders mark this magazine presentation of pictures and caption. The caption information for each picture is buried in a lengthy combined caption so that the reader cannot quickly relate words and picture: there is not even distinctive type or paragraphing to help in matching word to image. There is nothing for it but to read the whole caption from the beginning, and then the reader who persists that far is soon lost because even in the narrower leg at the top the type is set too wide. Nobody can read the second leg of the type with any comfort. For this width of setting the type needed to be twice as big and heavily leaded to enable the eye to transfer from the end of one line to the beginning of another. In fact, of course, the page cannot be rescued except by redesigning it.

'Early warning' legislation if necessary

THE GOVERNMENT WON SUPPORT FOR ITS INCOMES POLICY WHEN THE LABOUR PARTY CONFERENCE AT BLACKPOOL VOTED TODAY IN FAVOUR OF THE EXECUTIVE COMMITTEE'S RESOLUTION, WHEN AN EMERGENCY RESOLUTION OPPOSING THE PROPOSED LEGISLATION TO TOUGHEN THE INCOMES POLICY WAS DEFEATED ON A CARD VOTE BY 3,635,000

15

(15) This evening paper intro has too many words and in sans capitals the excess wordage produces a formidable slab of black type.

(16) Note the improvement in legibility when the intro was changed to fewer words in lower-case.

'Early warning' legislation if necessary

MR. GEORGE BROWN, Economics Minister, got his "early warning" plan for pay claims approved by the Labour Party conference at Blackpool today.

After a card vote had been demanded, delegates rejected by 3,635,000 votes to 2,540,000 an emergency resolution opposing the Government's proposed legislation for notification of union pay claims.

16

Back from the brain drain

David Wild, a British architect, went to the United States with his fam worked for one year in Chicago with Skidmore Owings and Merrill University in St Louis for a further year. Both jobs were better, fina offered, than any he had had in this country. Since his return to England last year he has been teaching, p ciation in London.) Why, then, did they come back? The pictures he took, some of which we show here of things he saw and heard there that produced a steadily mounting anxiety in him. The views exp Magazine. They are the reactions of one intelligent young man wh ment of America were not enough. We publish them to show tha drain controversy. "From the outset, a lot of people that we met in make us feel at home. The first visual impressions were quite overwhelming, but then an architect's particular preoccupation wi

12

at the age of 27. He
taught at Washington
in terms of the scope
the Architectural Asso-
ments, are fragments
are not those of the
the material induce-
wo sides to the brain
nt out of their way to
an sometimes obscure

his experience of immediate reality. On our first night, I walked into a bar and heard John Coltrane play-ing. His music, and that of many other jazz musicians I heard was, in retrospect, the most valuable experi-ence. That such beauty could be created in such surroundings is a question that preoccupies me still – is adversity necessary, as a stimulant? By the time we got back, however, after our two years in America, we were very depressed; in that time friendships had been established which we were sad to break. Just before we left there had been a massive demonstration in favour of the Vietnam war, in New York. We had had a post-card from London at the time saying 'Second-hand uniforms are all the rage' to which I replied 'Well, over here they're brand new'. I don't like playing the part of Cassandra, but with this, and the storm of racial violence which broke out, as anticipated, that summer of 1967, what can you say when you're introduced to someone who says 'Just back from the States? I say, it's a fun place, isn't it?'"

Fitness A measure of any society is its attitude to the old or infirm. I remember the storm of protest over the Medicare Bill which provides free medicine for those over 60. "But this is downright Socialism," I overheard one man say. Everywhere you can see the discarded old men: in the merciless glare of the neon lunch counters (centre), eking out a 12 cent hamburger so as to stay in the warmth, or shuffling past this church (below), built in an aban-doned cinema. And L.B.J. beams down at you from the hoarding which says. 'Remember – the future be-longs to the fit.' Like these marines (above) outside the recruiting station on North Avenue in Chicago? It is often remarked that the average American works hard; so would most people I think if they had to drive through scenes like this on their way to work every morning. And the poor

don't always meet with understanding. A car sticker put out by the John Birch Society reads 'I fight poverty – I work'. To many tidy-minded Europeans, it is the ugliness and brash-ness of America that is offensive. But to me the diversity and unashamed individualism of much American architecture could be a great strength. What concerned me was the increasing withdrawal from, parallel with the pollution and destruction of, the natural environment. The shores of Lake Michigan are littered each year with more and more dead fish, killed by industrial waste; Lake Erie is biologically dead; air pollution is countered by air conditioning units rather than at source – unfortunate for all those who can't afford it

Violence I did not have to go out of my way to take any of these pictures. The one on the left was taken at noon on the main street of New Orleans while I was out photographing buildings. A passerby, seeing my camera, directed me to the scene: "There's a guy back there with his head cut open – make a good picture. He's got tattooed arms too." Violence is common enough to be unremarkable. We had been in St Louis only two weeks when a 13-year-old boy, running from a stolen car, was shot and critically injured, literally outside our apartment window. The same week, another Negro youth was killed while handcuffed in a patrol car. The officer said he thought he was reaching for a weapon

Temptations of Emphasis

Overcrowding of display type is perhaps the most chronic feature of bad design all over the world in all kinds of newspapers. The headline needs white space to be read just as the eye needs light to see. Too much white is wasteful; too little is self defeating. This is as true for the Roman alphabets of the West, as it is for Japanese or Chinese newspapers with most of the headlines in vertically arranged characters, or with a bewildering mixture of horizontal and vertical heads, or of Urdu or Arabic newspapers in script with headlines written by calligraphers for blockmaking (despite the inevitable slowness of this procedure, many of these newspapers none the less waste inordinate amounts of space and time by having an excessive number of headlines).

(17) Display is even harder to read when it consists of frequent changes in character. Above left are a dozen changes of signal in display type and not enough light anyway. A considerable improvement would have resulted merely from keeping the strapline all in roman light face, leaving the sans punch for the banner. If the black-on-tint block had been white-on-tint there would have been a further improvement in inducement to read.

(18) The Tokyo evening adopted the American system of initial caps in all display letters, which is an added strain in scanning these crowded heads. The perfect symmetry of the top of the page, everything a mirror image of the other side, merely makes it twice as hard to read. Points of simple improvement: a pica of white between top lines of head and the title cut-off; separation of the sans italic heads in columns 2 and 3 and columns 6 and 7 from the main decks by running the lead text-type into this shoulder: anything to relieve the display heads all speaking at the same time.

(19) But note how much more clear and legible is the front page of the *Asahi's* morning edition in Japanese. There is reasonable white around the bold vertical heads—the character block with 10pt is a headline unit.

(20) Four decks are not needed on this Greek paper's lead. Setting the main head left would relieve the overcrowding by introducing white space on the right.

(21) Overcrowding aggravated by display-type ads at the top of the page in columns 1 and 6. The determination to write a full line only makes this juxtaposition more irritating. Note how much more readable is the set-left head in column 6 with reasonable white: much better still if it had been indented a pica at the left. The display ads should not be accepted in this position at the top of the page; and if they are, the make-up man must try to soften them by contrast (half-tone or white space) rather than by emphasising them by competition.

(22, 23, 24) are examples of less offensive crowding, but still avoidable. These are all irregular dog-leg headlines: the preferable style of heads in self-contained modular units with the text has the added advantage that it marries head and text instead of divorcing them, as the dog-leg does.

(25) What takes the eye? There is no focal point. There is a confusion of headlines at the top of the page. They are unreadable. The light face italic banner headline across eight columns leads into a single column head in column 1, but it is separated from its subsidiary head by a half-rule, and at a first glance it is not clear where you are supposed to read after reading the streamer. This banner is separated from the other headline stragglers by only a thin rule. The giddy effect of lots of display letters at the top of the page is aggravated by the picture titles, sticking out in bold. (It would have been better the other way round—bold for the main head, light for the intruder.) The unreadability of the main banner is due to four things: it is too wide to take in comfortably (even the small-scale reproduced here is hard to take in at a glance); it is too wordy; the style of initial caps interrupts reading; and it is cramped, with insufficient white. This is curious in view of the space wasted in subsidiary heads in column 1. Here, too, there is bad cramping. The second line of the second deck reads like a Sioux war-cry:

TORUNTOMORROW

The best first-aid here would be to separate the picture title-head from the main banner. Fold a piece of paper over the picture titling and you will notice an immediate improvement in the legibility of the main banner. For a permanent cure, of course, the banner and headline style would be jettisoned.

26A

26B

28

Remaking a feature page

(26A) On the layout the treatment for two features after the Papal encyclical on birth control looked all right. Across the top seven columns an artist's sketch of a Catholic city, beneath a reverse block which had been used with different wording on earlier pages; the text to go with the sketch in column 1; and the separate feature given a main headline below the sketch. But the page, when printed, failed. The heavy black and white of the reverse block, plus the heavy black and white of the five-column Franklin caps head sandwiched the black and white

of the sketch. Its fine lines were lost. There was too much competition on the page and not enough contrast. The rejig **(26B)** produced a much simpler, lighter display. The Franklin display line is reduced in size and spread. The Record by-line is put below the main head and retained in one light face without the extra bit of glitter of having the writer's name in Franklin. The Franklin side-heads with 6pt rules are dropped. The reverse block has gone. So has the second half-tone. The words relating to the sketch are tied on in the end four columns; again the type glitter is reduced.

(28) Tabloids, despite having magazine-size pages, cannot always play magazine games. Side-set headlines are therefore usually out, particularly where they are matched to legs of type running to the top of a page. In this example from the tabloid *Sun* (London) the reverse-block subsidiary line with the main headline is matched with the reverse-block headline below, which is addressed to constipation sufferers. The caption to the picture is in need of treatment, squeezed in between two unrelated reverse blocks and barely hanging on at all to Gina Lollobrigida in the half-tone. The half-tone of the gentleman who has been cured of his unfortunate ailment should have been separated from La Lollo by a column of text type.

27A

27B

Two versions of a page one with mostly the same elements differently organised. **(27A)** The panel across the top of the page announcing a major news story inside has become fussy and confused with three separate lines of display type, two arrows and three sets of thumbnail pictures. The two parts of the letter are needlessly separated by a column of type.

(27B) A quick revision reduces and co-ordinates the display elements in the panel. The gain in appeal is immediate. The Insight article is also in a more coherent shape. The loss: the temporary move of the long single-column picture into column 2 where it pulls less weight.

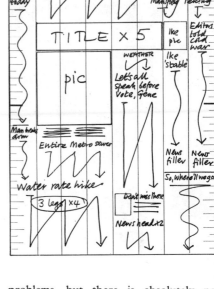

Water rate hike to 278% asked

31A

31B

(29) Why headlines should not be thrown haphazardly together. The intrusive Your Letters panel is not doing its job properly. It seems to be detached from the text above, but all the text here is letters. There is no invitation to begin reading. The worst confusion is in the relationship of the mid-page headlines.

It is easy enough to deal with these faults and gain greatly in legibility. For instance, the Tenants letter should be doubled-up under its headline, and the World letter doubled-up under that. The Your Letters panel should be moved. It could be made into an 18pt reverse block, single- or double-column, and inserted in the text type of the main letter. The letter headlined 'Leaving no stone unturned' in 30pt should be restyled as an italic caps 18pt to marry with column 1.

(30) After all that display effort, compare the cool way (right) in which the leisure page of the old broadsheet *Sun* differentiated its fare. The headlines are in one family, and all roman. There is white space where it is needed around display type, and the heads are cunningly separated. Where they might run together with the jazz and camera columns, there is a change of style, a black-and-white symbol with condensed 18pt underneath—again well whited.

This page is worth studying, too, for colour in a black-and-white newspaper. It is so rich in tonal gradation, an effect achieved by varying the colour of headlines (bold, roman, and condensed), and of symbols, and by contrasting the blacker elements with white space.

(31A) An attempt to emphasise everything ends up by emphasising nothing. There is no focal point in the *Montana Standard*. The three horizontal bold sans heads chop up the page. If their vigour emphasises anything, it is the puny antique quality of the paper's title, fading away like some Boot Hill tombstone in the weeds.

Clearly the worst feature of the anarchy here is the fragmentation of the Soviet–Czech story, which is in four separate places: columns 1, 2, 3, 4 top of the page and bottom; column 5 (Editors told); column 6 (Mansfield); and column 5 filler (Pekin sees plot).

Pulling the Soviet–Czech story together would force a certain coherence into the design of the page. A long story presents

problems, but there is absolutely no excuse for pretending it is a short story by dismembering it.

There are other design faults. The page is divided into two vertical four-columns. The excess column white in the two main Soviet–Czech stories merely emphasises the tightness of the other text setting.

(31B) is a revised page design for the *Montana Standard,* accepting its preference for floating its five-column titlepiece. All the Soviet–Czech material is pulled together at the top of the page, with the Editor story related in column 8. The resultant economy in display heads allows three more news shorts into the page. The new page organizes the news in a clear system of priorities.

30

164

32

33

Weekly and Local Newspapers

(32, 33) Local weeklies are among the general sinners, but weekly paper design should be different from daily paper design. Weeklies do a different job. They may not do it for a different audience but it is at least for a different market. The style for one weekly should vary from another; the country weekly will have remarkably different content from the urban or, again, the suburban weekly: cattle shows in one, court cases in another, school prizes in them all, but probably different area problems and different editorial attitudes. Given all this, however, the weekly paper must have the same disciplines as the daily. It must be legible. It must organise the news coherently and economically. The *Surrey Mirror* front page does not do this; the *Wigan Observer* front page does.

The treatment of the *Mirror* lead is a pale reflection of the banner of the nationals, and why the awkward arrangement across six columns into two? If this is meant to emphasise the importance of the story, it fails. The other heads on the page overpower the lead.

The answer lies not in having a big banner on the *Surrey Mirror*, but in sizing down the heads on the rest of the page and making more of a unit of the lead headlines and text. The *Mirror* could clearly put the space saved to good use: it has plenty of news and lively pictures. One effect of the inflated heads down-page is a feeling of unease when a pleasant but essentially soft story is given the weight normally associated with hard news (Spent 40 years looking after animals, columns 3, 4, 5).

The *Wigan Observer* is a model of restraint: it has several more stories on its page, yet saves 6in. on headline display space and still manages to give reasonable display. Typographically the page is marred only by the weak sans head in column 2, and has too much white in the single-column heads in columns 4 and 6.

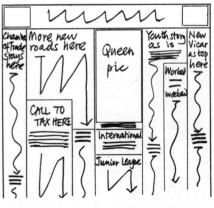

(34A) First, type. The paper's title type is admirably bold and clear, and the title is relatively uncluttered. But the type mixes on the page do not work. The light sans in New Vicar, column 4, and They Remember, column 4, bottom of the page, is too thin to do its work of bringing colour to the grey text of a news page. Its lettering is essentially prissy, too genteel a signal in itself and not even an effective light foil to the sans: the sans is overpoweringly blunt. The Bodoni Bold at the top of the page destroys what unity there was in the typography of the page.

Second, the plan. The position of the lead has not been thought out and the picture has been wasted. The Queen walks into the page, which is good, but the colour of the half-tone would have been better deployed among the greys of the text and to separate some of the higgledy-piggledy heads. The lead headline has been stretched to four-column, but white space, which would set it off, has been begrudged in legs 1 and 4. The run of the text, forced round to fill four legs, means that important top-of-page positions are given to fillers (Retiring and For Housing Emergencies).

Three, headline shapes. Two double-column heads (Polythene Drums and New Graveyard) lead into single-column heads

—but confusingly the single-column leg does not end where the text begins. In Polythene Drums: Temporary Move, the eye cannot read on naturally into the text below. It has to find its way back 1in. higher in the adjoining column.

(34B) Using the same shapes, but changing the position in the pages, produces the alternative tops for this page as shown.

166

Photo-composition

Photo-composition makes easy what is impossible with hot metal. Pictures or headlines can be printed at a tilt by the make-up man pasting the photoset headline or picture print at a tilt on the page. Shapes are unlimited. The cut-out or pierce does not involve cutting metal. You can have any shape you can cut in the print. The pierce is simply a piece of blank paper stuck on the photograph.

Printing a headline over a picture is merely a matter of the make-up man taking the photoset strip of paper of headline display and pasting that over the photograph. Varied tint screens can be laid over headings or pictures in the same way. The white-on-black heading is as quickly produced by photoset as the ordinary display line. Headline letters produced by the Photo Typositor can be spaced to join or overlap. And about 2,800 different type-sizes and setting styles can be obtained from a single film fount.

Very few newspapers have yet learned to use these freedoms properly. At one extreme, a traditional page is produced, avoiding superimposed headlines, reverses, tints, and cut-outs as if they were the invention of the devil. At the other, and especially in the so-called underground press, every conceivable gimmick is conjured up in a giddy defiance, not of society, but of all the laws of legibility.

36

(36) The pictures on a tilt destroy rather than distinguish the design. Does the designer want us to study the pictures, or not? Clearly he does, but it means a good deal of awkward swivelling of the neck. One feels sea-sick just looking at this photo-composition.

35

FLOP HAT
JUNGLE RATS *continued*

in base camp, on a high-speed trail or out in the boonies—he is in danger, too, then we have neutralized his advantage."
Former Secretary of Defense Robert McNamara cautiously acknowledged the far-ranging LURPs when he boasted about "Our armed reconnaissance," all but admitting that these units sometimes operate into North Vietnam and deep into Laos along the Ho Chi Minh Trail.

Many Army officials say that LURP patrols are more effective in cutting down the supplies reaching the Viet Cong than air bombing. Whatever their impact, they certainly tie up a lot of North Vietnamese troops in protecting the VC supply lines.

Faces blackened and wearing their camouflage fatigues, LURP patrols slip repeatedly into the jungle to keep an eye on the Viet Cong. Their goal is to see without being seen, to kill and kidnap in silence, with deadly consistency. The success of a LURP mission usually depends on the team staying completely hidden while its men monitor Viet Cong movements. In LURP language a team is "compromised" when it is spotted by the enemy. Then the handful of troopers must get the hell out fast before a larger Red force can surround them and cut them to pieces. Several LURP teams have disappeared into the jungles and never have been seen again.

Possibly the most dangerous LURP missions are now taking place in the Mekong Delta. The populous Delta contains nearly half of South Vietnam's people and many of them are hard-core

Former Secretary of Defense Robert McNamara cautiously acknowledged the far-ranging LURPS when he boasted about "Our armed reconnaissance"—all but admitting that these units sometimes operate into North Vietnam and deep into Laos along the Ho Chi Minh Trail

VC, or sympathizers. A LURP team can't expect to stay out for the four or five days of a normal jungle patrol without being "compromised." The Delta missions are shorter and more miserable. "You spend the night in a rice paddy with water up to your neck," a LURP leader explains. Since the water in paddies is muddy, filled with human excrement and sometimes garbage, "immersion foot" can be the least of a trooper's worries. "Don't make waves," has become almost a LURP battle cry in the Delta.
Normally in the jungle, LURPs operate during the daytime and rest at night, but it is just the opposite in the Delta. LURPs have

(35) Photo-composition makes this staggered setting easy—but try to read it. Because the eye has no fixed point of return at the end of a line of text or headline, this page is a fearfully hard read. Only dedicated people writing on design have been known to finish the course.

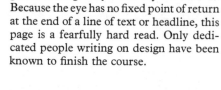

37

(37) Restrained but worthwhile page from photo-composition. The tilted election special black-on-tint produces just the right effect of an election sticker.

THE CROWDED SKIES

A week's sea voyage   five hours by jet. The air travel explosion needs no other explanation in a world determined to cram more living into life; airports can't grow fast enough for the accelerating passenger demand. This issue examines civil aviation. It looks in detail at the overcrowded London Airport of today, recalls the days when air travel was a leisurely adventure and describes plans for a new London Airport to cope with the 800-seater aircraft of the 1970s

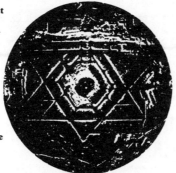
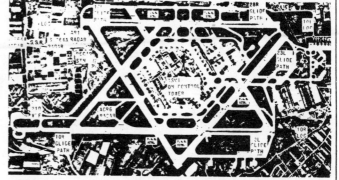

The radar screen (near right) is ASMI – Airport Surface Movement Indicator. It's part of the equipment of Heathrow's Aerodrome Control staff, who work on top of the Control Tower Building. Everything that moves on the airport's runways and taxiways is recorded on ASMI; it can be used to control planes in murky or foggy conditions. The aerial view (far right) clearly shows the two main east-west runways (the northern one's too short for the biggest jets) and the smears at their ends where rubber burns off wheels as planes touch down

Heathrow, intended for a wartime R.A.F. station, was opened in 1946 as the new London Airport. By the mid-fifties Nissen huts had been replaced by those redbrick buildings which now stand at its heart. There had been mistakes. Monumental buildings are too hard to alter as needs change. Putting everything in the centre left too little room for expansion – but who could have foreseen how much need for expansion there would be? – and meant that the only ground link with the outside world must be through tunnels. Compromise and ingenuity kept Heathrow working while its passenger load doubled every five years; enabled it to become the busiest international airport in the world. Soon the island layout will be scrapped and new adaptable buildings come into use. Throughout a 24-hour day this summer a SUNDAY TIMES MAGAZINE team watched London Airport at work. The British Airports Authority made the inquiry possible and enabled us to be searching and objective in our examination. This is the team's report. Remember, as you read it, that London Airport is more than a gateway; it is a city where 40,000 people work around the clock, and the watcher can only dip into its life. This is the city of Heathrow; London Airport.

1. TODAY'S CRUNCH

REPORTERS: Gilda Archer, Peter Crookston, Peter Dunn, David Francks, Peter Gillman, Nicholas Grimshaw, Derek Jewell, Brenda Jones, Meriel McCooey, Graham Norton, Philip Oakes, George Perry, Susan Raven, Godfrey Smith, Elisabeth Woolley.
PHOTOGRAPHERS: Allan Ballard, Duffy, David Steen, Michael Taylor, Bryan Wharton, Ian Yeomans

To this city, there is a brain . . .

"You have to have belts, braces *and* suspenders to make sure nothing goes wrong," says Ted Luff. He was explaining why all of Heathrow's complicated electronic equipment, which helps get aircraft safely up or down, is duplicated or triplicated, monitored, checked and double-checked 24 hours every day of every week.

There are, for instance, around 100 miles of cable under Heathrow's grass and concrete. "It's always possible a man will put a pickaxe through a cable," says Luff, who is chief telecommunications officer responsible for Gatwick and Stansted as well as Heathrow. He and John Muirhead,

job of Air Traffic Control. Ray Kirk, a brusque, wartime R.A.F. senior officer with a close-clipped moustache, sits at the centre of the spider's web which is Heathrow's intricate ATC system. His air of snap and pressure is understandable; as Board of Trade Chief Officer in charge of air traffic control there, he carries the can if anything goes wrong.

Kirk once nursed planes in and out of airports himself. Though his job now is mainly administrative, he plainly feels for his 150 air traffic controllers and control assistants. "See him?" he says, pointing to a shirtsleeved man in front of a radar screen in the Approach Control room. "That's the

to 3000 feet, heading two eight zero. Check your heading two eight zero . . .''

The world is covered by air routes ('airways'). They stretch out like interlocking fingers all over air traffic maps. Airways can be thousands of miles long; in the U.K. they go from 5000 feet to 25,000 feet up, and are 10 miles wide. No plane may move in an airway without having put in a pre-arranged flight plan which is passed on to ATC centres all over the world.

Once a London-bound plane is inside London ATCC's area, covering all southern England, it is guided to a holding point – the famous 'stacks' over Epsom and Garston, 12 and 20 miles respectively from Heathrow,

or below the correct glide path.

ILS, which avoids language difficulties between pilot and controller (and 48 out of 56 airlines using London Airport are foreign), is far more heavily used than the alternative or supplementary Precision Approach Radar.

PAR shows the radar director the path a plane is taking. Guide lines on his radar screen enable him to keep the plane on the centre line of the runway and on the correct glide path when 'talking down' planes in bad visibility. PAR is also used to monitor instrument landing system approaches in poor conditions and all approaches during 'parallel runway operations'.

Once Approach Control has estab-

38

The overcrowded display

(**38**) A magazine page, introducing a section on London's overcrowded airport. The typographic crowding of the feature may in some subtle way reinforce the title The Crowded Skies, but if that is the intention it is carrying allusion too far. The page invites the reader to turn over. Features—in magazines and in newspapers—often need a provocative introduction, a short puff or blurb in pungent prose to tempt the reader beyond the summary headline and into the text. Here there are three such introductions, far too much of a build-up, even if they were given room to be legible.

Worst of all perhaps is the combined caption on the left, which serves to explain both the illustrations with references to 'near right' and 'far right.' It would have been much more effective to concentrate on one dramatic symbol or illustration, with the directly related caption serving as one clear puff for the feature.

The display type, reminiscent of the Thirties, is unattractive in itself and inappropriate for an article on the Seventies.

Display without Pictures

In August, 1968, British newspapers had to manage without newly made illustrations because of an engravers' strike. It was a test of display ingenuity. Newspapers realised that what was missing in design terms was the colour and tonal relief provided by half-tones, and merely to make headlines bigger harshly aggravated the problem.

The right way to provide relief was by increasing body type-size, by better deployment of white space to separate head-

lines, by varying the colour of headlines and by the careful use of rules. The orderly *Guardian* front page **(39)** is made attractive by the creation of a display unit where the half-tone would normally go. The single most important feature of the panel is that it is set in generous white, separating the headlines and separating the bold, bastard-set from other text type. The bold type provides strong colour, but, because of the white, it is not harsh. And, finally, the strength of the neat 3pt rule is just right.

(41) The *Daily Mirror*, is less successful because the headlines in the centre of the page are monotonously bold with little white for relief, and the *Mirror*'s panel is more intrusive. The white space is lost to a strong vertical rule which does not fit neatly with the other rules.

(40) The *Sun*, on the other hand, succeeds by making a feature of a clean, well-whited neat panel, like the *Guardian*. Of course the single-column block, from stock, is a help, but not more than the subtle variation in headline weights.

10 Improvements and Innovations

No other format can offer man's first moon-walk headlined on page one, and at the same time elsewhere offer for sale a secondhand fur coat in 6pt.
—EDWIN TAYLOR

This final chapter consists of illustrations and comment on newspaper design of high standard, and experimental efforts and new efforts at innovation. The best here—notably Peter Palazzo's work—is suggestive of the way newspaper design might fruitfully evolve, but I have also included existing working examples which have won design awards. Though the standard wobbles here from time to time, these illustrations are evidence that good design can be produced under the pressures of time and space, and their variety demonstrates also that good design need not mean a deadening uniformity.

The Unpublished New York Forum

This appealing newspaper, *New York Forum*, was printed but never published or circulated in New York. The *New York Times*, which planned the paper in 1967, did not go ahead. It is always hard to judge a design which relates to past events, especially ly one produced as a trial, but the pages of *New York Forum* (and the earlier trial *New York To-day*), show considerable imagination and elegance.

There were forty broadsheet pages (22½in. × 14½in.). The intention was to limit the pagination of the paper so that it would be more wieldy than the daily or the excessively fat American tabloids. This would give larger editorial display potential inside, it being reasoned that a smaller paper would have smaller advertisements, presumably at higher rates. Key editorial pages were kept clear of display advertising—the three at the front, the editorial page, the arts page and the first sports page. The back was sold for

---

NEW YORK FORUM

FINAL
THURSDAY, AUGUST 3, 1967

WEATHER
Partly sunny today; showers tonight. Partly cloudy tomorrow. Temperature range: today 84–68; Wednesday 84–69. Temperature humidity index 75; Wednesday 78.

00c

Johnson Asks 10% Income-Tax Surcharge

By JOHN C. HILL

Lindsay Prods Banks: Aid Stores in Slums

By PETER MILLS

President Johnson briefs White House correspondents on proposed 10 per cent income-tax surcharge

'Hate' Unit Said to Get U.S. Funds

By TOM WILLIAMS

45,000 More U.S. Troops Will Go to Vietnam

By WARD ASHER

ANALYSIS

Between the Lines, Indicators of a Wider War

By FRANK McCULLOCH

INSIDE

- 37 Howard Traded to Red Sox — Catcher bitter, Sox happy.
- 10 Kraft Poll on Riots — 43 per cent think there will be more.
- 25 Hippies: a Dying Movement — Are too many turned on by cash?
- 12 Literary Agent 007 — Victor Louis peddles books and intrigue.
- 21 A Cultural Autumn — What to read, where to go, what to see when the air becomes nippy.
- 18 New York Schools — No one knows where the money goes.

- 14 SCIENCE
- 16 LIVING
- 18 OPINION/IDEAS
- 21 ARTS/ENTERTAINMENT
- 28 BUSINESS/FINANCE
- 37 SPORTS
- 16 EUGENIA SHEPPARD
- 17 ALISTAIR COOKE
- 37 RED SMITH

Priceless Gems Stolen In Jerusalem Shrine

JERUSALEM —

(From AP, Reuters and Staff)

The Rev. Kevin Mooney indicates statue of Virgin Mary in Church of the Holy Sepulcher, Jerusalem, from which relics were taken.

Drysdale Out of Action

Roquepine Returning

Jones Signs

SPORTS

RED SMITH

Rock 'n' Roll Gets Damascus Set for Travers

Grid Lam... Are Facin... Packers' ...

By WILL WALLS

Carlos Se...

By TED LITTON

advertising (a pity, it would have been better to sell page 2) but the display advertising was arranged as it ought to be in modular units, full pages, half-pages, and quarter-pages (four 11 × 2, for instance, stacked one on top of the other to produce two clear editorial columns).

'What we wanted to do was to establish a serious afternoon paper that was not a copy of the *New York Times*,' says Mr Abe Rosenthal, now managing editor of the *New York Times*, whose job it was to get the dummy out. That objective is a key to the design of the newspaper, for what emerged certainly looked different from the morning daily, 'the old grey lady.' The column grid was six columns at 14 picas, with a good pica of white between each (instead of 8 × 11 jammed in for the *New York Times*).

Broken or bastard measure was to be introduced occasionally (as in the 'News Watch' double-column, above left). Instead of twelve to fourteen stories on the signal-and-text front page there was to be a maximum of four or five, with mercifully fewer inconvenient turns than the daily. The layout was irregular, modified horizontal. Headlines and pictures were bigger than in the *New York Times*, but nothing extreme and certainly nothing above 48pt (compared with 30pt maximum then for the daily). The

NEW YORK FORUM — OPINION / IDEAS

Volume 1, Number 1

LETTER FROM HONG KONG

A PECULIAR CRISIS

THE SCHOOL BUDGET MYSTERY

THE LOOKING GLASS
By T.F.

AUGUST 3, 1967 — 37

Mets Get Koonce

The New York Mets acquired another pitcher yesterday—Cal Koonce, a 26-year-old right-hander from the Chicago Cubs for the waiver price of $20,000. Used mostly in relief by the Cubs, for whom he won two games and lost two this season, Koonce is headed for the same assignment with the Mets, who have already employed 19 different men to pitch for them this year. The Mets recently sent Bob Shaw, an important starter for them last year, to the Cubs on waivers, so this is one of those "unrelated but a natural consequence" deals popular at this time of year.

If the Mets decide to use Koonce as a starter as well, he does have that kind of experience. As a Cub starter two years ago, he defeated the Mets twice.

Generals Tie Atlanta

Unsuccessful for so long in home games, the New York Generals of the National Professional Soccer League continued to show improvement on the road by playing a 1-1 tie with the Chiefs at Atlanta last night. An Atlanta goal with 7:18 to go in the second half, scored by Ray Bloomfiled of Britain, prevented the Generals from being even more successful, as it matched a first-half goal scored by Julio Alas for New York. The tie left second-place Atlanta seven points ahead of fourth-place New York in the five-team Eastern Division, but it does leave an overwhelming margin under the system that awards six points for a victory, three for a tie and one for every goal scored up to three in a game.

...ward Traded to the Red Sox

...ward, the first Negro to ...New York Yankees, was ...o Boston Red Sox this ...return, the Yanks got the ...er price and two minor ...to be delivered at the ...eason.

Elston Howard, stunned by the news that he was traded to the Red Sox, prepares to clean out his locker at Yankee Stadium.

But Howard remained upset until a telephone conversation with his wife, Arline (who favored the move), and a business associate put things in a different perspective. He put off talking to Tom Yawkey, the Red Sox owner, who was trying to call him until he could make up his mind.

Howard played 1,426 games in 13 seasons for the Yankees. He started as an outfielder, then shared the catching duties with Yogi Berra, and finally became the regular catcher. From 1955 through 1964, he was a key figure as the Yankees won nine pennants in 10 years.

In spring training of 1965, he injured his elbow and required surgery that June. He never regained full effectiveness. This season he has a .196 batting average for 66 games, with only three home runs. But he had been hitting better in the last three weeks.

Only Mickey Mantle, who joined the Yankees in 1951, is left from the "old" Yankees. Whitey Ford, another Yankee of the same era, was forced into retirement earlier this season by an elbow ailment.

...ace Off the Track, Too

Can Clancy Lift Tennis Gloom?

By ANTHONY SCHIRS

SOUTH ORANGE, N.J.—Gil Clancy, the fiery Irishman who guided Emile Griffith to the middle-weight and welterweight championships, offered today to lead the United States Davis Cup team out of the gloom.

Although never a top tennis player, Clancy is a fan and a weekend performer.

"From what I've seen of the Davis Cup players," Clancy said during a visit to the Eastern Grass Court championships here, "they don't need a tactician as much as they need somebody who will sharpen their competitive spirit, who will make them want to win."

In boxing, Clancy, a physical education teacher in the New York City school system, is rated as a most competitive manager.

"I know that Clancy gets the most out of me, just the way he talks to me," said Griffith, who accompanied Clancy in viewing yesterday's third-round matches. "I don't see why he wouldn't do the same for tennis players. They'd shape up fast for Clancy, believe me."

Clancy suggested Pancho Gonzalez as an ideal coach for tennis tactics.

"But what the Davis Cup team has lacked," Clancy said, "is a captain who can stir up the players when he's sitting on the court with them during a match. I'd love a crack at it. I'd like to see some of these kids moping around if I'm out there with them."

---

headline style was Times Bold in upper- and lower-case, and in simple multi-line units rather than the system of decks still used by the *New York Times*. A good Gothic was used for kickers and for the admirably clear section-identification.

'I had dreamed for years of opening up the *Times*,' says George Cowan, who did a good deal of the design work on the dummy, and indeed the controlled use of white space around headlines, page folios and special text is one of the compelling attractions of the dummies. Rosenthal himself had more general ideas about *Forum*. He wanted to open the newspaper to non-newspaper people and he had no desire to confine them to the leader page. His scheme allowed for articles by outsiders in any part of the paper. Though *Forum* never made the streets, some of these ideas are apparent in the *New York Times* today. The Op-Ed page, above right, is one example; so is the use of white space and drawings.

In producing pages of such elegance and clarity it is essential that copy is either produced to required lengths, or accurately cast off and schemed: all is lost once the underlying discipline is 'bent' to accommodate a few odd lines. The writer is the ultimate beneficiary.

Sunday Asia

Here is the front page and the sequence of pages of a twelve-page broadsheet dummy for a new Sunday newspaper, *Sunday Asia*. The brief to the designer, Edwin Taylor, was to prepare a format and layout plan for a newspaper to be published in six centres in Asia for readers of English, in most cases probably as a supplement to an existing daily operation. It was to give emphasis to international and business news. It was to be dignified but alive. Since the brief required the paper to be able to accept international advertising on the basis of the 11-pica standard, Taylor kept to the 11-pica grid for editorial. Within that he prescribed a

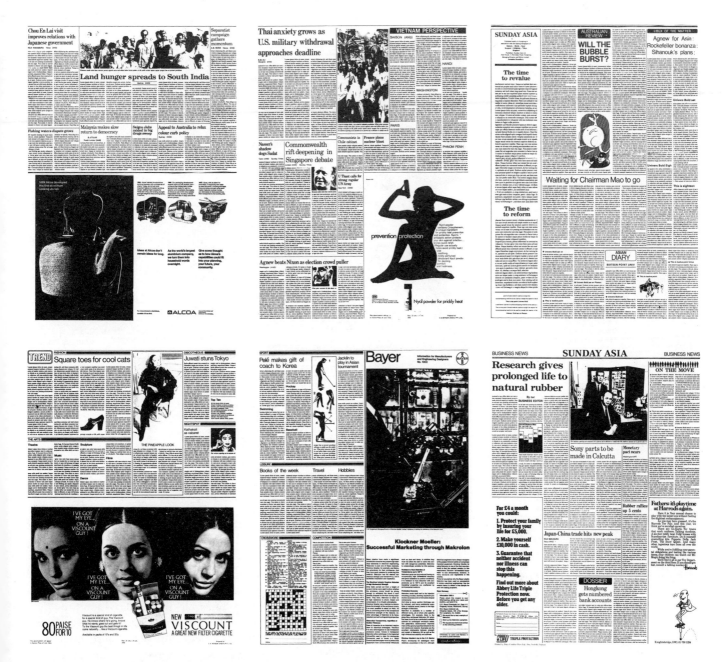

cool, asymmetrical, modular layout. He was helped by the promoters' insistence on carefully controlled advertising shapes and the requirement of no more than a dozen stories to a page. The headline dress was simple and restrained—variants of Century Bold roman, subsidiary lines in Helvetica, and feature pages in the best available grot.

So much for dignity: the vivacity was to come from good photographs, and especially careful selection and cropping of the smaller pictures, and from colour elements—6pt rules, Oxford thick and thin rules, and 18pt thick rules on the Trend page; white-on-black reverse blocks, white space, and line drawings.

A

B

C

The Asian

The Asian, a filmset-offset broadsheet of twelve pages, was launched in October, 1971, in Hong Kong, Manila and Bangkok, as the practical result of Edwin Taylor's dummies. It is, according to the publishers, the world's first regional newspaper, but it is included here for the quality of its design. The original design, shown on the two previous pages, was successfuly translated into the first printed dummy **(A)**. The layout has remained modular and asymmetrical with Times headline dress. The designer, Edwin Taylor, felt that neither of the two main headlines carried conviction, but especially the second lead in two lines of the wide Times 427. A subsequent live front page **(B)** is stronger at the top with the 427 more effectively deployed across three columns under the picture. The rest of the layout is not quite so arresting: it is more static because of the disposition of the first three columns; the typography of the Taiwan story in columns 6 and 7 had invited wordiness, and most of the headlines have not retained the well-judged white of the dummy between first line and cut-off.

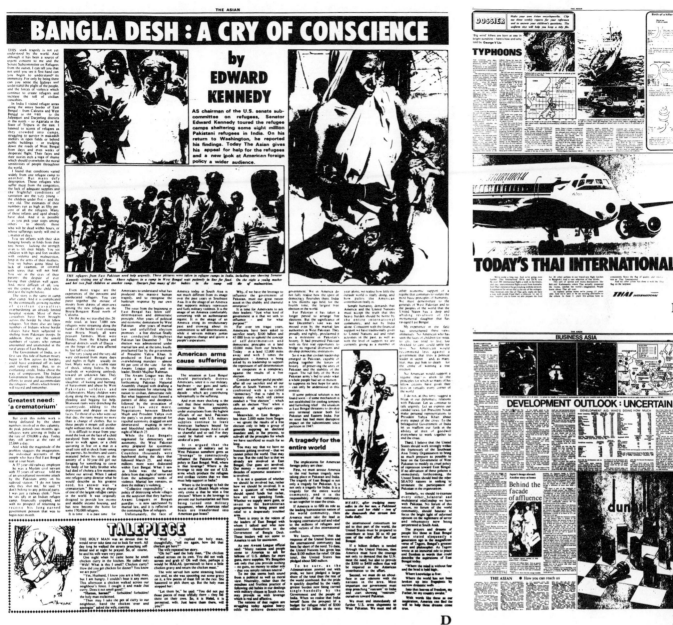

Since the composing and printing plant in Hong Kong is five miles away from the design and editorial department, this latter weakness can be put down to geography rather than graphic sense.

It is in the centre spread **(C)** and **(D)** of the second live issue and the Dossier page **(E)** that there has been a remarkable translation of the brilliance of the vision in the designer's dummies. What a perfect match is the cool leader page and the emphasis of the Bangla Desh presentation. The leader page with strong horizontal stress and restrained headline-sizing is calm without being dull. The column measure has been varied intriguingly, and spots of colour are well dispersed. Bangla Desh has an eight-column vertical emphasis, harsh headlining, and a coherent picture unit of great impact. But it is all very economical, and serves rather than stifles the text. Compare this page with the fireworks many layout men would have been impelled to set off, to the detriment of space and the message.

Business and finance were allocated the back page **(F)**—normally the most neglected page in newspaper design—and signalling it boldly.

A

The Sunday Australian

The *Sunday Australian*, started in 1971 and now merged, was notable for the clear identity of its four separate sections and the distinctive use of the neglected back page. The type is Century Bold Expanded mixed with Century Modern and ordinary Century. The logotype looks rather squashed and inadequate. (**A**). There is a very effective single-column guide to the rest of the newspaper, which is forty-eight pages in all. The first page of the first section suffers somewhat by failing to use its white space properly. The top-of-the-page horizontal spread could do with more white around the headline and a larger body type. The streamer on strikes would profit by more white. This could be borrowed from other areas of the page where it is not needed, especially between the decks of certain headings such as 'Striking Teachers' in column 2, and by taking one line off some of the descending headlines.

The back page of the first section (**B**) is devoted effectively to gossip, and a round-up of the world's affairs as other newspapers see it. The contrast of Oxford rules and elegantly serifed display type, all set in white, provides attractive colour. The leader page is (**C**). The front page of each section is identically introduced with bold titling underscored with a pica rule, all well whited. The first page of the Review section (**D**) makes it clear it is a page to be read and the text is admirably easy to read in its six-column format.

The graphics help a lot. The back page of this section is also bold and simple, giving a casual guide to leisure and pleasure and the crossword. The first page of the women's section (**E**) has an admirably bold photograph, but the use of the Record typeface is very uncertain, there being no fewer than four changes on the front page; and inside, the type has attracted a very inappropriate and ill-fitting 3pt rule. But again, the back page scores with a television guide, modelled on that of *The Sunday Times* of London by

F

THE SUNDAY AUSTRALIAN

G

being run horizontally tabloid style across the full depth of the page.

Page one of the Business Section **(F)** again marvellously identified as such, suffers from an awkward layout in this instance, and perhaps this is related to an unhappy conversion to a ten-column grid. In any event, the heavy lead sits unhappily in its position with the traditional lead position given over to a column headed in Century Light, and the photograph immediately above the lead is not related to it but to the story on the right about a mining boom. The back page of this final section is given to sport **(G)** again emphatically introduced. This also is in ten columns. The criticism here must be of a very unhappy mix of Century Bold and Record. They just do not mix well together in the way they are used here, and the white space is again very ill used; instead of being concentrated around the headlines it is too often driven through the lines of the Record, making them even more watery and the Century Bold even more harsh.

From the start, though, *The Sunday Australian* had the look of a substantial newspaper, the ambition but rarely the achievement of first issues. The design needed to develop with more typographical discipline, but it was promising.

The Underground Press

'They make a standard newspaper look, to me at least, about as exciting as the telephone white pages.' Mrs Ethel Romm[1], the wife of the publisher of the daily offset *Times-Herald-Record* of Middletown, New York, is writing about the psychedelic papers that began to bloom in the United States in the late Fifties and have been copied in Europe. Web offset printing had made it cheap to start a small weekly or monthly paper and easy to experiment with colour and photographic tricks.

Two very different kinds of underground newspaper have exploited the possibilities. There are the 'head' papers (such as *East Village Other, San Francisco Chronicle, Chicago Seed*, in the US) which aim to 'turn on' the visual senses. Then there are the political–literary papers which have a verbal message (*Village Voice, Los Angeles Free Press, Berkeley Barb, Rolling Stone* and many others in the US and *Private Eye* and *Ink* in Britain). The editorial quality of these papers ranges from the banal illiteracies of the drug cult to pungent radical reporting in the pamphleteering tradition. None of them is a newspaper in the ordinary sense of trying to report news objectively against the disciplines of deadlines and the requirements of providing routine information services. But they have mostly borrowed the tabloid format of newspapers and they are sometimes credited with generating a graphic revolution. What is their contribution to design?

Of San Francisco's eight-colour *Oracle*, Mrs Romm declares:

'Each *Oracle* page is redesigned as a composition first. The decorative area is given to an artist while the prose or poetry goes to the typist to set patiently on Varitype inside the pattern drawn. The text floats up the page in bubbles. Or it pours out in fountains. Colours blush over the page. . . . If only City Hall news looked like this, I might read it.'

The praise for what *Oracle* and others did for newspaper offset colour is merited; the

idea that there might thereby be any extra inducement to read text is hyperbole.

If City Hall news looked like that, you just could not read it. This is true of lots of the text in the 'head' papers. Text and content are so subordinated to visual fireworks that the words are illegible, vague configurations under several coats of coloured

IMPROVEMENTS AND INNOVATIONS

ink. If there is a graphic revolution here, it is a revolution in the opportunity for self-expression, or self-indulgence, and not in communication via the printed word.

Example **(A)** is taken from *Chicago Seed*, an irreverent 'head' paper. The text set in the telephone is the story of Free City Exchange, 'one of the first honest attempts to create an alternative switchboard.' The long variable lines fit the shape of a telephone but require dedication to read. The black text in the Recycling story is, in several parts, rendered invisible by being super-imposed on a black dustbin. The graphics have taken over.

The British 'alternative paper', *Ink* **(B)** did the same with news pictures on its front page, obscuring them with so much coloured ink that instead of the editors firing the reader/viewer with radical enthusiasm they have him reaching unsteadily for the Alka-Seltzer. It shows the temptations of colour because on its inside black-and-white pages *Ink* had good text (normally $14\frac{1}{2}$-pica, unjustified), bold half-tones and simple strong display dress.

The traditional press could do with the occasional spree, but mediocre as its own text setting is, it has nothing at all to learn from the 'head' papers about the typography of newspaper design. Nor do the run of literary–political papers offer anything in typography. Some, such as the small but lively *Great Speckled Bird* of Atlanta **(D)** have flamboyant yet readable text (19-pica columns, unjustified), but the bigger political–cultural papers all do their thing in the same strait-jackets as the traditional press, with advertising shapes as grim, and often without proper distinction between advertising and editorial. But note **(B)** the forceful illustration.

The *Berkeley Barb* **(E)** has been called the world's ugliest newspaper and the inflated Franklin headlines with wavy or smudged rules are certainly among the more repulsive specimens. The thriving *Village Voice* sets unwelcome records in the number

D

E

and mystery of its text continuations—one is expected to turn, like a literary legionaire, from page 1 to page 20 and on to page 38. The content is for the most part worth the effort, but it is not a contribution to newspaper design.

Despite these limitations a contribution does emerge, notably from the 'head' papers. What is there as a persistent quality, give or take a point or two of paranoid fever, is a sense of graphic excitement. It is suggested in line art, photographic montages, and editorial comment presented as a comic strip, in the images of pop art.

Now this is not very impressive stuff. It is, for the most part, not professional, not sophisticated. It is certainly not *avant-garde*. Better experimental graphics were produced in New York by the *Pushpin Monthly Graphic*[2] in the Fifties, and are produced today, marvellously miles ahead, by *New York Magazine;* and as for front covers, the London *Economist* scores more for consistent wit and originality than any of the underground papers, except perhaps *Private Eye* on its grown-up days. But the enthusiasm of the amateur effort in the 'head' papers does come through, and there is, in the individuality and vivacity, a moral for the traditional press, for the most part so greyly corseted in its wire-set columns.

The exception in the underground press to my strictures on its typography, and my qualifications about the value of its graphics, is *Rolling Stone*. The words are printed—such regression—in black ink on white paper. They are laid out with a subtlety that evades most other papers, above or below the ground. They are usually in self-contained editorial units in four 13-pica columns with handsome margins, all contained within a panel border of Oxford rules. There are no impediments to reading, no bold type, no drop letters, no art director's freak-outs.

There is white space to relieve the eye, and to draw one in, *Rolling Stone* presents superbly selected and sized half-tones.

Rolling Stone is one of the more stable elements on the underground scene (and there is much flatulent dispute about which papers are real underground and which are 'straight'). For the rest there is flux, and anyone who wants to explore further will be assisted, as I was, by an excellent American study, *The Underground Press in America*.[3]

F

Jim Marshall

JONI TAKES A BREAK

"Inside I'm thinking, 'You're smiling phoney. You're being a star.'"

Crocuses bloom before the snow melts

BY LARRY LeBLANC

TORONTO—Canadians are stunned by the vague, awesome level that Joni Mitchell has reached. She was the least-known of the Toronto group of folksingers of the Sixties.

Joni returned to Toronto, this summer, to appear at the Annual Mariposa Folk Festival on Toronto Island (15 minutes by ferry from downtown)—her first public performance in more than six months. She has an undisputable genuine affection for the Mariposa event. One reason is it is possible to find a degree of privacy here among old friends. In the afternoon workshop she freely doodled a dulcimer, smiled, and hummed in rhythm with her hands.

She appeared shortly before eight, backstage, dressed in a short robe, belted loosely around the middle which clung without tightness to all of her. In the shelter of the trees along the lagoon we talked. The sun was gone, there was a shadow all across the grassy prairie-like opening and a small cloud of insects hovered over.

A few feet away Gordon Lightfoot sat on a park bench and said how great it was to be a spectator for a change.

David Rae, who at last is emerging from the relative obscurity of guitarist to Lightfoot, Ian and Sylvia, and Joni, were there, cheerier than ever. Jack Elliott, with significantly smiling eyes, pulled his broad-brimmed cowboy hat over his forehead, put his thumbs in pockets and waited his turn at the bottle being shared by Mississippi Fred McDowell, J. B. Hutto and Lightfoot.

Joni sat watching, curiously and quiet, nodding hello now and then. With her chin resting on her crossed legs, she seemed just a little self-conscious, but most inwardly serene. So bright with high soft cheekbones, great bright blue eyes, bittersweet blond hair dribbling down past her shoulders; she has a broad smile worth waiting for and a tremendous vanilla grin which makes her always magical.

Carefully, almost cautiously, she picked the words to describe self-exile from the pop scene.

"In January, I did my last concert. I played in London and I came home. In February I finished up my record. I gave my last concert with the idea I'd take this year off, because I need new material. I need new things to say in orde to perform, so there's something in it for me. You just can't sing the same songs.

"I was being isolated, starting to feel like a bird in a gilded cage. I wasn't getting a chance to meet people. A certain amount of success cuts you off in a lot of ways. You can't move freely. I like to live, be on the streets, to be in a crowd and moving freely."

She confirmed that she was still uneasy of the great army of photographers scrambling around her, of the crowds fawning on her at every turn, wanting something, wanting to touch her. In the center she worked hard to smile constantly, answer the seemingly endless questions, and make that magic.

"It's a weird thing," she said solemnly. "You lose all your peripheral view of things. It has its rewards but I don't know what the balance is—how much good and how much damage there is in my position. From where I stand it sometimes gets absurd, and yet, I must remain smiles, come out of a mood where maybe I don't feel very pleasant and say 'smile.' Inside, I'm thinking 'You're being phony, you're smiling phony. You're being a star.'

"I was very frightened last year," she said quite directly, wiping some hair out of her eyes. "But if you're watching yourself over your own shoulder all of the time and if you're too critical of what you're doing; you can make yourself so unhappy. As a human you're always messing up, always hurting people's feelings quite innocently. I'll find it difficult, even here. There's a lot of people you want to talk to all at once. I get confused and maybe I'll turn away and leave someone standing and I'll think—'oh dear.'

"I've changed a lot," she said. "I'm getting very defensive. I'm afraid. You really have to struggle."

She paused, frowned and laughed. She leaned forward, suddenly, and said: "I feel like I'm going to be an ornery old lady."

Last January she made the surprise announcement of her self-imposed retirement, and canceled two important gigs—in New York's Carnegie Hall and Constitution Hall in Washington. She took a vacation instead.

"I've been to Greece, Spain, France and from Jamaica to Panama, through the canal. Some of my friends were moving their boat from Fort Lauderdale up to San Francisco. I joined them in Jamaica and sailed down through the canal. It was really an experience.

"On the plane to Greece we — I travelled with a friend, a poetess from Ottawa — met a man who was studying in Berkeley. He was a fairly wealthy Greek, very into the family. They're very family-oriented people. He invited us to his home for supper. In that tradition, his sister, cousins and aunts were there. It was very formal. They had a maid who brought the dinner and prepared all the national dishes of Greece kinds in our honor.

"From the peasant on up, when they have guests in the house, they're hospitable and lay on their best feed. Then he took us to a couple of nightclubs with Greek musicians playing. It was a very sophisticated introduction to Athens. Not sophisticated like New York sophistication, but on that level of their culture.

"He would always say, 'We must be spontaneous. The Greek is spontaneous. Let us dance, drink some wine, throw the gardenia to the singer.'

She giggled, bringing to her freckled and tanned face a smile that almost closed her eyes. She remarked she was delighted with Crete. It was a beautiful country, she said.

"I hiked in boots through the fields. It's very rugged, very simple, so basic. People live from the land much more. The seas are very small, very countryish. Peasants walked donkeys. There were very few cars.

"Even the poorest people seem to eat well: cucumbers and tomatoes, oranges and potatoes and bread. They ate that well. They lived in concrete huts with maybe one or two chairs, a bed where the family slept and a couple of burrows and chickens."

After a brief pause, she added, "To me, it was a lovely life, far better than being middle class in America. I lived for five weeks in a cave there. The only trouble was it was very commercialized. The magazines were writing it up. As a result, you had a lot of prying tourists all of the time. Even that was kinda funny, because most of the people living in the caves were Canadians, Americans, Swiss and French. They'd say, 'Oh, here come the tourists.' It was kinda funny, the Greeks being the tourists."

Then she described the Matelan surroundings. "It was a very small bay with cliffs on two sides. And between the two cliffs, on the beach, there were about four or five small buildings. There were also a few fishermen huts.

A New York Dummy

These are two pages from early dummies of a projected new paper in the United States. The intention was to produce a serious paper which would cheerfully leave spot news to TV and concentrate on interpretation and investigation. Its paging would be limited so that the breakfast reader did not feel he had to handle the products of half a lumber mill before getting at the essential information. The broadsheet dummy ($22\frac{1}{2}$in. × 17in.) is notable for the hypothetical combination of a lengthy investigative report with, in counterpoint, a quick summary of national and international news, set across 30 picas and rather lavishly decorated. There is strong colour on the page. The centred title is picked out in blue or red, the index in top left is bold (some would say extravagant for a small paper) and the headline dress works on the front where it is predominantly upper- and lower-case. On the inside page the expanded caps used on subsidiary lines is too slow and that

graphic symbol, 7in. by 3in., of Jewish stars and Soviet sickles would not last a minute at that size in real production.

The text is a readable $14\frac{1}{2}$ picas, giving six columns inside, but the unjustified setting here is questionable. Unjustified setting is a controversial subject (*see* Book Two), but one can say here that if the main text were set justified, the retention of unjustified for the summary index would be worthwhile.

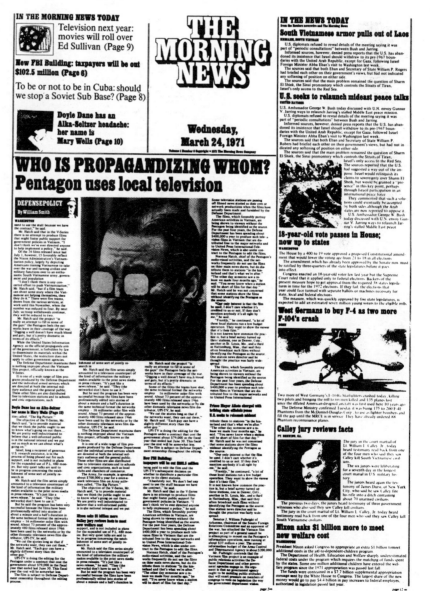

The newspaper images shown include three front pages labeled **A**, **B**, and **C**:

A — *New York Herald Tribune*, Late City Edition, Sunday, January 1, 1961. Headline: "Hands Off Laos, U.S. Warns Red States"

B — *New York Herald Tribune*, The Late City, Sunday, October 14, 1962. Headlines: "Congress Adjourns — Same Old Feuds", "Reds Warn: Crisis Time In Germany", "Vigorous Vatican Council In This 'Changing' World", "GALLUP POLL — INVADE CUBA NOW?"

C — *The Sunday Herald Tribune*, section 1, October 1962. Headline: "Invitation to Debate"

Peter Palazzo and the Sunday Herald Tribune

Peter Palazzo was charged with giving a really radical new look to the Sunday edition of the *New York Herald Tribune*. He provided a format which was both elegant and exciting, based on a new editorial concept of the task of a metropolitan Sunday.

(A) The front page of the *Herald Tribune* in 1961, not very different from the *Herald Tribune* of the 1940s, with headlines in Bodoni Bold in several decks and text in eight columns of varied news items.

(B) The *Herald Tribune* of October, 1962, which marks a change in emphasis. There is rather more analysis on the front page, and columns 1 and 2 have been given up to a double-column news summary.

(C) The Palazzo transformation. The edi-

torial emphasis has been shifted to the presentation of a single story, and this has been projected with a striking panel dominated by two strong photographic images. The news summary has been

retained, but the Bodoni side-heads are no longer labels. They say something; they have been enlarged and set in white. The title, too, has been cleaned up and set in a neat box with an unmis-

takable numeral: there was similar treatment for each of the other sections to identify them individually but unite them as sections in the same newspaper. Some other front pages are illustrated.

Peter Palazzo has described the approach which resulted in these scintillating newspaper-magazine pages. 'My first overall functional objective was to design all the Sunday sections for individual identification and unified appearance. This was done by layout treatment and by the almost exclusive use of one typeface—Caslon (whoever was doing the design of the paper would make no difference; its identity would remain through the typeface). I chose Caslon because of the instant impression of integrity it gives to the news' [Bodoni had to be retained for a time for economy].

'My second objective was to devise some system of modular layout. A number of contemporary papers making design changes appear to be departing from the modular layout which newspapers have always used for reasons of efficiency. This modular system is very useful, it seems to me, because it acts as an automatic organiser for many news items on the page; I believe that much visual chaos has resulted from its abandonment. At the *Tribune* I've attempted to return to a complete modular system and to create added readability simply through the judicious use of white space, good typography, and a restrained use of pictures and artwork'.[1]

But Palazzo recognised that changing the design meant, to some extent, changing the traditional approach to news: 'a large graphic presentation of a news story on Sunday meant more careful editorial planning and editing of stories in a feature magazine way.' The design editor of the *Tribune* had a hand in editing the pictures and was present in the composing room working with type and blocks; indeed everyone on the paper had to be involved and understand what was happening.

THE SUN SAYS

Peace or propaganda?

MR. DEAN RUSK, U.S. Secretary of State, is fully entitled to ask that countries which clamoured for America to stop the Vietnam bombing should now press Hanoi to take positive peace steps.

Mr. Rusk pointedly declared: "We shall be interested in what others do to insist upon action by Hanoi which will move us towards peace."

The North Vietnam Government have in fact drawn back their own forces to permit a lull in the fighting. But President Ho Chi Minh continues his violent talk.

Yesterday he described the end of the bombing as "only an initial victory" and urged his people to "sweep every aggressor out of the country." He called on the Communists in South Vietnam to carry on their offensive unremittingly.

DELICATE

If this incitement keeps the fighting going in South Vietnam, as well it may, it could gravely jeopardise all hope of stopping this tragic war.

Russia, as Ho Chi Minh's ally, is in a delicate position. She has welcomed the bombing halt, but must now bring strong pressure on North Vietnam to act with moderation.

There is a limit to the concessions President Johnson can make without a reciprocal gesture. North Vietnam's friends must make her understand the danger of pushing "victory" propaganda too far.

Football fouls

FOOTBALLER A fell to a tackle by Footballer B. He got up and aimed what appeared to be a vicious kick at Footballer B's shin. Footballer C then knocked down Footballer A.

An unhappy episode in a match seen by at least nine and a half million viewers on television

WHERE NIXON, HUMPHREY AND WALLACE STAND —AND WHY

1 DAY TO GO

The making of the 37th President

		VIETNAM	ARMS RACE	FOREIGN RELATIONS	CALL-UP	GUN CONTROL	LAW AND ORDER	CIVIL RIGHTS	UNEMPLOYMENT
Hubert Humphrey	The Democratic candidate, aged 57, started political life as Mayor of Minneapolis in 1946. Then he served in the Senate from 1949 to 1964 and became Vice-President four years ago.	HAS favoured stopping the bombing of North Vietnam if the Communists would respect the demilitarised zone. If that condition were satisfied, he would agree to gradual withdrawal of U.S. troops and free elections in South Vietnam. The National Liberation Front could participate in elections if they renounced force.	WANTS the Senate to ratify immediately the Anglo - American - Russian treaty banning the spread of nuclear arms. Wants real reductions in military spending. Would like an agreement with Russia on reduction of missile stockpiles.	FAVOURS closer relations with Russia, especially in areas of trade and cultural exchanges. Wants to strengthen the United Nations as an agency of peace. Favours annual summit meetings.	WANTS a lottery system of selection for 19 - year - olds with right to complete their education first.	FAVOURS stronger federal controls in favour of gun owners.	SUPPORTS recent court rulings in favour of defendants in criminal proceedings. Favours greater effort to rehabilitate criminals rather than locking them away. Urges federal grants to increase local police salaries.	CALLS for more education and jobs for Negroes. Sympathises with current trend towards militancy in civil rights movement. Is more associated to Negroes than any other candidate because of his long advocacy of civil rights.	WANTS federal programme of retraining and relocation to facilitate full employment.
Richard Nixon	The Republican candidate, aged 55, served in Congress from 1947 to 1952. Was Vice-President under Eisenhower for eight years and ran unsuccessfully for President against John F. Kennedy in 1960.	SAYS the war must be ended by America's military, diplomatic and economic might. Has not spelled out details of his plan but he is on record as opposed to the bombing halt until North Vietnam made reciprocal move that would protect U.S. lives. Has taken a hard line on the war in the past.	WANTS the Senate to delay ratification of the treaty banning the spread of nuclear arms because action at this time would "put the seal of approval" on the Soviet seizure of Czechoslovakia. Wants major build-up of U.S. missile strength.	FAVOURS building up NATO and entering into security arrangements with Asian and African countries so that in any future wars they will furnish the men and America the arms and money. He favours summit meetings but only if America can negotiate from strength.	WOULD end it after the Vietnam war. Wants all-volunteer army with higher pay as incentive.	DOES not think stricter registration would have much effect, calls for more state and city licensing. Warns that gun control can disarm law - abiding citizens. Wants a law providing for compulsory prison term for all who use guns in committing crimes.	SAYS much of the blame for so-called crime in the streets is due to court rulings freeing individuals on legal technicalities. Wants a tough Attorney - General. Says that crime cannot be curtailed by social legislation.	CALLS "civil rights" an extended term. Favours anti-discriminatory housing regulations but would prefer that they be handled by state and local authorities and local individuals. Opposed enforced movement of children by bus to schools to correct racial imbalance.	FAVOURS tax credits to industries to locate in the ghetto areas.
George Wallace	The candidate of the American Independent Party, aged 49, was elected Governor of Alabama in 1962. His wife Lurleen succeeded him in 1966 because of a law forbidding a second term. She died last May.	WANTS to give the peace talks a chance, but would go all-out for military victory without nuclear weapons if the talks fail. Opposed halt to the bombing without reciprocal action by North Vietnam.	FAVOURS delay in Senate ratification of treaty banning spread of nuclear arms. Criticises the nuclear test ban treaty. Says the Russians have never adhered to it. Wants a speed-up in installation of anti - ballistic missiles. Opposes any disarmament agreement.	FORESEES the time when America might have to withdraw from the United Nations because the UN has become involved too much in domestic affairs of other nations. Warns of world-wide Communist plot to subvert weak nations. But favours summit talks with Russia.	WANTS the call-up to include all men regardless of their economic or social status. Eventually would like volunteer army.	OPPOSES federal regulation of gun owners.	CRITICISES leniency of courts. Would fight crime in Washington by calling out 30,000 troops and stationing them apart with fixed bayonets. Wants local police to have a free hand to deal with criminals and rioters.	OPPOSES any federal civil rights law which supersedes State laws. Would seek repeal of all anti-discriminatory housing regulations. Wants individual States to decide whether schools should be segregated.	WOULD encourage industries to locate in rural areas. Thinks it is a problem for private enterprise.

£ THE SUN SAYS
Continued from Page One

WHAT DEVALUATION WILL MEAN TO YOU

WAGES by Geoffrey Goodman

HOMES by Robert Adam

PRICES by Jack Waterhouse

PETROL by Barrie Gill

EXPORTS

CARS

HOLIDAYS by Arthur Eperon

DEFENCE by Brian Woosey

Mr. 14%, taking a sample of the opposition

The Sun

These are two brilliant exploitations of the possibilities of graphic tabulation by the *Sun* of London in its broadsheet days. The panel on the different policies of the three candidates for the Presidency is notable for white space, the consistent use of type, and the balance of the design. Note that there is no attempt to fill each sub-section with type. The type is left to hang asymmetrically in its white. Colour is provided by half-tones, the flag and the blunt numeral 1. Of course the feasibility of the design depended on the succinct editing of the type; it is an example of successful co-operation between designer and writer.

The devaluation tabulation was spread across two pages, linked, despite the gutter, by the strong wording, the panel rule, and the consistency of the design.

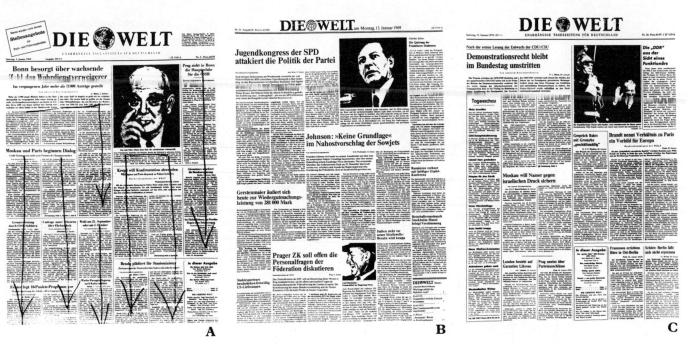

A

B

C

Die Welt

In Chapter 7, the international section on front pages for the Tet offensive in Vietnam, I wondered how long *Die Welt* would resist 'the appeal of a warmer display signal.' At the beginning of 1970 *Die Welt* did change, abandoning Bodoni for Times Bold, following a redesign by Professor Kurt Weidemann. The old front page of *Die Welt* (A) retained decks of heading and fine cut-off rules between decks; the subsidiary stories on the page were headlined in a restrained, not to say invisible, manner. The six-column modular layout, as demonstrated by Professor Weidemann's pencil, tended to be static. His proposal (B) was for a non-modular asymmetrical page, with white replacing column rule, simpler headlines and stronger down-page headlines, and a considerably cleaned up title area. The philosophy was accepted by *Die Welt,* though the implementation was somewhat different (C). Column rule was (rightly) retained; so broadly was the modular layout. But the other changes were effected— simpler, bolder headlining in Times Bold, a cleaner title-piece (though not quite as good as Professor Weidemann's), and the summary column in column 8 headlined Tagesschau. This is in sans. The one blemish in the new page is the introduction of an italic bold sans at the top of column 8, inexplicably in a page whose reasoning is clarity, order and consistency.

The London Observer

The pages (right) from the London *Observer* illustrate the range of good design possible in a traditional newspaper—coherent bold-ness and flexibility on the front news page, and imagination in the front of the Review section. The *Observer,* several times a design award winner, has always on its news pages demonstrated how bold simplicity is super-ior to elaborate contrivance. The strict vertical symmetry of a few years ago, with double-column lead headlines in 36pt and in decks, has been replaced by a freer hori-zontal layout using two weights of the square Century Schoolbook in lower-case with immaculate white spacing and generous picture sizing. The *Observer* was the first British newspaper to exploit Schoolbook, Note that big self-confident title, designed by art editor Ray Hawkey to increase point-of-sale attraction; one coat of arms was dropped to allow the top of column 8 to be used for trailers for inside attractions. Raymond Hawkey also designed the Review front. The display type here, unlike the news pages, varies from week to week to respond to the feature and its treatment.

ESTIMATING CHURCHILL

THE OBSERVER, JANUARY 31, 1965

THE MAN I KNEW by Lord Attlee

A blazing row

Monologues

Superbly lucky

Tonypandy

£8,700 for £3 monthly

THE OBSERVER

Lord Hill gives pledge on BBC orchestras

Rhodesia bishops denounce Smith

It's not good enough, Wilson warns TUC

Bomb hoax halts premier's train

4 killed in mercy plane

Steel prices decision near

China plots war says Brezhnev

Thorpe wants Clyde inquiry

Frontier to close in Gibraltar blockade

THE OBSERVER
WEEKEND REVIEW January 10, 1965

IAN NAIRN 20 THREATENED TOWNS

our critic-at-large on architecture and planning, spotlights a score of national assets now in danger from developers, planners—and the people who live there.

Huntingdon · Gravesend · Carmarthen · Ashton-under-Lyne · Deal · Harwich · Bishop Auckland · Hanley · Lowestoft · Macclesfield · Mansfield · Hartford · Newark · Rochdale · Slockport · Stockton-on-Tees · Shaftesbury · Wimborne Minster · Worcester · Radstock

What everyone should know about languages

A scientist looks into his own grave · Eliot's influence by Philip Toynbee

Two new regular contributors
MALCOLM MUGGERIDGE on books
GEORGE MELLY on pop and blues
ERIC NEWBY in MOSCOW

A

B

C

Presenting the TV Guide

The design of the night's or week's TV guide in most newspapers has all the public service passion of a post office clerk near to the end of his night shift on a holiday weekend. Of course it requires thought to organise a time-and-channel guide, especially when there may be as many as thirteen channels with variable times and programmes, and in most offices the presentation has all too obviously become a chore.

Connecticut's *Bridgeport Post* (**A**), burying one-line references under a tobacco display ad, is not untypical. It is too depressing to show samples of the small-type horrors or confused guides, with excessive changes of signal, so here are two that try and succeed.

le to the week's television   Compiled by Elkan Allan

D

E

F

G

(B, C) are Peter Palazzo's design of the week's TV Guide for *New York Magazine*. The day is divided into time units, each indicated by italic numerals, inset in white. Each channel was then given a bold numeral followed by the programme titles, with details in roman. In all this there was no change of type face or size and there were no words in caps. And the format was easily adaptable to longer or shorter entries.

The example (D) is from *The Sunday Times* of London (which has, as mentioned, been imitated by the *Sunday Australian* and others). It began as an editorial idea of doing more about TV: the layout followed as the idea developed from (E, F, G) programme listings and a 'film strip' which were at first run separately and then combined. The page now gives detailed listing of Sunday's TV times with a selective preview of the following week. Instead of running the text north to south on the broadsheet pages, the originators (Edwin Taylor and Oscar Turnill) gave the feature the benefit of an arresting east-west presentation across the width of the broadsheet page on its side. Strong reverse blocks distinguish each day with heads in 14pt Ludlow Black (which words well at such small sizes) and the formula has been worked in a surprising number of combinations without ever violating its essential logic. The selective preview is very selective and can stand being run continuous text; if there were more entries it would clearly have to follow Sunday's time-listings style.

A

B

Birmingham Post

The restyling of the *Birmingham Post,* a leading British provincial morning newspaper, took four years. The effect the designers say they wanted as 'that of turning up the contrast on a television set—the same content but brighter to look at.' They succeed in rather more than a bright appearance. The best of the new pages is much more legible, much more intelligible, and more consistent in its news judgments.

(A) The old page one. Nine-column format. Bodoni Bold for news headings, partly set in traditional all-cap decks with fine rules between each deck. The headlines in the top left corner have muffled impact because of the overcrowding, the fussy attribution of the main statement, and the intrusion of the Castro story. There is not enough white space between the main spread of headlines, and the cut-off from the title and a subsidiary

line of the title *Birmingham Gazette* in blurred black-letter crowds down on the cut-off from above. The page plan has confusions: it is immediately clear what the three-column block down page refers to; it is not immediately clear which story owns the three-column block down page. The headlines are all centred, except the 7–8 story of kidnapping which, for some mysterious reason, is set left.

(B) The first stage of the change. The heads are still in Bodoni Bold, but the decks have gone, so has the *Birmingham Gazette* sub-title. The main head has been set in lower-case: compare it with the other page one for its capacity to communicate a signal and a quick summary. The top three heads are set left. A striking new departure is the presentation of campaigns and exhortations. The top four-column panel is a campaign

C

D

against drinking and driving, the graphics prepared by the *Birmingham Post*. It makes its point boldly but the style marries with the rest of the page. A criticism of the layout would be that it does not make effective use of the bottom section of the page.

(C) The change complete. There is a new range of headline styles in Century Extended and Century Bold, set left, and bold treatment for an effective picture. The main headlines are marvellously clear (though the Bodoni, retained for italic heads, i.e. Davis Cup, column 8, is rather lost). The bold panel in columns 1 and 2 is a poster-style index to the rest of the paper and a much better puller than the old-style index in column 2 of the first specimen. But its position is questionable: it could be overlooked as a normal paid advertisement. If it had been moved in by one

column, with text type in column one, it would have been immediately recognisable as editorial.

(D) An issue of the *Post* where the style of the third illustration is adapted for big news. The attempt here is to report news and reflect the mood of the event, the agony of remorse felt by a nation which had its violent streak exposed. The running double-column story forms the basis of the page, in news content and make-up structure, and the eight-column picture-strip suggests the sequence of tragedy. There were also four inside pages on the news. These demanded a strong cross-reference panel (column six), much more successfully placed than the preceding example. It is noticeable without destroying the main heading; it neatly divides the Kennedy story from the adjacent second lead.

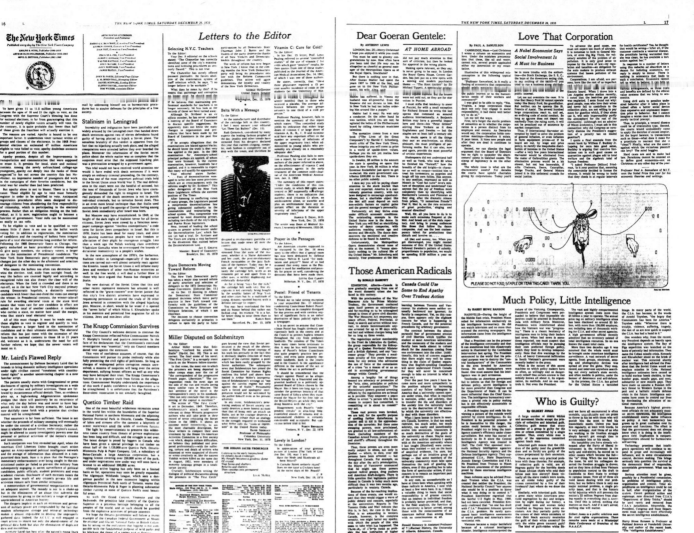

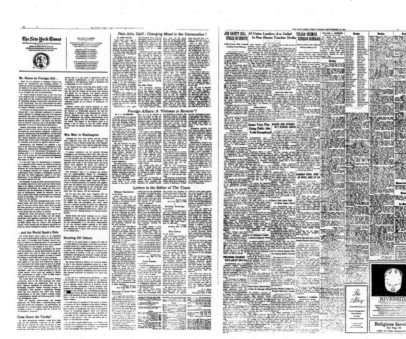

A

B

New York Times

(A) *New York Times* leader or editorial page and its facing page (the Op-Ed page) redesigned by Louis Silverstein from **(B)**; there the leader columns were impressive, but that was all. There was no conviction in the display of the other articles and letters, and the Op-Ed page was a ragbag—the death notices in the end four columns an appropriate accompaniment for the sombre news display which disappeared after the fold in a run of fillers headlined with watery sans.

In **(A)** the Op–Ed page has been cleared of death notices, peripheral advertising, and news, and given up to columns and articles by outsiders, freeing the leader page for a handsome presentation of letters. The effect of this editorial decision has been maximised by the presentation. The Op–Ed page is divided into six wider columns for optimum legibility, and laid out in clear modular units with single-line headings of Bookman roman upper- and lower-case 36pt.

But perhaps the main distinction is the artwork. Day after day Silverstein contrives to add vivacity, grace and point to the page by the choice and commissioning of drawings. The wider columns for the letters on the leader page, and the occasional spot colour from a half-tone, has transformed that page, too; all it needs, one feels, is a daily live headline instead of the static 'Letters to the Editor.'

Right: Another redesign by Louis Silverstein at the *New York Times*. The old page (C) was clean enough, but its basic single-column was too narrow for easy reading, its artwork was routine, it gave insufficient emphasis for a large paper to announcing what was inside, and to distinguishing Thomas Mullaney's column from the rest of the news.

(D) The new front page is modular, based on five wider and more readable columns, plus a two-column display unit for index and Mullaney's column. Distinct elements on a page should have distinctive signals, and three here have that in well-judged, res-trained typography—the inside contents, the column, and the consumer's news story. The reader is guided, not bludgeoned, by the 14pt Gothic kickers set right above the Bookman heads, with well-whited 3pt and fine rule running parallel, just the right amount of colour. The summary index at top left is confidently bold (though the captionless two column is a problem). And, again, perhaps the finest part of the new front page is the quality of the drawings specially commissioned for the page. Communication is more than headlines, half-tones and text.

Western Daily Press

The front page should reflect the paper's assessment of the important news of the day. The essential difference in the old and the new *Western Daily Press* is not so much the change in display type from Bodoni to Century Bold and Franklin. It is in the undeniable fact that the new layout functions effectively as an organiser of the news. The newspaper has an idea of its news priorities and uses the page vigorously to express them. The old layout is full of dither. It is hard to know where one should begin.

The bomb hoax story, given undue prominence in column 4 for its worth, is the only story at the top of the page. It is related to the lead on the left—and so are all the top three pictures. Anyone interested in this story has to wander all over the page.

The midpage gives accidental prominence to one of the weaker stories (Sunday soccer) and a strong position on the fold in columns 6, 7, 8 is given to a 36pt caps headline which communicates not news but only the promise of news (From the World's News). Theoretically, the new design can be criticised. The space taken by headlines is inflated, but having opted for *Daily Express* style banners the *Western Daily Press* has to resist looking anaemic by comparison. And the dashing, flamboyant style is in keeping with the paper's new role as a vigorous crusader for the West Country.

The new design also offers an attractive summary of the news in the rest of the paper (in picture captions at the top), and an effective new title. It is a pity the title area is cluttered, but the slab serif lettering is undeniably powerful.

The *Western Daily Press*, incidentally, had a spectacular revival under its editor Eric Price: in 1960 it sold only 12,000. Redesigned and reinvigorated, it rose to 50,000 within three years.

Oxford Mail

Leader pages should lead. Most American newspapers, for all their design faults, have long since reserved what they call their 'editorial page' for editorial. The leader page of the *Oxford Mail*—typical of many evenings in many countries—used to start with three columns of display advertising. This not only forced the leading article into a subdued and subordinate position, it announced that the paper set more store by display advertising than its own opinions. And the uncontrolled typography of the display advertising reduced the chances of the page looking as if someone had thought about it. The leader page of a newspaper wishing to be taken seriously (and most newspapers presume to be taken seriously here) should be orderly, clear, noticeable, and have maximum legibility.

The redesign of the *Oxford Mail* achieves these objectives. The display advertise-

ments and the crossword have been transferred to another page. The leader is set double-column and the top of the page is also freed for a main article. Since the page is built up of a few self-contained units, rules have been omitted without making it too difficult for the reader to find his way around. The page functions better; and, despite the absence of any sizeable half-tone, it looks better, too.

The Journal

This Newcastle-based provincial morning used to be a straight imitation of the post-war *Daily Mail*—seven- or eight-column streamer in Century Bold caps, with strapline over-heavily underscored and second deck, a column 1 editorial, and the inevitable gothic condensed 'kicker' heading **(A)**.

Then it followed *The Northern Echo* in questioning the traditional streamer and substituting a vertical weight for horizontal; the old streamer disappeared to be replaced by a three-column caps lead. In the initial stages **(B)** this was less forceful than the old streamer and the page was less well organised —note the awkward position of the Stop Press. But later **(C)** *The Journal* adopted a much more effective treatment of the lead story. Compare this lead treatment with the original seven-column banner. The caps banner is noticeably weaker, fringed by other headlines and robbed of some of its colour by the letterspacing used to make the wording fit the space.

By contrast, the Century Bold Extended lead in lower-case set left, bringing its weight down page, stands out on its own.

The white space is not diffused through the letters; it is concentrated, and so is the message of the headline. There is no doubt that it is easier and quicker to read and grasp the import of this new lead. The simpler treatment saves space: the two decks of the vertical lead save $2\frac{1}{2}$ column-inches on the old three-deck lead. The rest of the page, with two strong horizontal heads acting as midpage supports, illustrates again that it is not necessary to call in Gothic condensed to have variety and impact. Century Bold lower-case heads, properly whited, are sufficient.

The Journal also abandoned banners on its inside pages and made the leads simple three-lines, all in lower-case and in good proportionate relationship (usually 48pt and 36pt Century Bold). *The Journal* came second to the *Observer* in the 1968 Design Award contest.

The Sunday Times

Leader columns are text columns. That is the way we think of them, but there are occasions when the opinion requires visual illustration. This was one *Sunday Times* attempt to combine the emotional appeal of a photograph with the logic of the textual argument. It was effective because the photographs by Snowdon were quite brilliant, because they were designed into the leader column, and because the presentation was a surprise. The leader column was then normally text down the first two columns or a strip across the top of the editorial page. To exploit two pictures in this instance meant contriving a link between the gutter of two broadsheet pages, which was achieved by rules and by maintaining the same depth on both pages. The traditional way would have been to run the pictures on the same page, or facing, or on page one. They would still have been effective, but fewer people would have read the leading article.

A

B

C

Sunday Times Business News

(A) *The Sunday Times Business News* with Franklin only on the front page. This is an extremely bold type and an excess of large sizes produced an overwhelming effect as well as taking a great deal of space. The text type wandered all over the place in irregular units, and the lack of organisation was compounded by the omission of column rules. The poster-style index as a double-column panel is lost on top of the ad in cols 7 and 8.

(B) Stage one of a redesign. The text is presented in clear, self-contained rectangles, organised by column rules. The Franklin heads have been sized down and the changes in size limited.

(C) Stage two of the redesign. The Albertus title, unique to *Business News*, is replaced by a bolder but more compact Century Bold used as the logotype for other sections, thus linking the separate sections. Record is introduced as a colour contrast with the heavy Franklin.

The Sunday Times gave restrained and effective display of a feature after three US astronauts died in an Apollo space capsule. The consistent Franklin display type unites the page and is subtly varied in size, character and spread. Note the simplicity of the wording in the three main display decks, and the handsome white space in the top panel. This piece and the picture would have been strengthened as a unit if the whole thing had been enclosed in two equal rules top and bottom—two 6pt rules, say, running the full width of the page, underneath the picture, and, at the top, replacing the cut-off.

The existing 6pt rule under the panel would have been displaced, of course.

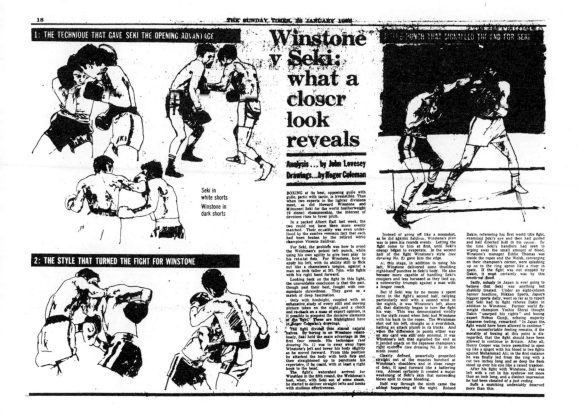

Improving a good effort. The idea (above) was to analyse the techniques of the boxers in a big fight. An artist was commissioned to sketch the essential maneouvres and the text was intended to emphasise the analysis of the drawings. The first layout provides a striking feature, but there are two basic failures of communication. First, to understand the sketches you have to find the reference points in the running text. Second, the separation of the third sketch by text and headlines spoils the flow of the action and the understanding of the analysis. The best aid to quick communication would have been to write the text solely as a set of individual captions. This was not possible, however, and the compromise solution is to present analytical captions in three boxes (right). The sketches are then pulled together to form an uninterrupted sequence. Note the detailing—distinctive Bodoni Black type for the numbers 1, 2, 3 over each sketch, and again in the three box captions. There are two other refinements. The reverse blocks are dropped because their colour competes too much with the sketches. And the awkward shape of the original headline is changed: it creates a pattern which distracts attention from the essential patterns of the sketches.

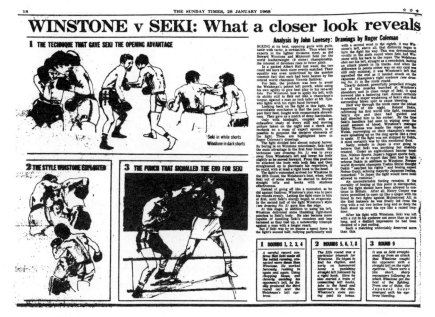

Award-winning Designs

The newspaper design awards in Britain and America have stimulated considerable improvements in both countries (though the Americans are certainly too complacent in the judgment that standards are now so high that the Ayer Cup Award can be safely discontinued).

The British design contest has been sponsored since 1954 by Linotype and Machinery Limited and organised by *Printing World*. It is administered by a committee representing Linotype, *Printing World*, the Newspaper Society (the organisation of provincial owners), the Council of Industrial Design, and the British Federation of Master Printers. The three judges are nominated annually and normally consist of two printers or typographers or journalists plus an eminent layman interested in design. They are assisted by a technical adviser, the newspaper typographer Allen Hutt. They make their choices from up to 400 newspapers divided into various award categories. Only newspapers which enter are judged. They are invited to submit one copy from a short past period during the year, specified by the organisers. Some of the national newspapers have held aloof from the contest for several years, which is a pity because it is a fruitful agency for improving standards of design.

Birmingham Post

This three-page picture special in tribute to West Bromwich Albion's Wembley Cup victory won the *Birmingham Post* a Special Award in newspaper design. This is how pictures should be treated—cropped into big clear simple rectangles. Text on picture pages, as here, should be enlarged in sympathy. The judges rightly commended the ingenious and striking reverse-block levels which linked the pages.

Perhaps the Design Award's most important effect has been the assault, stimulated by the technical adviser, Allen Hutt, on antique and cluttered mastheads. Year after year Allen Hutt has inveighed against the grubby, overcrowded title-pieces under which newspapers have seen fit to parade their news (and especially against bad Black Letter title-lines such as the elaborately white-lined variety and its fussy Victorian successors). Many newspapers, even small weeklies, are not distinguished by titles of clarity and character.

A second benefit of contests is that, despite the furious argument the judgments provoke, they are slowly enabling some minimal common standards of good design to be agreed. Here are the front pages of some winning newspapers. The words in quotation marks are comments by the judges.

The Journal, Newcastle

(No. 2 of Class 1, daily or Sunday news-papers.) 'It handles an all-Century head-line style excellently, in clean and consistent fashion throughout. Avoiding the temptation to oversize it maintains a sound balance in its inside page leads and second lead headings: they are simple three-liners, all in lower-case and in good proportionate relationship (usually 48pt and 36pt).'

Barrhead News

(Commended, Class 3.) 'A web offset Glasgow surburban tabloid (repro-proof-ed from hot metal) makes a simple headline show with Grot No. 9, includings its Italic, though the overall effect is rather dull; its title-line is notable, appropriately presented in a large lower-case of Scotch Roman aspect. In fact it is not a Scotch but Stephenson Blake's Modern No. 20 blown up to around 96pt. and looking very well indeed.'

South Wales Echo

'A conventional rotary letterpress job, Cardiff's evening is thoroughly well hand-led. It is a good example of a broadsheet sans make-up using the keyboard for lots of its run-of-paper single- and double-column headings (in varying sizes of Intertype Vogue Extra Bold Condensed).'

Evening Echo

(No. 1 in Class 2, evening papers.) 'One of the Thomson computerised photo-set web-offset evenings at Hemel Hemp-stead. It is a dashing and dramatic effort presenting a powerful local front page. Small criticisms may be made: though the combined Anzeigen-Univers sans style is agreeable there are some ugly headline juxtapositions and word spacing in head-ings need attention; the short title line looks rather lost in its surrounding white.'

Eastern Daily Press

(Commended, Class 1.) 'Retains the clarity and order of its Bodoni Bold display in the now unusual seven-column format.'

Shropshire Star
(Commended, Class 2.) 'Britain's pioneer web offset evening. We noted particularly its admirable use of spot colour (bright blue) for its Weekend Woman double-page spread.'

Evening Star, Burnley
(Commended, Class 2.) Medium Gothic lead with a serifed contrast producing a powerful front page. 'The *Evening Star* has been greatly improved with a normal across-page title instead of its previous double-column reverse (always a mistake with a broadsheet).'

Evening News, Edinburgh
(Commended, Class 2.) Combines a Square Grot lead with a serifed contrast. 'We thought the *Evening News* hand-drawn italic title line rather coarse.'

Merthyr Express
(No. 2 in Class 3.) 'The Medium Grot italic title-page strikes an unusual but pleasing note; the news pages are open and lively, but with a reasonable restraint in display, playing on the Sans variations of Tempo Heavy and Grot No. 9, with italics.'

The West Sussex Gazette
(Commended, Class 3.) 'The first product of the first computer-set, web offset plant in Britain to use a cathode ray tube photo-setter (the Linotron 505). The *Gazette* demonstrates the commendable clarity of this kind of setting in a text face of some delicacy (Times). Heading display in Times Bold, Univers and Bodoni Italic (all photoset) is pleasing though the open lower-case of this version of Bodoni may strike some as peculiar.'

Yorkshire Gazette and Herald

(Commended, Class 3.) 'Has previously won commendation especially for its attractive title-line: its Bodoni display style is set off by a heavy front-page sans, lead, hand set in the not often seen Granby Extra Bold.'

The Guardian

(Commended, Class 1.) 'Sound as ever with a startlingly effective full-page-depth double-column half-tone to illustrate the Ronan Point tower flat disaster.'

Crosby Herald

(Winner, Class 3: weekly, bi-weekly or tri-weekly.) 'A simple (and it might be said) traditional effort, letterpress printed, but outstandingly good. It made a welcome contrast with some of the headier web-offset offerings or the cramped old-fashioned weeklies. The *Herald* avoids the sin of gross oversizing of headings, still too common a weekly fault—and with no right reason. Its Century Bold news style, with Medium Gothic for spot contrast, is handled in workmanlike fashion. Above all, its picture sizing, in large, simple rectangles, agreeably disposed, is a model that other weeklies would be well advised to emulate.'

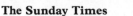

The Sunday Times
These pages on the six-day Middle East War of 1967 won the London *Sunday Times* the Newspaper Design Award. The paper's front page was entirely devoted to it, with a double-column summary in the first two columns (normal Century Bold headlines and Franklin side-heads for reports from various centres). The judges commented: '*The Sunday Times*, we felt, soared above all others in the Daily/Sunday class and amply deserved its bronze plaque as No. 1. Its winning issue was the one at the end of the breathtaking week of the Israel–Arab War. It told the whole story, and in depth, in a brilliantly linked series of news feature pages. Boldly pictured, these pages were presented with heavy black reverse labels, with large-sized Gothic condensed lower-case dis-

play, as dramatic and harsh as the story itself. The presentation blasted the reader with authority although the total effect was calm and measured. Nowhere was there a hint of the rush, toil, sweat, back-breaking stonework and unbearable tension which must have accompanied the production. It was a professional job of the very highest order.'

Looking back on it one sees that some pages succeeded more than others. Two of them after the fold barely surfaced above the greyness of the large areas of classified advertising; and it would have been nice if the scale and drama of the picture on the section's first page could have been carried through.

But the 'if only . . . .' of page design will, I suspect, always be one of its tantalising attractions for newspapermen.

Bibliography

ARNOLD, Edmund C. *Modern Newspaper Design*. New York: Harper and Row, 1969.
Strictly American, but descriptively comprehensive.

BARNHART, Thomas F. *Weekly Newspaper Make-up and Typography*. Minneapolis: University of Minnesota Press. London: Oxford University Press, 1949.

EMERY, Michael C, SCHUNEMAN, R Smith, and EMERY, Edwin. *America's Front Page News 1690–1970*. New York: Doubleday and Co; Minneapolis: Vis-Com Inc, 1970.
Fascinating 15in. × 10in. reproductions.

EVANS, Harold M. *The Active Newsroom*. Zurich: International Press Institute, 1961.
Written for Asian newsmen after a series of seminars in India and Pakistan; contains some simple basic pointers for text editors, news editors and layout men.

GILMORE, Gene, and ROOT, Robert. *Modern Newspaper Editing*. Berkeley, Calif.: Glendessary Press, 1971.
Has a chapter (pp. 73–107 with illustrations) which is a crisp summary of American practices in layout.

GLESSING, Robert J. *The Underground Press in America*. Bloomington and London: Indiana University Press, 1970.
Sympathetic account which has a chapter on 'The Graphic Revolution.'

HUTT, Allen. *Newspaper Design*, Second Edition. London: Oxford University Press, 1967.
Scholarly study, especially good in descriptive passage on mechanics of newspaper production, text setting and discussion of title-pieces.

LEWIS, John. *Typography/Basic Principles*. London: Studio Vista, 1966.
Short but perceptive general guide with some insights of value to the newspaperman.

MCCLEAN, Ruari. *Magazine Design*, London: Oxford University Press, 1969.
Collection of illustrations, with captions, of the best magazine practice. Any newsman can learn a lot from these pictures about typography, photographs, graphics, and especially the use of white space.

MCLUHAN, Marshall. *Understanding Media*. London: Routledge and Kegan Paul, 1964.
One does not have to accept all the marvellously arrogant argument or assertions, but print men who think about their work cannot fail to be usefully provoked.

ROBERTS, Raymond. *Typographic Design*. London: Ernest Benn, 1966.
Not directly written for newspapermen, but is a lucid general guide, and Chapters IV and V are relevant.

SAUSMAREZ, Maurice de. *Basic Design: the dynamics of visual form*. London: Studio Vista, 1968.
Intended for young artists but journalists can peep with profit.

SELLERS, Leslie. *Doing it in Style*. Oxford: Pergamon Press, 1968.
A–Z manual for journalists, PR men and copywriters; has a pungent few pages on newspaper design.

SELLERS, Leslie. *The Simple Subs Book*. Oxford: Pergamon Press, 1968.
Lively short treatment by former British popular-paper executive. Has a chapter on typography.

STEER, Vincent. *Printing Design and Layout*, Third Edition. London: Virtue and Co, 1951 (?).
Intended for general designers and printers but has some valuable insights for newspaper designers.

WESTLEY, Bruce. *News Editing*. Cambridge, Mass.: Houghton Mifflin Co, 1953.
Trenchant guide to the best American practice has three chapters on make-up and typography.

WILLIAMS, Ian (ed.). *Newspapers of the First World War*. Newton Abbot, Devon: Times Newspapers Ltd and David and Charles, 1970.
Full-size reproductions of selection of British and US dailies.

Newspaper design is occasionally discussed, and the wider professional questions often discussed, in the following magazines:

Annually
The Penrose Annual, London, edited by Herbert Spencer, and published by Lund Humphries, 12 Bedford Square, London. There is usually a contribution of importance for newspapermen.
The *Annual Report* of the judges of the Award for Newspaper Design, published jointly by Linotype and by *Printing World,* Lyon Tower, High Street, Colliers Wood, London SW19 2JN.

Quarterly
Vidura : Published by the Press Institute of India, Sapru House Annexe, Barakhamba Road, New Delhi 1, India.

Seminar : Review by Copley Newspapers, published from 776 Ivanhoe Avenue, Post Office Box 1530, La Jolla, California 92037, USA.

Columbia Journalism Review : 602 Journalism, Columbia University, New York, NY 10027, USA.

Weekly
Editor and Publisher : 850 Third Avenue, New York, NY 10022, USA. Trade journal.

UK Press Gazette : Bouverie Publishing Co, 2–3 Salisbury Court, Fleet Street, London EC4Y 8AB. Trade journal.

References

CHAPTER 1

1 *The New Architecture and the Bauhaus* (Boston, Mass: Charles T Bronford Co).
2 *The English Newspaper* (Cambridge University Press, 1932), p. 317.
3 *Typographic Design*, by Raymond Roberts (London: Benn, 1966), p. 59.
4 Guild of British Newspaper Editors' Conference at Grangeover Sands, Lancashire (1970).

CHAPTER 2

1 *America's Front Page News 1690–1970* is a superb collection of historic front pages, edited by Michael C Emery, R Smith Schuneman and Edwin Emery, published by Vis-Com Inc, Minneapolis, and distributed by Doubleday and Co, New York, 1970.
2 *The English Newspaper 1622–1932*, by Stanley Morison (Cambridge University Press, 1932). Fewer illustrations but an illuminating text.
3 *Newspapers of the First World War*, published by Times Newspapers Ltd and David and Charles (Newton Abbot, 1970); basically a collection of British and American pages reproduced full size.
4 The technical changes within newspaper printing are discussed by Michael Twyman in his illustrated history of English printing, *Printing 1770–1970*, published by Eyre and Spottiswood, London, 1970. *See* pp. 50 *et seq.*
5 *Printing the Times since 1785*, by Stanley Morison (Printing House Square, London, 1953), p. 63. Morison is not named as author but it is his work.
6 *Printing The Times since 1785*, p. 70.
7 Memo to Executives, September 14, 1970.

CHAPTER 3

1 *The English Newspaper 1622–1932*, by Stanley Morison (Cambridge University Press, 1932), p. 163.
2 *The English Newspaper*, p. 301.
3 *The Guinness Book of Records*, by Norris and Ross McWhirter (London: Guinness Superlatives Ltd, 1969), p. 108.
4 *The Penrose Annual 1968* (London: Lund Humphries), p. 106 *et seq*.
5 Some of the local reasons for this are discussed by Allen Hutt, p. 70 the 1960 *Penrose Annual*, who noted the contrary movement, back to broadsheet, among monopoly evenings. The weekly trend continued in 1969 with Edwin Taylor's redesign of the *Diss Express* into tabloid.

6 *See* for instance the comparisons in *Graphic Design, Visual Comparison* by Alan Fletcher, Colin Forbes, Bob Gill (London: Studio Vista, 1963). And the *Annuals of Advertising and Editorial Art and Design* of the Art Directors Club of New York (Comet Press Inc).
7 As reported by Ben Bagdikian in *Esquire*, March, 1967. *See also: Economic Trends in the Daily Newspaper Business 1946–1970*, by Bureau of Business Research and Service of the University of Wisconsin.
8 In an address to the American Society of Newspaper Editors, Washington DC, April 21, 1967. Speech reprinted in *UK Press Gazette*, May 1, 1967.
9 *Modern Newspaper Design*, by Edmund C Arnold (New York: Harper and Row, 1969), p. 336.
10 *Modern Newspaper Design*, p. 340.
11 Article by Christopher Johnson, Managing Editor, October 25, 1968.
12 'Can Newspapers move from the Stone Age to the Space Age?,' *The Penrose Annual*, volume 60 (London, Lund Humphries, 1967), pp. 106–118.

CHAPTER 4

1 *The Penrose Annual*, volume 60 (London, Lund Humphries, 1967), pp. 106–118.
2 Clay Felker, *Dot Zero*, volume 1, No. 223, p. 12 (New York, May, 1967).
3 Address to the Chicago Chapter, American Association of Newspaper Representatives, January, 1971. *See also: Editor and Publisher*, March 20, 1971, p. 12.

CHAPTER 5

1 *The Underground Press in America*, by Robert J Glessing (Bloomington and London: Indiana University Press, 1970), p. 49.
2 *Editor and Publisher*, April 20, 1968, p. 48.
3 *Principles of Typography*, by Stanley Morison (Cambridge University Press, 1967).
4 Robert Fichenberg at p. 7 in *What's Happening in News Display*, November, 1968, by the Associated Press Managing Editors' news display committee.
5 George N Gill in the APME booklet, ref. 4.
6 *Modern Newspaper Design*, by Edmund C Arnold (New York: Harper and Row, 1969), p. 268.
7 *Newspaper Design* (London: Oxford University Press, 1967), p. 137.

8 *Pioneers of Modern Design* (Harmondsworth: Pelican, 1960), p. 214.
9 Article in *Print Magazine*, September/October, 1964 (pub. Robert Cadel, 527 Madison Avenue, New York).
10 *News Editing*, by Bruce Westley (Boston: Houghton Mifflin, 1953). *Functional Newspaper Design*, by Edmund C Arnold (New York: Harper and Bros, 1956).
11 *Modern Newspaper Design*, p. 320.
12 *News Editing*, p. 270.
13 *ASNE Bulletin*, No. 471, January 1, 1964, p. 8.
14 For a fuller discussion *see: Printing Design and Layout* (3rd edition) by Vincent Steer (London: Virtue and Co), p. 13 *et seq*.
15 In broadsheet form the *Sun* was successor to the old *Daily Herald*. It was taken over in November 1969 by the Australian proprietor, Mr Rupert Murdoch, and converted into a circus-layout tabloid.
16 In lectures Reiley urges layout men to follow four rules for effective layout: '1. Harmonious layout in rectangular patterns, avoiding zig zags. 2. Accents in the corners (hot spots). 3. Abundant white space. 4. Elimination of ornaments.'
17 *Functional Newspaper Design*, p. 171.
18 *Functional Newspaper Design*, p. 176.
19 *Printing Design and Layout*, Third edition, pp. 22–23.
20 Designed by Edwin Taylor. *See also* Chapter 9 of this Book.
21 *Printing Design and Layout*, Third edition, p. 27.
22 *Typography/Basic Principles*, by John Lewis (London: Studio Books and New York: Reinhold, 1966), p. 28.
23 Judges' Report for 1965.
24 Judges' Report for 1966.
25 *Better Looking Newspapers* (Philadelphia: N W Ayer and Son Inc, 1960).
26 Ed Arnold at p. 10 in *What's Happening in News Display*, November, 1968, by the Associated Press Managing Editors' news display committee. This is a fascinating pamphlet with an admirable concern for raising professional standards.
27 *The Penrose Annual*, volume 60 (London: Lund Humphries, 1967), p. 104.

CHAPTER 6

1 Inverview in *Campaign*, May 14, 1971, p. 21.
2 Page 22 of ref. 1.
3 Interview in *UK Press Gazette*, June 7, 1971, p. 18.

CHAPTER 7

1 Courtney R Sheldon, managing editor, *Christian Science Monitor*, in *What's Happening in News Display*, November, 1968, by the Associated Press Managing Editors' news display committee.
2 Discussion paper by Yoshiumi Fujita, then chief make-up editor and later vice production-manager, The Mainichi Newspapers, during the Eleventh Asian Seminar of the International Press Institute, Seoul, Korea, November, 1965.
3 *L'Evolution des Formules de Présentation de la Presse quotidienne* [The Evolution of Display Patterns in the Daily Press], by Raymond Manevy (Paris: Editions Estienne, 1966), p. 71.
4 George N Gill in *What's Happening in News Display* (ref. 1).
5 *See*, for instance, *Newspaper Editing, Make up and Headlines*, by Norman J Radder and John E Stempel (New York: McGraw Hill, 1942).
6 *Get More Out of Your Newspaper*, by Theodore M Bernstein (New York: New York Times, 1966).

CHAPTER 8

1 Kenneth C Reiley, associate editorial consultant, Copley Newspapers, California, has written an entertaining account of his work with *El Tiempo* in: *Seminar*, the quarterly journal of the Copley Press, La Jolla, California, No. 18, December 1970, pp. 33–37.
2 The Monotype Corporation publish a good working sheet in association with the printers, Oliver Burridge & Co Ltd.

CHAPTER 9

1 In 'Psychedelic by Offset,' *Editor and Publisher*, November 11, 1967, p. 68 *et seq*.
2 Produced by the Pushpin Studios, 114 East 31st Street, New York 16.
3 By Robert J Glessing (Bloomington and London: Indiana University Press, 1970).

CHAPTER 10

1 *Print Magazine*, September/October, 1964 (pub. Robert Cadel, 527 Madison Avenue, New York).

Index

Journals Cited